Turning the Tide

THE HISTORY OF EVERYDAY DEPTFORD

Deptford Forum Publishing Ltd
441 New Cross Road
London SE14 6TA

First published 1993

Reprinted 2000

© Jess Steele 1993

The right of Jess Steele to be identified as the author of this work has been asserted by her in accordance with the Copyright, Designs and Patents Act 1988

Design and Layout by Nïxx
Typeset by Community Desktop Publishing
Cover by Lionel Openshaw
Printed by Darwin Press, 77a Blackheath Rd, London SE10 8PD

ISBN 1 898536 00 7

British Library Cataloguing in Publication Data
A catalogue record for this book is available from the British Library

PREFACE

Struggling my way through this book has been harder for me than I hope it will be for readers. Like Nathan Dews who wrote the last history of Deptford more than a century ago, "I must frankly confess that had I known the labour the work would entail in research and preparation when it was first suggested to me, I fear I should not have commenced with so light a heart as I did."

This is not a finished product; this is just the beginning of talking about Deptford's history. I would have liked more time but Deptford can't wait anymore. We are involved in another moment of change, perhaps the biggest since the closure of the Dockyard in 1869. Let's take up the City Challenge and get some real Action on the Estates, armed with a fuller knowledge of our past, and go beyond them to take Deptford proudly into the 21st century.

Bane of my life, Deptford – town in the marshes, straddling the deep ford, beached-up inner city 1990s slumland – has also become an abiding love and I hope this book reflects that. I've met the best of characters, long-dead heroes and those struggling through the present, I've wandered streets and markets, driven my battered Datsun through even more battered industrial estates, gone to look at buildings in the bits most people never see. Although too often only part-time (debt notices bring on writers' cramp and words won't pay the rent), I have submerged myself in Deptford's past and searched for the heart of its present.

There is a glory in Deptford. It does not reside in old buildings and famous visitors, though they please and entertain us. Rather it lived and lives on the spirit and creativity of the people. I wouldn't take for granted the adaptability of powerless people or trivialise the harshness of their lives but while the text doesn't shudder from a less romantic view of Deptford people and politics, I take this opportunity to pay my tribute to the good times and to the struggle for community in a world that believes the concept is dead.

Jess Steele, October 1993

Local history is a bugger to write! It slips
and slides between neighbourhood and nation.
Its single threads cross centuries with
disarming disregard for the conventional rules
of historical periods. They tangle with each
other mercilessly; disappear, reappear, lie
forgotten, rise unbidden. In the end, it is up
to the writer to decide on a structure, to put
down anchor and tether up the good ship
Deptford so the world may have a look.

ACKNOWLEDGEMENTS

Names flash in front of my eyes and I want to write them down to say thank you and well done: to Dr Jim Sharpe, the Deptford boy with a passion for history and crime; to Cari, Beth, Karen, Clare, Adrienne, Vanda for listening to my terror; to my mother who put up with me (and put me up); to Simon, Julian and the other Deptford entrepreneurs who inspired me; to Christine, Deptford's one-and-only bookseller; to Bob, Peter and Nïxx for meeting my panics with hard work; to Juliet Desailly who struggled with me and to Jani Llewellyn with respect; to all the friends and friends-of-friends who were interested to hear that Deptford had any history; to Lionel who was on the front line; to Richard at the heart of it all; and to the Deptford folk past and present for whom I write.

Above all, this book goes to my father with all my love. Thanks for everything, and especially for living in South East London! And then a final tribute to my battered and beloved Datsun which was older than the Tory government but died in service 4 April 1993.

"To acknowledge our ancestors means
we are aware that we did not make
ourselves, that the line stretches
all the way back, perhaps, to God; or
to Gods. We remember them because it
is an easy thing to forget: that we
are not the first to suffer, rebel,
fight, love and die. The grace with
which we embrace life, in spite of
the pain, the sorrows, is always a
measure of what has gone before."
– Alice Walker

"Those who cannot remember the past
are condemned to repeat it."
– George Santayana

Deptford Forum Publishing will continue to publish material about the area until not one Deptford resident wants to leave!

Photos courtesy of Lewisham and Greenwich Local History Libraries, Sophie Lake, South East London Mercury, the British Library, Keith Cardwell and especially Bob Bray. Photo cataloguing by Catherine Townsend. Initial map sketches by Yola Sanders.

Research on Gut Girls and the Albany Girls' Club by Iris Dove.
Research on Victualling Yard by Josephine Birchenough.
Information on archeological findings around the Dover Castle provided by South East London Archeological Unit.

In a work with a 2,000-year span it is impossible to acknowledge individually all the hours of research other people have done. I only hope the book itself is thanks enough. Any mistakes are my own fault though time caused havoc with research plans. I would be grateful for corrections and further information.

CONTENTS

PART ONE

DOWN BY THE DEEP FORD

The Town in the Marshes

"Once upon a time..."

Deptford has a special and spectacular 2,000-year history. It is a tale of firsts, from the first frigate to the first urban railway. Long known as the Cradle of the Navy, it was also the birthplace of the monorail, steam navigation, assembly-line production, navy biscuits and large-scale power generation. It has been owned or controlled by a series of England's most powerful people and its crucial position on the major Roman road from Dover to London made it the scene for some of the most dramatic moments of English history.

Yet Deptford began, like any place, in obscurity. A little island of nearly solid ground sloping back from the Thames and surrounded by bog-swamp, it was known as Meretun, the town in the marshes. The marshlands stretched south of the Thames from Southwark to Greenwich and out as far as Clapham Common. Cockle shells which gave their names to Fossil and Shell Roads in the 19th century show how far southwards the high tide could intrude.

Walter Besant describes how merchant traders from the north would come through the Isle of Bramble, later called Thorney (now Westminster), and over on the ferries which crossed the river back and forth all day. Reaching Southwark they faced a long, stinking trek, often wading through the marshes with slaves, pack-horses and mules, until they got out of it for a rest on the higher ground of southern Deptford.

Eventually, as Besant puts it, "some genius had the idea of building a causeway". There was probably more to it than that and it is likely that many died in its construction.

A more modern city built on swampland at the cost of many lives was St Petersburg, begun in 1703 when New York was already 70 years old. This was the work of Peter the Great after his return from Deptford, and its sombre beauty was captured in the title "the city built on bones".

On a modern map the 12-foot wide causeway would have stretched from the southern end of Westminster Bridge to the beginning of the Old Kent Road. It was made by driving piles into the mud at regular intervals, forming a wall of timber within the piles and filling up the space with gravel. The causeway made travel easier and Southwark grew up as an area of inns (a quick pint after the ferry crossing!) but also of wealthy villas along the line of the causeway, hugging it close to keep away from the treacherous marshes. The ground lay low either side of the causeway and muddy Thames water gathered in stagnant pools. At this time there were no markets or industries but Southwark was famous as a place of rest and entertainment. Already by the 12th century there were 18 licensed brothels in and around Southwark.

Meanwhile the Thames was being embanked. We do not know exactly when this happened but it was a massive earthwork stretching out as far as the Essex coast, enclosing the swamps. Finally South London was free to develop. With less flooding the marshland turned slowly into fertile pasture and arable land, allowing settlements to develop all along the river.

This was the beginning.

Roman Deptford is not easy to discover. We know that a Roman camp at Southwark stretched in a line of forts to the Thames at Lambeth and to the Ravensbourne at Deptford Bridge. The Via Wathalunga (Watling Street), the Roman road from Dover to Chester, forded the Creek and veered southwards to avoid the riverside area which suffered frequent flooding. A portion of Roman tessellated pavement and brickwork was found in 1866 some three feet below Deptford High St near New Cross Rd, and in 1735 Roman urns were found in a New Cross garden. It is possible that we may soon find the remains of a Roman sailing vessel used to load up 'clunch', the hard chalk from the New Cross area used by the Romans. Something similar was dragged up from under Blackfriars Bridge in the 1960s.

An archeological dig at the Dover Castle site on Deptford Broadway in 1992 uncovered positive signs of Roman occupation in the form of pottery and even a saddle–shaped quern (a stone hand–mill) of Iron Age type. The South East London Archeological Unit also found two Saxon graves. It seems that the Saxons, who invaded Britain in the 5th and 6th centuries, revived the Roman settlement by the old Dover Rd.

The first recorded event connected with the area was in 871 AD when Aethelred the Unready and his brother, the future King Alfred, fought the Danish fleet which had sailed up the Ravensbourne. With the help of Olaf of Norway, the Danes were defeated and the Creek "ran red with blood" but they returned many times over the next centuries and it is thought that the name Ravensbourne came from the black ravens on their flags. In 1012 they were responsible for the martyrdom of Archbishop Alphege at Greenwich.

In 918 AD King Alfred's daughter Elfrida, who had married a Flemish Count, bequeathed her lands in Lewisham, Greenwich and Woolwich to the Abbey of St Peter of Ghent in Flanders. For most of the next 500 years the Abbot received rent from the area, until the lands eventually reverted to the Crown of England under Henry V in 1414.

By 1570, when Lambarde the famous Kentish judge wrote his *Perambulations of Kent,* the name Meretun had been lost. He noted that the settlement was called West Greenwich in ancient evidence and, in Latin, Vadum Profundum (which means deep ford). Many different spellings of the name can be found including DEPFORTH, DEADFORD and DEBTFORD but they all refer to the difficulty of crossing the tidal River Ravensbourne.

It is safe to say that the early inhabitants of riverside Deptford started to build rafts to catch fish and that slowly these became more sophisticated. Over the years the rafts would be shaped and the sides built up to keep the water out, a keel would be added to keep the whole thing on a straight course, a mast with hides hung on it would follow. Deptford had produced its first ship. The small settlement of fishermen-boatbuilders would soon be bringing back more fish than they needed for their families and may have begun to barter it for other necessities locally. Some may even have taken it to sell at the first

London markets like Queenshithe and Billingsgate in the streets running down to the inlets at the water's edge.

View near Deptford Common, Kent. 1771. Deptford has a long farming tradition, not lost until the late 19th century, when "many with little regard or respect for farm work streamed into the neighbourhood" (Buckley, 1991) and it became necessary to put constables on the corners of fields to stop people taking short cuts.

In the meadows near the river and beyond, cattle, sheep and pigs grazed peacefully. Slowly the grinding of corn and meal developed. The earliest Ravensbourne mills were water-powered. The Domesday Book (1086) mentions eleven of them and Rocque's map of 1745 shows five in the short stretch of river between Deptford and Lewisham.

The Tide Mill to the north of Deptford Bridge was the starting point of the small concentration of flour milling at the end of Deptford Creek which lasted until the 1960s. The mill relied on the flow of high tide water and would have had gates like lock-gates on a canal which opened as the tide rose and were pushed closed by the pressure of water as the tide withdrew. The Deptford Tide Mill dates back at least to the 12th century (Ch.1). In 1585 it was bought by Christ's Hospital who owned it through to the 19th century when it was known as the Old Flood Mill. In the early days the mill-keeper was responsible for maintaining Deptford Bridge which was no easy task with all the cart wheels digging out huge ruts on this major road. The old mill building was carried away by the terrible flood of 1824 but was rebuilt within four years and taken over by J & H Robinson who made it the first flour mill on the river to be powered by steam. By the mid-19th century corn was coming into Britain from the American prairies and the Tide Mill's river access was an important advantage. Robinsons' mills dominated the Deptford skyline until demolition in the late 1970s. The red-brick Skill Centre which replaced them at a cost of £3.4 million is now defunct (Ch.14).

The Tide Mill was joined at the Deptford Bridge site in the late 18th century by S & P Mumford. The Mumfords' building which survives (grade II listed) dates from 1897. From the 1930s smaller mills like Robinsons' and Mumfords' faced increasing competition with the building of massive mills. They banded together into the Association of Flour Millers, aiming to compete with Rank and Spillers but within a decade the Association was bought out by Rank Hovis McDougall. The Ravensbourne mills had a

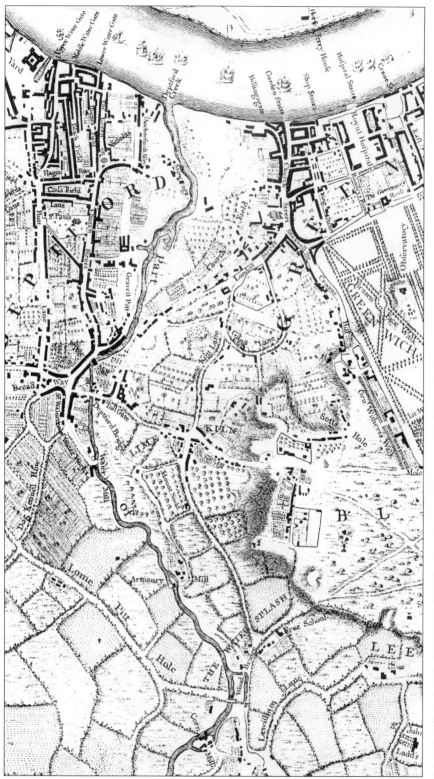

Detail of Rocque's map of London and surrounds (1745-6). Three of the many Ravensbourne mills are shown here: the Tide Mill, oldest of them all; the Brook Mill, which was to become part of the Kent Waterworks south of Deptford Bridge; and the Armoury Mill, mentioned by Lambarde in 1570.

The narrow streets and courts behind the riverfront were full of all the trades of the water from sea-captains to anchorsmiths, from shipwrights to coopers. The three watergates offered access to watermen for all those whose business or pleasure took them to the river. To the west, the square building was the old storehouse of the royal dockyard and further upriver the old Red Houses had just become the official victualling yard of the navy (1742).

By the Creek was the Stowage where the East India Company had their provision and repair yards until 1782 and the Gravel Pitt where the House of Correction had become St Paul's parish workhouse in 1726.

tradition of creative diversification but although Robinsons' turned to the production of animal feed and Mumfords' specialised in cake flours both fell victim to the vast scale of modern milling.

Deptford Tidemill in 1841, following the rebuild of 1828 after severe floods had carried off the old building. The earliest record of a 'flood myll' on this Creek-side site north of Deptford Bridge is found in a court record of 1293. but in 1157 Wakelin de Maminot was paying a yearly rent on a Deptford mill which was almost certainly the old Tide Mill. It is likely that it had stood there since before the Domesday Book (1086) The chimney in the background suggests that this new mill was at least partly powered by steam.

Further upstream was the water mill known as Brook Mill. In 1588 a leatherseller called Thomas Miller sold it to a London mercer, Henry Brooke. Eighty years later it was purchased by John Evelyn. In 1701 two local citizens – William Yarnold and Robert Watson – were given a 500-year charter to raise water from the Ravensbourne and pipe it to the manors of Sayes Court and East Greenwich. This was the beginning of the Ravensbourne Waterworks which survived precariously throughout the 19th century as the Kent Waterworks Company, absorbing local companies throughout North Kent until the formation of the Metropolitan Water Board in 1903.

Another water mill marked on Rocque's map is the Armoury Mill. Two hundred years earlier Lambarde had mentioned "a mill for the glazing of armour". The economy of the area was finely tuned to the old-established arms market of Deptford and Woolwich. Another example is the bakery of Mill Lane which made bread and biscuits for the royal dockyard from 1835. It helped feed the troops and sailors of the Crimean War as well as supplying two special London markets, the London workhouses and Pentonville Prison.

Windmills were built along the banks of the Thames, including a line of them on the Isle of Dogs which eventually led to the name Millwall. A windmill also stood at the entrance to Deptford Creek and remained there until the 19th century. To the north east of the present Deptford Park, Windmill Lane commemorated the old Clayton windmill which can be found on 18th century maps and was probably much older.

In the marshes reeds and rushes grew abundantly and the industry of rush-work flourished in early Deptford. Rushes were mainly used for thatching but there was also demand for rush mats to take the edge off cold stone or plain earth floors. Basketmaking is one of the oldest industries in the world and the marsh reeds would certainly have been used for this purpose. As late as 1844 there were osier-grounds below Deptford Bridge growing willows for cane-work.

Another early industry was brickmaking using the clay of the Lower Thameside. Burnt or sun-dried bricks were used in England from the time of the Roman occupation but building with brick seems to have lapsed for nearly 1,000 years after that. When it returned to fashion the riverside brickfields of the Deptford area were quickly worked out but the industry thrived for many centuries around Loam Pitt Hole, where roads like Undercliff were cut into the hillside along the lines of old brickfields and troublesome foundations are the modern legacy of ancient brickworking.

EARLY DAYS

1

From Odo to Evelyn

"Then, over all, John Evelyn's honor'd name..."

The history of the lands of Deptford presented here shows how important some of its holders have been in national politics. We move quickly from the greedy Earl Odo to the barons' revolt which led to Magna Carta, from the infamous Earl of Suffolk to the discontented Lord Lieutenant of Ireland. In John Evelyn's time Deptford was a site of struggle between Monarchy and Parliament and the squire had to buy back the manor of Sayes Court from the Parliamentary rebels.

In the reign of Edward the Confessor the manor of Deptford or West Greenwich was held by Count Harold (later King). After Edward's death the Saxon lords elected and crowned Harold who claimed to have been chosen by Edward on his deathbed and was the brother of the former queen, Editha. Despite his popular election, Harold could not avoid the pretensions of William, Duke of Normandy. Neither Harold nor William had particularly good claims but the true heir, Edgar the Atheling, was a young boy, weak in mind and body. The contest was decided on the battlefield where William's claims were bolstered by the Pope who proclaimed 'a holy war' against Harold.

After the Battle of Hastings in 1066 at the 'hoary apple tree' site which later became the town of Battle, William marched towards Dover wreaking havoc on the way. Failing to take London, he ravaged the country around to starve the city into surrender. The route taken by the troops can be traced by examining the reduced values of manors brought about by the devastation. In our area it seems that the Duke advanced to Lewisham and through southern Deptford to Camberwell. The policy of terror was successful and William was crowned on Christmas Day, 1066.

The Conqueror's half-brother Odo (the Bishop of Bayeux who commissioned the Bayeux Tapestry) annexed Deptford to his principality of Kent. He became enormously wealthy, mainly through extortion, and harboured a secret desire to be Pope. He bought a palace in Rome and prepared to move there, accompanied by Hugh 'the Wolf', Earl of Chester. William heard of the scheme, arrested Odo and seized his treasures, charging him with "untruth, and sinister dealings". When Odo exclaimed that he was a minister of the Lord and only the Pope could judge him, William retorted "I arrest you as Earl of Kent, not as Bishop of Bayeux".

After Odo's fall the manor of Deptford passed to Gilbert de Maminot, one of eight barons chosen to guard Dover Castle. King William had given 56 knights' fees to distribute to trusty persons who could help defend such an important place. Twenty-four of the fees were passed to Maminot who made Deptford the head of the barony and built his castle there. Some stone ruins of the castle were probably still visible in the 18th century near Sayes Court. Deptford was to provide 112 soldiers for the defence of Dover, 25 of them to be stationed at the castle at any one time and the rest to be ready in an emergency. For seven centuries Deptford continued to pay a 'castle-guard rent' for the Dover obligation.

Dover Castle viewed from the north in 1772. Deptford was part of the lands given to Gilbert de Maminot in return for providing soldiers to defend the castle. The print shows "the amazing assemblage of embattled walls, towers, dikes and mounts constructed for its defence".

In 1145 Wakelin de Maminot promised part of the manor of Deptford to the monks of Bermondsey Abbey. Although never confirmed this gave the monks a chance to interfere with future claims and the next Maminot compensated them with 10 shillings yearly rent out of the 'Mill of Deptford' (presumably the Tide Mill).

The last Maminot died in 1191 and his sister Alice brought Deptford to her husband Geoffrey de Say, one of the chief barons to pay the enormous ransom demanded by the German Emperor for the release of Richard the Lionheart. He granted Deptford to the Knights Templars for their part in the Crusades but his son – also Geoffrey – swapped it with them for Saddlescombe (now Sedlescombe) in Sussex. This Geoffrey was involved in the revolt of the barons which led to the signing of Magna Carta at Runnymede in 1215. King John retaliated by seizing the lands. Deprived of his castle at Deptford, Geoffrey joined the son of the King of France when he invaded Britain. Luckily for Geoffrey, King John died unexpectedly in 1216 and the manor returned to the de Says, remaining with them for many years. The family became "mighty among the barons of their day and generation" and they gave the name Say's Court to their Deptford home. Writing in 1884, Nathan Dews commented that "the name is preserved despite the vast changes and alterations Deptford has undergone". Even today, after many more changes, part of the site is still known as Sayes Court Gardens.

In 1436 the manor came back into national importance when it fell into the hands of William de la Pole, Earl of Suffolk, who was to become the country's most influential man after the King. Extremely ambitious, de la Pole courted Henry VI for lands and titles. He was sent to Sicily as a proxy bridegroom to 'marry' Henry to Margaret of Anjou and conduct her back to England. He brought her with great ceremony to his house at Deptford. The following day she was taken to Blackheath where she was met by the mayor, aldermen and sheriffs and a great crowd who took her to the City with marvellous pageants for which Suffolk demanded a large tax in Parliament.

Almost from the day of the marriage, Suffolk and the Queen monopolised the government. They were constantly together and people said he was more like her husband than the monkish Henry. Suffolk continued to acquire power and privilege: lordships, castles, estates and titles, until finally he was made Lord Chamberlain and Lord High Admiral of England. He was the most powerful man in England but was very unpopular among every class in English society and discontent spread throughout the country. A hostile meeting was even held in the Broomfields, Deptford, on Suffolk's own land. Defeats in France, the loss of the Norman provinces as presents to Margaret, and the murder of Humphrey, 'the good Duke of Gloucester' and a one-time contender for the position of King's favourite, were all attributed to Suffolk. When he added insult to injury by assuming the title of Duke, Henry personally interfered, sentencing him to five years exile. The populace flew to arms on hearing this and more than 2,000 people gathered in London against him. Libels against the Queen and Suffolk were nailed to the doors of St Nicholas' Church at Deptford Green. Suffolk escaped but was caught at sea between Dover and Calais and beheaded with six strokes of a rusty sword.

The Vicar of Deptford from 1423 was Richard Wyche. A boyhood friend of John Wycliffe, the heretic, Wyche was known locally as 'the Lollard'. He was burned for heresy on Tower Hill in 1439.

Suffolk's son was only seven when his father died. He later married Elizabeth, sister of Edward IV, and was reinstated. Their son, John, who held the manor of Deptford, was made Earl of Lincoln and Lord Lieutenant of Ireland. When Richard III fell at Bosworth in 1485, John became a prisoner of Henry Tudor. He escaped to Flanders and joined the mercenaries of the Duchess of Burgundy to support the cause of Lambert Simnel, pretender to the English throne. They gathered a further army in Ireland and landed in Lancashire in May 1487. More than half of them were killed in the battle with the King's troops at Stoke. The Earl's body was found on the battlefield and Deptford was forfeited to the crown.

Henry VII granted the manor to Oliver St John but it reverted to the crown in 1514 when Henry VIII gave it to his beloved Jane Seymour. On her death the stewardship of Sayes Court was awarded to Richard Long, an unscrupulous courtier who had helped Henry to break his marriage to Anne of Cleves. The next steward was Sir Thomas Speke and then Sir Thomas Darcy. In 1554 Queen Mary granted the manor to Sir Thomas Pope and it ceased to be crown property. By 1568 it was in the possession of William Chaworth of London, clothworker.

Meanwhile the manor of Hatcham had been settled by an early Saxon called Haecci. It is described in the Domesday Book as containing land for three ploughs, nine villagers and two smallholders, six acres of meadowland and woodland for three pigs. The manor was annexed by Odo and, like Deptford, came to the Maminots before being granted to Gilbert de Hachesham (who took his name from it). It returned to the crown under Edward III who granted it in 1370 to the Convent at Dartford until the dissolution of the monasteries by Henry VIII. Mary I granted it to Anne, the widow of the

'Good Duke' Somerset, Lord Protector of England whose "good meaning and honest nature" had brought nothing but trouble until his execution in 1552.

In 1614 Hatcham was bought by the Haberdashers' Company to provide an endowment for their school and almshouse at Monmouth. In 1630 it was leased to Randolph Crew who was caught up in the age-old boundary squabbles when he was obliged to pay 'Ship Money' to both Kent and Surrey. He appealed and his case was heard by Charles I himself at Greenwich in 1637 when Hatcham was judged to be in Surrey.

The manor of Brockley, granted to Michael de Turnham by Henry II for a rent of 12 pence a year, was later sold to Countess Juliana, wife of Wakelin de Maminot. She founded a monastery near the present St Peter's Church (Wickham Rd). Though the monastery was only occupied for 20 years the White Canons held on to 'Brokele' until the dissolution of the monasteries when the lands were given to Cardinal Thomas Wolsey. When Wolsey fell from favour in 1529, having failed to get Henry VIII his divorce from Catherine of Aragon, the estates were forfeited to the King. In the following centuries the manor passed through hands which have left their mark in the road names. These included the 18th century Drake family who owned Shardeloes House in Amersham. The two Drake brothers married the daughters of William Wickham. They also owned St Donnatt's Castle in Glamorganshire and their cousin was Rector of Malpas in Cheshire. Later Drake family marriage partners included a Miss Ashby whose family's country seat was Breakspears in a village called Harefield. Another marriage brought in the Tyrwhitt connection, but Tressillian is more obscure. In the 19th century remains of the old monastery were found in a meadow belonging to Mr Myatt of Manor Farm, Deptford, along with several old coins, a Deptford token dated 1665, an antique key, an ancient buckle and an old well.

The manor house at Sayes Court was in the possession of the Browne family from 1568 and their good services were rewarded with extensions of the grant in 1585, 1610 and 1632. Christopher Browne, lord of the manor in Elizabethan times, held the title Clerk of the Green Cloth. This meant he was responsible for providing meat for the royal court when the Queen stayed at Greenwich Palace and the slaughteryards near the manor house reeked at these times.

The next inhabitant was Sir Richard Browne who had been a gentleman of the Privy Chamber of Charles I. He was sent to Paris before the Civil War and he stayed at the French court as the representative of Charles I and his son until the Restoration of the Monarchy in 1660. Browne was worried about Sayes Court when he heard that the King might have to sell his fairest parks and lands. He wrote to the Secretary of State begging him to advise His Majesty not to sell "certain pastures called Say's Court at Deptford" or at least to offer Browne himself first refusal since it had been long in the custody of his ancestors "and is the place wherein he was borne".

Sir Richard did not return to Deptford for many years and it was John Evelyn, the famous diarist, who became the next resident of Sayes Court. Evelyn was born at the family estate of Wotton in Surrey in 1620. He lived through all the great events of the 17th century: the 'eleven-years tyranny' when Charles I ruled without Parliament; the turbulent times of the Civil War; the Protectorships of Oliver Cromwell and his son Richard; the colourful Restoration of Charles II; the many crises of James II's reign and the Bloodless Revolution which brought William and Mary to the throne.

Portrait of John Evelyn, the diarist, who lived at Sayes Court 1652-1694 and kept up his interest in the area until his death in 1706. His diary is full of fascinating detail and stories, although most of it was rewritten for the benefit of his heirs and lacks the spontaneity of his friend and fellow-diarist, Samuel Pepys.

From the age of twelve Evelyn used "to set down matters in a blank almanack". He went to Balliol College, Oxford, "rather out of shame at abiding longer at school than from any fitness". The build up of ominous political forces convinced the 21 year old Evelyn to leave England for the continent. The French and Dutch were besieging Genappe and the young traveller volunteered his services. For a week, to test his taste for the soldier's life, he "trailed a pike" and then abandoned the military career. After his return to England he studied a bit and, in his words, "danced and fooled more".

When the Civil War broke out in 1642 Evelyn joined the King at

Brentford but was advised to leave since capture would ruin himself and his brothers without advantage to His Majesty. Instead, he retired to Wotton and began his long gardening career. Soon he visited Sir Richard Browne in Paris and his diary of June 1647 states baldly: "We concluded about my marriage." This was to Browne's daughter Mary, who was only 14 at the time. Sir Richard sent Evelyn back to England to try to negotiate with the Parliamentary soldiers for possession of Sayes Court. The matter was not finally resolved until 1653 when Evelyn purchased the house for £3,500.

In 1648, with Charles I imprisoned in Carisbrook Castle, Evelyn noted that "there was a rising now in Kent, my lord of Norwich being at the head of them and their first rendezvous in Broome-field, next my house at Say's Court". The rising ended disastrously. Evelyn's diary describes the lead up to the King's execution in January 1649. Evelyn himself kept a fast on the day and, unlike most Londoners, he stayed away from the scene, commenting miserably on politics – "Un-king-ship was proclaimed, and his majesty's statues thrown down" – and the weather – "now was the Thames frozen over, and horrid tempests of wind".

Evelyn finally settled at Sayes Court in 1652 "there being now so little appearance of any change for the better, all being entirely in the rebels' hands, and this particular Estate...very much suffering from want of some friend to rescue it out of the power of the usurpers".

On the evening of 30th May 1593 Christopher Marlowe, poet, playwright and secret agent, was killed in Eleanor Bull's house in Deptford. The jury at the inquest convicted Ingram Frizer of manslaughter in self-defence. Within a month he was pardoned by the Queen and there were no further enquiries. Marlowe's death has usually been described as a tavern brawl over a woman or the payment of a bill but this cannot be true. Eleanor Bull, born Whitney, was registered not as a common alehouse keeper but as the well-to-do widow of an arms-bearing gentleman, Richard Bull, the sub-bailiff of Sayes Court. It is likely that her house at Deptford Strand offered rather select board and lodging. Marlowe was in no position to be enjoying time out with theatrical friends. Since college days he had been deeply entangled in the web of the Elizabethan secret service. According to Charles Nicholl, he was now being framed for the sake of courtly rivalry at the highest level: a pawn in the battle between the powerful Earl of Essex and Marlowe's own patron Sir Walter Raleigh.

The background to Marlowe's murder is impeccably traced by Nicholl in *The Reckoning*. In short it goes as follows:

In April 1593 anti-immigrant libels began to appear in the streets of London. The most vicious of them was signed 'Tamburlaine', a Marlowe character, and was full of references to Marlowe's other work. Nicholl believes the libel can be traced to Richard Cholmeley, "just one more figure in this story of bad company".

Cholmeley was arrested after an informer drew up a series of *Remembrances* against him, portraying him as a militant atheist with a company of 60 followers ("the damnable crew") aiming to set up an atheist commonwealth. The *Remembrances* include this allegation: "He saith... that one Marlowe is able to show more sound reasons for atheism than any divine in England is able to give to prove divinity, & that Marlowe told him he hath read the atheist lecture to Sr Walter Raleigh & others". The Earl of Essex intervened to save Cholmeley because he knew the atheist pose was a pretence. Essex knew the real truth because it was of his own devising – to discredit Raleigh through his controversial follower,

Christopher Marlowe. Raleigh's own actions – speaking in Parliament against proposals to extend privileges to the immigrant Dutch traders and later making a speech for religious tolerance – were easily twisted to portray him as a vicious libeller and an atheist. The anti-immigrant libel and the *Remembrances* shifted both these accusations onto Marlowe.

While this trouble was brewing Marlowe was down at Scadbury at the house of his old patron Sir Thomas Walsingham. On 18th May a warrant was issued for him to appear daily before the Queen's Council. Considering the place of torture in Nicholl's tale it is surprising that Marlowe was not hauled off to prison. His protection on the Council came from Sir Robert Cecil who had used Marlowe in his own dodgy dealings and would be happier to see the Essex camp discredited than Marlowe placed under the heavy hand of legal investigation.

The Essex faction were disappointed. Marlowe had been accused and taken but remained untortured and unconfessed. What they needed was some harder 'evidence'. The confession under torture of Marlowe's old room-mate Thomas Kyd and the famous Baines 'Note' detailing all Marlowe's heresies could have provided this. However, Nicholl believes had Marlowe lived he could have outplayed the charges, claiming he was not really an atheist at all, just a faithful dealer in an underhand world using these 'damnable opinions' only as a cover to do the Queen's business. "Marlowe knows the rules. He is the target of this smear campaign, but he is a moving target" (Nicholl, 1992) The Essex camp knew the rules too and must have worried that Marlowe's political agility would allow the momentum against Raleigh to falter or even backfire. Suddenly Marlowe has become not a victim but a danger. He needs to be silenced to allow the fabricated evidence to play its role in the political destruction of Sir Walter Raleigh. The Baines 'Note' was produced on 27th May. Three days later Marlowe was dead. As Kyd put it, *mortui non mordent,* the dead cannot bite back. The men in the chamber at Widow Bull's that day were no innocent bunch of old mates. Rather they were a group typical of the underside of Elizabethan life – loan sharks, schemers and experienced agents of the Elizabethan secret world. Their paths had crossed many times, they understood and mistrusted each other. In all the accounts Robert Poley and Nicholas Skeres are shadowy figures caught up in the action only as witnesses, yet Skeres was a servant of the Earl of Essex and Poley was a government agent working under Sir Robert Cecil. Poley was a somewhat unexpected guest, recalled from the Low Countries by Cecil in a flap about what Marlowe might confess under pressure. 'Sweet Robyn' is the most sinister of the 'gentlemen' who walk Eleanor Bull's garden. As Cecil's man he is Marlowe's ally, but only to a point.

As an Essex man, Skeres is Marlowe's enemy and Nicholl believes the Deptford meeting was a confrontation between these two, fixed for Skeres by his accomplice Frizer. Skeres must try to persuade Marlowe to turn evidence against Raleigh. If this fails, Marlowe must be silenced forever. The meeting in Deptford was not arranged for murder. Rather, as the day dragged on and wine headaches descended on the men, time began to run out. "Persuasion becomes threat, and threat flares up into anger. 'Divers malicious words,' are spoken, not about a 'sum of pence' but about matters of life and liberty, truth and betrayal. In the heat of the night, in the irrecoverable fleeting logic of the moment, the situation resolves itself. Someone pulls a knife. There is a brief struggle, and Marlowe is killed by a savage blow to the head...Marlowe's death was a decision. It was a point the day reached, by a process of dwindling options."

Nicholl has told the story in its best form yet but there are many uncertain areas. Whatever the truth, Marlowe's body lies peacefully in the churchyard at St Nicholas' Church, or at least we think it does, nobody knows where exactly...

2

The Dover Road and the Mighty Thames

*"Deptford Creek: deep, awkward and
indeed often dangerous" – Bartlett*

Local history always reflects the physical geography of an area.
Deptford's position between the greatest river and the oldest road
in southern England gives it its special character. The meaning of
these features for everyday lives has changed with each passing
century but they are the threads along which Deptford's history and
character have formed. John Burns called the Thames "liquid
history". The travelling tradition along the London to Dover road
should earn some similar title suggestive of movement for our A2.
These two physical features are connected by a great meandering
Creek, the mouth of the River Ravensbourne. For so long the
industrial focus of Deptford, today's Creek is lost under concrete and
mud except at the mouth where the water flows under a layer of oily
slime. If we are to reclaim Deptford's history and move forwards to a
better environment, the Creek must be given a high priority.

Map of the River Thames, 1849. There was a lot more of Deptford by this time than is shown in this drawing but the stretch of fields behind the riverfront between Deptford and Rotherhithe and the open ground of the Isle of Dogs are accurate.

The Ravensbourne River emerges "a crystal rillet, scarce a palm in width"
on Keston Heath. As it meanders towards the Thames it "wanders in Hayes
and Bromley, Beckenham Vale, and straggling Lewisham" before its flood
storms under Deptford Bridge and goes on "to swell the master current of
the 'mighty heart' of England". This sparkling Ravensbourne of the 17th
century did not last and by mid-18th century Samuel Johnson scorned it
in the *Gentleman's Magazine*:
  "But, oh! how changed with changing years,
  'Tis now the vilest stream on earth
  Polluted from its place of birth!"

Nathan Dews believed the Romans would have felt undignified using ferries and it is possible that they built a bridge over the deep narrow gully which cut across the crucial Watling Street. In the 5th century Deptford Creek was a favourite resort of the warlike Teutonic tribes who eventually became the Anglo-Saxons. Four hundred years later the Danes began their regular visits. The Roman bridge may well have been destroyed for strategic reasons by one of these invading fleets moored in the Creek below.

Certainly a wooden bridge was in existence in 1345 and when it was rebuilt around 1570 it was made partly with stone. The bridge needed repairing many times over the centuries, not only for ordinary wear and tear on such an important route, but also from damage by the many floods to which it fell victim. In 1809, for example, the waters rose above the archway, carrying off the parapet and much of the bridge itself. The stream rushed in torrents washing away the body of a man as well as many pieces of furniture. All over Deptford flooding remained a great danger and local landowners were often taxed for repairs to the Thames bank and the marsh-walls between the town and the Ravensbourne.

Deptford Bridge, 1840. This view shows the bridge before the removal of the central pier which was stopping the flow of the river and causing terrible floods.

The Great Flood, New Year's Day 1651
A terrible storm whipped up at Deptford and became so violent that the waves forced their way into the shipyards, scattering great trees and piles of timber that 20 horses could scarcely move. Soon there were seven feet of water in the lower town and rising. The inhabitants fled to the upper town, leaving all their property "to the mercy of the merciless waves". One poor woman was busy turning a goose on a spit and keeping an eye on her two young children. Seeing the water rising she ran to get her husband but before their return the house was three feet deep in water, the cradle floating, the goose swimming and the other child was up on a high table.

Those who could not escape in time had to be rescued by boats from the upper windows of their houses and some were said to have drowned. The flood caused enormous damage. More than 200 cattle drowned in the meadows of Deptford. Ships lying anchored in the Thames broke away and crashed into each other though the damage was kept in check by the hard work of the mariners.

Three black clouds were seen on the evening before the flood which may have resulted in an old chronicle which warns: "When you discern the sun to be eclipsed and the appearing of three black clouds, then expect great inundations, loss of cattel, changes and dreadful revolutions, even as a signal from heaven, to purge nations and commonwealths from oppression and tyranny, and to restore to the freeborn their just freedom and liberty, that so peace may abound within the walls of Sion, and each man enjoy their own again."

Among the many people who must have crossed old Deptford Bridge were a number of rebel armies. The first of these was the Peasants' Revolt in 1381 against the new poll tax. There has been much debate about the kind of person who participated in this rebellion. They included many poor priests, urban artisans and even some people who had been appointed to collect the offensive tax but instead helped to lead opposition against it. The enormous casualties of the Black Death earlier in the century had meant that those who survived were in a better bargaining position and standards of living had risen considerably. It was not despair which sent the 'peasants' marching to London but raised hopes. In general these protesters were not the most wretched or hot-headed of the population. Many of them were middle-aged and held offices in their villages. They tended to come from stable, well-established families and they were more likely to serve on juries than appear before them. They knew the risks of rebellion, and yet they marched on. With all this in mind, we may conclude that their grievances were real and deeply-felt.

The rebels came from Essex and Kent and they may have been in liaison with discontents in London. They joined up on 11th June and elected Wat Tyler as their leader. They sent word to Richard II that they were coming to destroy the traitors around him and that they wished to speak with him at Blackheath. When he did not turn up they forced onwards across Deptford Bridge and into the City with the help of the London commoners and the aldermen. They burned houses and beheaded a number of lawyers. At Mile End the two most hated of Richard's advisers were killed but it was the interview with Richard at Smithfield which brought the revolt to a head. Tyler was stabbed to death by the Lord Mayor and new help for the government came from loyalists in London. The rebels dispersed having accomplished virtually none of their aims but leaving a deep mark on all contemporaries and a fascinating example to future revolutionaries.

In 1450 Jack Cade revived some of their aims and methods when he led a formidable movement of the 'men of Kent' (the 'radicals' of the century). The rebellion included a knight, a mayor and many gentlemen and expressed the discontent of a broad section of the community. As in 1381 they gained access to London Bridge and the City but, though they put the heads of two of the King's advisers on poles and paraded them about the place, they were forced to surrender after a bitter struggle. Cade was captured and died of wounds.

In 1497 Henry VII was demanding huge taxes to deal with the pretender Perkin Warbeck who had landed in Scotland to a ready welcome from the Scottish King, James IV. In Cornwall, far away from these problems, the taxes were considered irrelevant and fell hard on the poorer section of the mining community. Typically, resentment was directed at the King's evil advisers. The rebels made a remarkable march across England and by the time they assembled at Guildford they were said to number 15,000. They continued their march around the south of London and the army being prepared for Scotland by Lord Daubeney had to be diverted. Guns were placed at Deptford to defend the passage of the river and Daubeney gained Deptford Bridge. Though he was captured by the rebels he was soon released and the Cornishmen were "with no great difficulty cut in pieces and put to flight". More than 2,000 men were slain at the bridge. Henry characteristically fined all those who survived and that year made nearly £15,000 out of fining rebels.

Deptford was again the scene of rebellion when a Kentish gentleman, Sir Thomas Wyatt, anxious about the coming marriage of the Catholic Queen Mary I with Philip of Spain, conspired to keep her off the throne. In February 1554 Wyatt and his 2,000 men camped for three days at Deptford before setting off to Southwark and then on a roundabout route into London. Wyatt's appeals to patriotism whipped up popular fear of the Spaniards and made the danger seem local and immediate for the Kentish people. In London, too, the populace was uncertain and the rebels advanced as far as Ludgate before the Londoners finally decided for the government. The gates were closed against the meagre 300 men who had remained with Wyatt to the end and the rising was defeated.

Passing through Deptford is a long tradition and not only for rebel armies. Chaucer's Pilgrims came this way from the Tabard Inn at Southwark to St Thomas à Beckett's shrine at Canterbury. The Pilgrims' host addressed the company:

> "Lo Depeford, and it is half-wey pryme!
> Lo Grenewych, ther many a shrew is inne!
> It were al tyme thy tale to bigynne."

or, in a modern translation:

> "Look, it's half after seven, and Deptford's here!
> That's Greenwich, full of scoundrels, over there!
> High time you told your story, so begin."

It is rather sad that Chaucer had them pass over Deptford Bridge at 7.30am: no chance to stop for a rest at the Christopher (Ch.4). The fact that Chaucer was living in Greenwich at the time of writing may explain the location of the 'scoundrels' there rather than at Deptford.

Great processions of London's dignitaries regularly passed through Deptford to Blackheath to welcome foreign leaders or home-coming English kings such as the victorious Henry V in 1415 after the Battle of Agincourt. Perhaps most exciting for local people would have been the triumphant procession of King Charles II at his Restoration in 1660. Deptford had shared in the turmoil of the Civil War. In 1647 there was fighting nearby when a party of horsemen came upon Colonel Robert Pye's (Parliamentary) troops quartered at Deptford. A letter describing the incident laments: "Here is blowes struck, here is blood shed, the Lord direct the Parliament, and the

City, and the Army, to study how to compose these fresh divisions lest poore ENGLAND be whelmed in the redde Sea of the subdivision." In the following year a more serious fight occurred at New Cross when Kentishmen led by the Duke of Lennox were victorious against the Parliamentary forces.

The dockyard was held by the Royalists during the Kentish rising of 1648, giving all Deptford great opportunities for plunder in the confusion. Such victories were short-lived, however. The dockyard was retaken and the new moral order imposed by Parliament was shown when the men were ordered to attend a weekly lecture on 'saving truths'. With Sayes Court overrun by Cromwell's soldiers in 1652, Evelyn lamented that "all was now entirely in the rebels' hands".

Although Royalists in Deptford and everywhere were horrified by the execution of Charles I in 1649 there was some comfort to be found in the miraculous healing powers of his blood. Mrs Baylie's 14 year old daughter had suffered for many years with the disease known as the King's Evil (scrofula) which had "putrified and corrupted, not only the unseen parts of her body, but her face and her eyes". Her mother had tried everything but nothing could help until a London wool draper called John Lane turned up with a handkerchief which had been dipped in the royal blood on the day of the beheading. No sooner had Miss Baylie applied the hankie to her sores and wiped her eyes with the bloody side, than she recovered her eyesight and became "lusty and strong" and many hundreds of people came to see the miracle!

Under the rule of Oliver Cromwell theatres had closed, dancing was forbidden and England had taken on a rather gloomy air. The new King took great pleasure in such 'frivolities' and the contrast must have been felt all over the kingdom. Although Charles did not keep his promise to give over the Sayes Court lands forever, Evelyn seemed well pleased when the King came "to honour my poor villa with his presence" in 1663.

Whales in the Thames

1658: "A large whale was taken betwixt my land abutting on the Thames and Greenwich, which drew an infinite concourse to see it, by water, coach, and on foote, from London and all parts. It appeared first below Greenwich at low water, for at high water it would have destroyed all the boats; but lying now in shallow water, incompassed with boats, after a long conflict it was killed with a harping yron, struck in the head, out of which it spouted blood and water by two tunnells, and after a horrid groan it ran quite on shore and died." (Evelyn)

1699: "After an extraordinary storm there came up the Thames a whale fifty-six feet long." (Evelyn)

1842: A young fin whale, about 20 feet long and weighing more than two tons, was killed off Deptford Pier one Sunday by a number of watermen. A printer in Flagon Row, Deptford, quickly printed up a number of bills to advertise this 'Extraordinary and Suprising Novelty' which was to be seen at Mr William's butchers on the corner of Old King St nearby.

1965: That November there was great excitement when a school of about 20 whales (between 6 and 25 feet long) was sighted in the Thames off Woolwich Pier. Billy Smart's Circus tried to catch one, enlisting skin-divers, a gigantic nylon fishing net and a rubber dinghy to inflate under the unfortunate captive and tow it to shore. They planned to take the whale to a temporary pool on Clapham Common on the way to a permanent aquarium at Windsor. All was frustrated though when a policeman pointed out that anything caught in the Thames becomes the property of the Queen and that the Whaling Industry Act states that you cannot catch a whale in British territorial waters. The whale-catchers were last seen edging the whales gently out of the Thames, hoping to catch one in the open sea.

"Sketch of a Species of Whale caught in the river Thames off Deptford, between 4 and 5 oClock in the afternoon of Sunday the 23d Oct! 1842. It measured 14 feet 6 inches in length, the mouth 3 feet 10 inches long, the tail measured the same from point to point, and it weighed about two tons. It was taken to premises adjoining the Bull and Butcher in Old King Street, Deptford where it was exhibited on a stand erected for the purpose".
(By permission of the British Library)

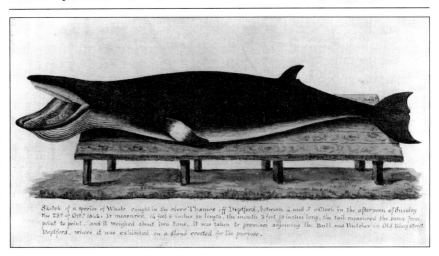

Sketch of a species of Whale caught in the river Thames off Deptford, between 4 and 5 oClock in the afternoon of Sunday the 23d of Oct." 1842. It measured 14 feet 6 inches in length, the mouth 3 feet 10 inches long, the tail measured the same from point to point, and it weighed about two tons. It was taken to premises adjoining the Bull and Butcher in Old King Street, Deptford, where it was exhibited on a stand erected for the purpose.

SECTION TWO

CRADLE OF THE NAVY

3

A King of England and a Drunken Czar

"Deptford, navy-building town" – *Alexander Pope*

In Chaucer's time the land between Shooters Hill and London was one long stretch of woodlands and common, covered with gorse and brushwood. The strip of land running down to the river west of Deptford (now Woodpecker Rd) was known as the Woolfacre and was probably an oak forest. There were two settled areas: a fishing village along the banks of the Thames called Deptford Strand and a cluster of houses near the bridge known as Deptford Town or Upper Deptford. For centuries throngs of pilgrims, merchants, soldiers, players and travellers passed through Deptford and some dramatic moments enlivened an otherwise calm and quiet existence on the Dover Road.

Down at the river, shipbuilding was already an important industry by the Middle Ages, providing for an ever-growing merchant trade. Ships were always armed against enemies and pirates. With no separate navy at that time, when it came to defence all kinds of vessels were pressed into service. As early as 1326 local tax-collectors were ordered not to trouble the men of East and West Greenwich since they had sent out ships to serve with the King's Admiral. In the 1420s Henry V's ships, the *Thomas of the Tower* from Wapping and the *Katrine* from Greenwich, were brought to a 'dook' at Deptford for rebuilding. Though the term dock was in common use, these 15th century versions were primitive structures. The vessel would be hauled up

The Royal Dockyard, 1810. Showing the old storehouse with its clocktower (See Epilogue) and the launching slips to the west.

onto the mud of the foreshore and a brushwood and clay fence built behind to keep out the tide during the repair.

In 1513 Henry VIII established the first naval dockyard at Deptford. Henry was born in the royal palace at Greenwich and knew the area well from his trips up the river to London. Crowned at the age of 18, he would have been just 22 years old when he founded the royal dockyard and stores at Deptford Strand and set the future of the little fishing village.

From its foundation growth was so rapid that in less than 40 years the King's Yard at Deptford became the chief Thames dockyard, though it later faced stiff competition from Chatham and in the early 17th century there were plans to abandon the Deptford yard altogether. During the 1620s, however, six large men-of-war were built at Deptford in five years and no one spoke of withdrawal again for 150 years. Royal dockyards, even in peace-time, were the most considerable industrial units in the country.

The Redrith (Rotherhithe) waterside had long been an important landing place below London Bridge and it began to merge with Deptford where much of the expanding population worked in the boatbuilding yards, the docks and the gunpowder mill. The dockyard brought prosperity and fame to Deptford and it set the tone of life there for many centuries. Parish registers from the 1590s onwards suggest that for every person who died in Deptford there were ten who came to the riverfront to get work or join their families. Besides shipwrights came those skilled in, or willing to learn, the many trades of a bustling waterfront town, including a rowdy population of sailors with tales of scurvy, starvation and overcrowding as well as tropical adventures in the lands beyond Deptford's imagination.

Deptford's tenements and lodging-houses overflowed but not all the inmates were related to the sea. Greenwich was Queen Elizabeth's favourite residence and the downmarket fringe of the royal retinue spilled over into Deptford where foreign musicians and minor courtiers waited out their time, dreaming of royal favour.

The King's Yard covered some 30 acres and contained a double wet-dock, three slips for naval vessels, craftsmen's workshops, a storehouse, a double mast pond, timber-sheds and officers' quarters. In early dockyards the timber was usually dumped in the nearest available space and the workforce had to manoeuvre themselves around these huge obstacles created with little or no warning. Since these great timber piles had no means of ventilation, much of the wood would be lost through rotting. Not until 1772 were special seasoning and ventilation techniques introduced.

The timber-sheds were no more than open-sided buildings enclosing a saw pit. A piece of timber was placed across the pit supported by beams. A pair of sawyers with a two-man saw would go to work on it, one in the pit and the other standing above. It was hard work and a normal day lasted from 6am to 6pm. Each man was given an allowance of eight pints of strong beer per day. It is not surprising that drunkenness was a common complaint from officers.

A rope-walk was established at Deptford "replete with all the most up-to-date devices for spinning hemp and making ropes and cables".

Rope was needed in vast quantities for rigging: a 74-gun ship needed a total of around 30 miles of rope. The spinning-houses were an extraordinary shape since they had to be as long as the longest piece of rope needed.

There were sail-lofts at the dockyard, too, and many skilled sail-makers. Tar, pitch, tallow and oils were also needed and thriving trades grew up around these. The earliest anchors were simple baskets of heavy stones but later a class of skilled anchorsmiths emerged in Deptford forging strong iron anchors. Another occupation, now sadly extinct, was concerned with the making, painting and gilding of the figureheads without which no vessel was complete. One of these figureheads, in the shape of a cherub, supports the pulpit at St Nicholas' Church and dates from around 1620.

Some of the greatest shipbuilders of the time worked at Deptford. They included the Pett family, master shipbuilders since the reign of Edward VI. The woodlands they owned in Kent provided timber for the ships and the area is still known as Petts Wood. Peter Pett was master shipwright at Deptford until 1589 and his son Joseph held the same position. Phineas Pett, born at Deptford Strand in 1570, was apprenticed to Richard Chapman who built the *Ark Royal*. Pett went on to work on the preparation of Drake's ship for the Caribbean expedition of 1595. He was the first scientific naval architect and, at his lodgings in Deptford Green, built a huge-scale model of a ship which attracted the attention of the Lord High Admiral, Howard of Effingham. Peter Pett, nephew of Phineas, introduced the fast-sailing warship known as the frigate to the English Navy.

Another Deptford shipbuilder was the pious Jonas Shish who, according to John Evelyn, used to kneel in his own coffin every night to pray, though Pepys called him "illiterate, low-spirited, of little appearance or authority". His ships included the *Loyal London* which was sunk by Dutch fireships in the River Medway in 1667. Jonas trained many of his children in boatcraft and his son succeeded him as one of Deptford's master shipwrights.

Corruption was rife in the dockyards and remained so for many centuries. Wages for ordinary shipwrights were low though food and lodging allowances were provided. For master shipwrights there were many supplements to the basic shilling a day. Early in the reign of Charles I England was at war with Spain and France and, as the wars dragged on and the government coffers ran dry, the dockyards fell into chaos. The unpaid men stripped the ships and storehouses of anything they could eat or sell or burn for fuel. Accusations and rumour flew about, fed by envy and backbiting. The dominance of the Pett family, who were in control in all the Kentish yards, made one workman witness scared to speak out "for fear of being undone by the kindred". In 1634 Phineas Pett was accused of inefficiency and dishonesty. The charges were dismissed at a hearing before the King and Prince of Wales but it was said that Pett was on his knees throughout the long trial. That same year the storekeeper at Deptford was charged with selling off the stores: he had not been paid for more than 14 years!

The corruption in the dockyard, which continued without halt until its closure in 1869, is shown in the notorious subject of 'chips'. Under Henry

VIII there had been a 'chip-gatherer' to collect the waste fragments of wood. Later the custom grew of allowing the workmen to take broken pieces of wood out of the yards. By 1634 workmen were cutting up timber to make chips, carrying great bundles of them out three times a day, and even building huts to store their plunder. A lighter was seized at Deptford containing 9,000 wooden nails each about 18 inches long. The strong notion of customary rights was clearly expressed when the offender maintained that these were a lawful perk. The authorities tried to meet these practices on their own terms by paying the men a penny a day instead of chips, but they simply took the penny and the chips. The Navy Board was always ready to pay informers but when two Deptford labourers asked for 150 guineas in return for information they were told £25 was enough. The list of abuses in 1729 included drawing lots for sail canvas which could be made into breeches. An informer said he had known 300 yards of canvas at a time to be taken by the master sail-maker. In a sudden search at all the dockyards that year Deptford and Woolwich came out worst and the back doors of officers' houses, which opened directly onto the dockyard, were ordered to be bricked up.

In the year after the Dockyard was established, Henry VIII gave a royal charter to the Guild of Trinity House. This organisation had been founded in 1511 by Thomas Spert as a voluntary association of English mariners, a kind of early trade union. Now it was made official with the aim of "the Reformation of the Navy, lately much decayed by the admission of young men without experience, and of Scots, Flemings and Frenchmen". Skilled pilots were needed to navigate the bigger ships now becoming common through the shallows of the Thames. By mid-16th century Trinity House had the right to license Thames pilots and the duty to keep the river clear of obstructions. Soon markers were erected to help guide boats. The Guild received all the tolls of 'beaconage and buoyage' but it was not until the 1730s that a lightship was established. Eventually Trinity House took over responsibility for the provision of lighthouses all round the English coast.

Thomas Spert was Sailing Master of the ill-fated *Mary Rose*. He transferred in 1513 to control the rigging-out of the new *Henri Grace à Dieu*, possibly the first vessel to be correctly called a battleship. He later skippered the ship which took Henry VIII to his spectacular meeting with François I, King of France, at the Field of the Cloth of Gold in 1520. This meeting earned its name because the competition between the leaders to see who could be most splendid made the humble field in which the conference took place glitter with gold. Henry's banners were painted by Holbein; his clothes were cloth of silver, ribbed with gold and studded with jewels. A prefabricated castle was built of wood and canvas painted to look like brick and stone, with diamond-paned windows and fountains flowing with red, white and claret wine. The shimmer of cloth of gold and silver fell on drunken heaps of vagabonds, ploughmen, labourers and beggars who came from miles around for this greatest of royal shows.

The royal charter had confirmed the Trinity Guild's property held at Deptford, including almshouses beside the Corporation's Hall near St Nicholas' Church. This consisted of 25 almshouses which were later known as Rose Cottages and used for ordinary housing. In 1672 Trinity Hospital was built in Church St on land given by Sir Richard Browne, Evelyn's father-in-law, who became the Master in that year. These 56 apartments for 'decayed seamen' or their widows were demolished in 1877. Although the HQ of the Corporation moved in the 17th century, a grand procession came back to Deptford every Trinity Monday to elect a new council. Landing at Deptford Green they would march to the Hall where the 'Loving Cup' was passed round with finger biscuits, before a trip to St Nicholas' Church for the customary sermon. The Duke of Wellington, Master from 1837, kept up the ceremony but it lapsed soon after his death in 1852. The last Master to be elected in Deptford was Prince Albert, Queen Victoria's husband.

Entrance gate of Trinity almshouses in Deptford Church St, 1871. The Trinity Hospital, as these almshouses were known, was built in 1670 and demolished in 1876. The inscriptions on the tablets either side of the crest refer to a parish paving agreement.

The first recorded royal visit to Deptford appears in the diary of Edward VI (Henry VIII's sickly son). In 1549 Edward went to Deptford to watch a sham fight which marked the appointment of Lord Clinton as Admiral of England. A large ship with a mock castle whose captain and 40 soldiers were dressed in yellow and black was attacked by men in white on four pinnaces using "clods, scuibs, canes of fire, darts and bombardes". The attackers burst through the outer walls of the main ship and forced more than 20 men to leap out and swim in the Thames. Then came a man dressed as the Admiral who attacked the castle and took the captain prisoner.

During Edward's reign the street leading to the yard was paved, having been "so noisome and full of filth that the King's Majesty might not pass to and fro to see the building of his highnesses ships".

The dockyard was the site for the provisioning and launch of most of the English voyages of discovery. Not all of these were exactly successful. Hugh Willoughby set out from Deptford in 1553 for China with three ships. The crews of two of them died from cold and starvation and the last ship crawled into the Russian port of Archangel. Willoughby arrived at Moscow and founded the Muscovy Company but he never made it to China. St Nicholas may be the patron saint of sailors but sometimes the Divine works in mysterious ways!

Internal problems kept the English crown from whole-hearted state support of expeditions until the new-found security and optimism of Elizabeth's long reign and the enthusiasm of Howard of Effingham, her Lord High Admiral. Effingham caught the public imagination as a great hero in commanding the fleet which defeated the Spanish Armada in 1588. He was also involved in the infamous 'singeing of the King of Spain's beard' in 1596 when he and the Earl of Essex crept into Cadiz harbour and set fire to the Spanish fleet. Effingham's house at Deptford Green became the Gun Tavern. In 1807 it was converted for use by a firm of anchorsmiths and later became a private shipbuilding yard.

The most famous of the Elizabethan sea-heroes is Francis Drake whose ship the *Pelican* was renamed the *Golden Hind* on its return to Deptford loaded with treasure after his trip around the globe. Elizabeth came to Deptford Dockyard in April 1581 and dined with Drake aboard the ship. It is now known that his attacks on Spanish ports had escalated political tension between England, Spain and France and that the Queen spoke her mind about this rashness before handing the sword to the French Ambassador who knighted Drake. So many people clambered across the wooden dockyard bridge to see the Queen that it broke and more than a hundred people fell into the river, though no-one was hurt. Drake's career finally ended in 1595 on his Caribbean expedition where he died along with Sir John Hawkins, explorer and Treasurer of the Navy who had lived in the Treasurer's House at Deptford Dockyard.

Elizabeth ordered that the *Golden Hind* be preserved at Deptford and it seems to have remained here for nearly a hundred years as a memorial, eventually becoming a floating snack-bar. A chair made from one of the planks was given to the Bodleian Library at Oxford and is now in the British Museum. The only other remnant is a table known as 'the cupboard' made from a hatch. In 1977 archeologists working from a 17th century Dutch tourist map which marked the location of 'Captain Drackes Schip', began digging into the lawn on the Pepys Estate hoping to find the ship. The chance was a million to one but the dig caught popular imagination and was big news for a while. Now there are new attempts coming from those who believe the *Hind's* final resting place was Deptford Creek. Grand plans to turn the nasty red-brick Skill Centre on Deptford Bridge into a heritage centre may discover something during excavation. It is more likely though that the *Golden Hind* on view as we move into the next century will be a museum reproduction built by heritage centre workers dressed as 16th century dockers. If that brings jobs and visitors to Deptford it will be better than a plank of the original.

On a summer afternoon in 1583 young Thomas Appletree was mucking about with some choirboys in a boat off Deptford showing off his shooting skills. Their fun was cut short when one of his shots struck an oarsman in the Queen's barge less than five feet from Elizabeth herself. Appletree was condemned to hang on the river bank at the scene of the crime but news of his long, tearful speech at the foot of the gallows reached the Queen and the royal pardon was delivered in the nick of time.

In 1589 Sir Walter Raleigh sailed from Deptford with a volunteer crew attracted by his reputation. That same year a less famous privateer, Thomas White, found himself with a strange booty. Capturing two Spanish ships he found them laden not only with chests of quicksilver but with a more unusual cargo – over 2 million 'indulgences'. These were certificates from the Pope forgiving the purchasers for their sins and letting them off the penance. The indulgences scandal had been central to the criticism of the Roman Catholic Church during the Reformation. It was thought that the King of Spain had bought up the load for 300,000 florins in order to sell them to his Mexican subjects for 5 million in gold! Poor White cannot have found much use for them in England: Elizabeth I had been excommunicated by the Pope.

Another seafarer of the time was Captain Edward Fenton whose forlorn attempts to find a north west passage into the south seas brought him into dangerous contact with the Spanish more than once before he settled down at Deptford to regale fellow-seamen (and anyone else who would listen) with his stories in the local pubs.

In 1700 a visitor to Deptford described the inhabitants as 'amphibious creatures' and noted that all the pub signs related to the sea so that the 'salt-water novices' could understand them.

A more successful Elizabethan venture with a base at Deptford was the East India Company whose charter to compete with Dutch traders was awarded at the dawn of the 17th century. Within 6 weeks their first expedition sailed. This company was the last of the Merchant Adventurers. Their ships were built and fitted out at Deptford on land at the Stowage bought with the profits of their first adventure. After 1620 they contracted out to private local yards but they retained their headquarters and large depots in Deptford until 1782 when they transferred to Blackwall. During this time both the incoming cargoes and the job opportunities gave a new importance to Deptford which was developing rapidly.

The 1977 archeological dig did not find the *Golden Hind* but it did turn up some cowry shells used as currency in the African slave trade. An even more unusual piece of cargo was imported in 1732 when "a Tyger at Deptford, on board the *Cadogan* from the East Indies, broke his chain which obliged most of the Sailors on Board to get out of his Way...He jump'd from Ship to Ship and cleared all before him, till a Sawyer belonging to the King's Yard, knocked him down with a Handspike and killed him on the spot".

Another Deptford name which crops up everywhere is that of Samuel Pepys. A close friend of John Evelyn, Pepys was another prolific diary writer. His tremendous energy helped to regenerate the Navy during the 17th century and he was often at Deptford in the course of his work. In 1661 he wrote "...then we put off for Deptford – where we went on board the King's pleasure-boat that Commissioner Pett is making; and indeed, it will be a most pretty thing". Later that year he went with the King by barge to Deptford and on the way back to London, he says "we pulled off our Stockings and bathed our legs a great while in the River".

Pepys had been a civil servant for the Commonwealth during the 1650s. He was sent to France with the fleet that was to bring Charles II home at the Restoration in 1660 and he began work for the Navy Board soon after. James, Duke of York, the King's brother, was appointed Lord High Admiral, but from 1673 he was debarred by Parliament because of his Catholicism. In a plan said to have been suggested by Pepys, Charles II took control himself, setting up a Commission of the Admiralty and appointing Pepys himself to the key position as its Secretary. Working directly under the king, Pepys set about his new task with zest. He achieved epoch-making results in founding a professional officer class, constructing a larger navy and bringing in a new sense of discipline and purpose.

In 1679, under pressure from the Whig opposition in Parliament, the King dismissed his Commissioners and their Secretary, replacing them with a board of Whig politicians and "sporting himself with their ignorance" according to Pepys. In 1684, once the political crisis known as the 'Popish Plot' had died down, Charles resumed control and appointed Pepys as 'Secretary for the affairs of the Admiralty', a high-level post no-one ever held before or since. During the reign of James II the Navy Board was replaced by Pepys' own Special Commission. Though Pepys began his official career at the dockyards by learning the multiplication table he became one of the most remembered men of the 17th century and his legacy was a naval power unmatched anywhere in the world. It is a fitting tribute that when the pressures of the Napoleonic Wars forced the Navy Board to reform its procedures in 1805 eighteen volumes of Pepys' naval papers were borrowed for consultation.

In 1670 Pepys was concerned about security at the dockyard. He explained to the King that between the end of the working day and the setting of the watch and again in the morning after the watch retired but before the workers arrived, the dockyard's safety was committed to two Look-Outs. He complained that "many doubts arise upon discovery of Stores imbezled whether the said imbezlements were made in the tyme for which the Look-Outs were answerable or that of the Watch and...it has been very difficult...to discover upon which of the two justly to charge the neglect". Pepys' proposal to extend the watch to cover the extra hours was approved by the King and the Look-Outs were laid off. Despite such attempts to improve the security and efficiency of the yard malpractice remained a fact of dock life. Perhaps we should consider it a kind of 'social crime'. When workers' wages were a year or 18 months in arrears it is hardly surprising that they stole supplies and chips of wood to keep the home fires burning.

Pepys' cousin, Thomas, had leased the manor of Hatcham for less than £3,000, but it is unlikely that Samuel visited often since he found his cousin "a sorry dull fellow...without a turd (sic) of kindness or service to be had from him". He is known in the Diary as 'the Executor' and 'Hatcham Pepys'. The family name is preserved throughout the area including the Pepys Estate, Pepys Rd and, until the 1980s, Samuel Pepys School on the far side of Telegraph Hill.

In 1691 Mary Evelyn wrote to her husband with the suggestion that their good friend, Samuel Pepys, may wish for a country residence and could take Sayes Court when they retired to Surrey. She remarked "he should be preferred to any other for his neatness and friendship". This did not work out and the manor house passed to Draper, their son-in-law, when they left Deptford in 1694.

The tenants Draper found were grand enough for the house, but far from the Evelyn ideal of 'polite'. The first was Captain John Benbow who had his own house in Hughes Fields but stayed at Sayes Court for some months. Later, as Vice-Admiral Benbow, he was shot in the leg during a three-day skirmish with a French squadron while protecting the British colonies in the West Indies. He continued to command the action from a hammock slung on the quarter-deck and he lasted long enough to court-martial the officers who had deserted him during the battle.

The second of the Sayes Court tenants was Peter the Great, Czar of Russia. As a child Peter had found a 100 year old English boat long-forgotten among his father's foreign stores. He became hooked on ship-craft and it remained the love of his life, though he later boasted that he was proficient in 14 trades. In 1697 Peter left his country in the hands of a committee and set off on his 'Great Embassy' around Europe to study techniques which would help to modernise the Russian empire. No Czar had ever been outside Muscovy before and Stalin, who also put much energy into westernising Russia, labelled Peter's reign "a peculiar attempt to jump out of the framework of backwardness".

Peter went first to Amsterdam where he worked in the shipyard and took the proper cultured tourist trips to lectures and laboratories, mills and museums. He even visited van Leeuvonhoek who had invented the microscope. While in Holland Peter met William of Orange who had gained the English crown in 1688. William invited the Czar to London where he rented Sayes Court. In an early version of the 'Spinal Tap' nightmare, Peter's cronies behaved like a rock band on tour. Evelyn's servant wrote to his master at Wooton: "There is a house full of people *right nasty*. The Czar lies next [to] your library, and...is very seldom at home a whole night."

Peter and his mates used portraits for target practice and Evelyn's favourite holly hedge – a great shimmering barrier about 400 feet long,

The Grand CZAR of Moscovy.

R. White sculpsit 1698.

nine feet high and five feet wide – was spoiled by the Czar's habit of trundling a wheelbarrow through it daily for exercise (or, in other stories, having his men race him through it in a wheelbarrow for entertainment late on drunken nights!). These stories came to light after Benbow, worried that he would get charged for the damage, petitioned the Lords of the Treasury for a survey. The King's Surveyor at the time was none other than Sir Christopher Wren whose estimate of the total damages came to over £350 and included "3 wheelbarrows broke and Lost...Eight Fether beds and twelve pair of blanketts very much dirtyed and spoyled". Wren was helped by George London, the King's Gardener, who observed that "during the time the Zar of Muscovie inhabited the said house, several disorders have been committed in the gardens". Mr London's tone is very disapproving of "his Zarrish" and his list includes the comment: "All the grass worke is out of order, and broke into holes by their leaping and shewing tricks upon it." A Treasury warrant of 1698 paid Evelyn damages for the house and gardens and Benbow for his own damaged goods.

During his time at Deptford, Peter's greatest delight was to take out a small boat with a few of his men as practice for them to command the navy he had planned for back home. After the day's work they would resort to a pub near Tower Hill to smoke pipes and drink beer and brandy, before rolling back to Deptford for the wheelbarrow games. Peter did learn some skills at the dockyard and one of the yard's journeyman shipwrights, who was a young man at the time of the visit, insisted that "the Tzar of Muscovy worked with his own hands as hard as any man in the yard". It is said that William Penn, the Quaker founder of Pennsylvania, visited Sayes Court and that his quiet manner persuaded Peter to attend services at the Quaker Meeting House in Butt Lane (Deptford High St) "where he conducted himself with great decorum and condescension, changing seats, and sitting down and standing up as he could best accommodate others." A plaque remains on the site of the old meeting house (demolished 1907) as a memorial of this uncharacteristic sobriety.

4

Deptford and the Ducking Stool

"We all came out of the parsley bed" – *John Evelyn*

Although Deptford's connection with the Thames was fundamental, the town was never only water-based. 17th century Deptford stretched southwards along the river terrace hillock whose sides are marked by Church St and Butt Lane (Deptford High St). Passing through fields and market gardens, these straggling lanes joined Deptford Broadway, a triangular country green on the London side of Deptford Bridge. Around the Broadway were riverside meadows and osier-beds of willows used for basket-making. From the Broadway, Mill Lane followed the Creek further before ending abruptly beside the Brook Mill. On Lewisham High Rd (now Lewisham Way) huge rabbit warrens were maintained and the royal buck-hounds were kennelled in Dog Kennel Row (Friendly St). When James I visited the area, the dockyard workers were contemptuous of his obvious preference for hunting rather than ships.

At the head of Deptford Green and giving its name to Church Street stood the ancient parish church of St Nicholas, the 'Westminster Abbey of the Navy'. The church certainly dates back to the 12th century: the right to choose its vicar was granted by Countess Juliana de Vere to the White Canons around 1183. The lower part of the tower is the oldest portion of the present church, possibly dating from the early 15th century. The rest was pulled down in 1697 and what Evelyn called "a pretty new church" was built on the site. It is likely that all the seafarers mentioned in the last chapter would have prayed at St Nicholas', also known as 'The Admirals' Church', before setting out on their voyages. Certainly Trinity Monday celebrations always included a sermon at the church.

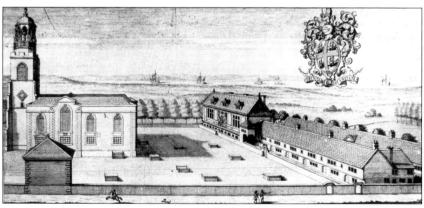

St Nicholas' church from the Stowage with Trinity House (demolished 1786) and the old Trinity almshouses to the east. This is the oldest known view of the church. The belltower on the summit disproves the theory that St Nicholas' used to have a beacon to guide ships in the area.

In early January 1837 a strange petition appeared on walls all around old Deptford. It came from the Bells of St Nicholas imploring the parishioners to rescue them from their "ruthless oppressor", Churchwarden Godwin. It seems that Godwin had removed the "graceful appendages which formed the line of communication between us and our Harmonic Friends the Trinity Youths", ie. the bell-ropes. The ropes must be saved from "the

Degrading contamination of any DEALER IN OLD JUNK" which may well have been Godwin's occupation since the petition goes on to say "the period is fast approaching when our Oppressor must sink into his original sphere and his brief Authority expire". This emotional plea ended "from our Soundless, Ropeless, Silent Tower of St Nicholas". A vestry meeting, called by the other churchwarden, Godfrey Hill (who must have been the Bells' ghost-writer), resolved that Godwin had acted outrageously in preventing "the Ancient Custom of Ringing in and out the Old and New Year" and that the ropes were to be returned immediately.

While riverfront Deptford was protected by St Nicholas, the patron saint of seafarers, it was St Christopher who succoured the footsore travellers on the Dover Road. The oldest hostelry in the area, surviving uninterrupted from at least 1400 to 1990, was the Christopher Inn on the northern side of the Broadway. The building was bought from the vicar of West Greenwich and Robert atte Wood of Deptford by two masons, Henry Yevele and John Clifford. Yevele built Westminster Hall and has been described as 'the Wren of the 14th century'. Both were bridge wardens for the Bridge House Estates, the organisation responsible for London Bridge whose lands in Deptford and Lewisham helped to pay for maintenance of the Bridge.

In 1460 Ralph Reynold was paid to paint the pub sign and 80 years later John Heyth, painter, received 16 shillings and 8 pence for "a great signe of Saynt Xpofer with a crosse beam and the sparres to the same for the Inn at Deptforde". A local chalk man was paid 6 pence for transporting the posts and beams for the sign by water.

In 1463 the publican was William Fox but, in debt to the Bridge House by 15 shillings, he departed suddenly one night leaving nothing behind. The Christopher was a sizeable inn with two stables, a hayloft, a barn and two garden plots. Its perfect position on the road to London provided excellent travelling trade but the appropriate name – St Christopher is the patron saint of travellers – was lost when it became the Castle in 1675. In 1757 it was renamed the Dover Castle and the following year the landlady, Mrs Seabrooke, married another local publican.

In September 1990 the Dover Castle blew up. The details of this tragedy are difficult to discover, though conspiracy theories abound. At least it allowed archeologists a perfect digging spot and the Saxon 'cemetery' that they unearthed is considered by the Museum of London to be a major discovery, the first to be found so close to the city.

West from the Broadway along New Cross Rd one came soon to Wolfacre Lane (Clifton Rise/Woodpecker Rd) This ancient woodland had long ago been plundered for timber by shipwrights, gunsmiths, blacksmiths, glass and pottery makers. Since around 2,000 oak trees were required to build a 74-gun wooden ship, the old forests met their doom in this 'navy-building town'. Between 1619 and 1665 the 120 acres of sloping woodland of southern Hatcham disappeared almost completely. With its home supplies exhausted, timber by the thousand tons came to Deptford from far and wide.

Wolfacre Lane joined Deptford Road (Evelyn St) near the present Deptford Park and the land to the east was the Broomefield, bounded by Loveing Edwards Lane in the south. Nearer the river, south west of the King's Dockyard, the Sayes Court mansion, expanded and

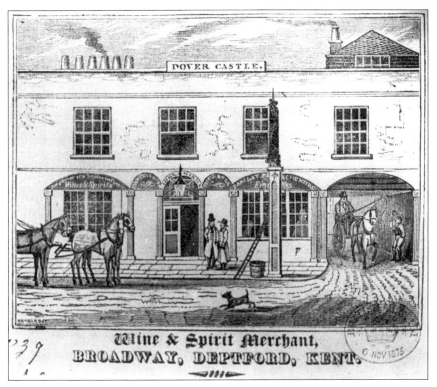

DOVER CASTLE.

Wine & Spirit Merchant,
BROADWAY, DEPTFORD, KENT.

partially rebuilt by Evelyn in the second half of the 17th century, stood proudly in beautiful gardens for which their owner was justly famous. The house was interesting enough for Charles II to insist on seeing every room when he visited in 1663 and Evelyn continued to add to it, but the gardens were his lifelong pride and joy.

Evelyn's idea of a complete garden included knotted flower-beds, herb-gardens, trellis-work, parterres, compartments, borders, banks and embossments, labyrinths, cabinets, cradles, close-walks, galleries, pavilions, porticos, lanterns and other relievos of topiary and horticultural architecture, fountains, water-jets, cascades, pools, rocks, grottos, mounts, precipes and ventiducts, gaxon-theatres, artificial echoes, automato and hydraulic music. He accepted that "it would still require the revolution of many ages with deep and long experience, for any man to emerge a perfect and accomplished artist-gardener". For a man who had changed a 'rude' orchard and rough pasture into a landscaped park – with a glass beehive built to resemble a city, an aviary where birds seemed to fly free, carp ponds and bowling greens – this was great modesty. He saw a garden as a place "the most resembling Heaven" and his work is littered with such phrases as "A garden is the pit from which we were all dug; we all came out of the parsley bed".

Evelyn's time as lord of the manor fully met his own brief to provide a sorely-needed friend to the parish. He was a stockholder for the East India Company, a Trustee of Addey's Charity and he may have worked with Henry Wise who laid out the avenues in Greenwich Park. He contributed toward the reconstruction of New Cross Rd in 1671 and the rebuilding of St Nicholas' Church in 1697. During the plague year of 1665, when 406 Deptfordians died, he arranged for large hulks to be bought and anchored off Greenwich to isolate the sick. After the Great Fire the following year he prospected in the fields near Lewisham Way for suitable brickmaking clays to rebuild the City of London. Towards the end of his life he drained the outlying parts of his estate, planning the lines of road and letting off building plots for development. Though he left Deptford in 1694 he retained his interest until he died on 27th February 1706 at the grand old age of 85.

Another of Evelyn's achievements was the discovery of the wood-carver Grinling Gibbons (1648-1721). Evelyn met him by accident while walking near a poor solitary thatched house in a field near Sayes Court. "Looking in at the window I perceived him carving that large...crucifix of Tintoretto. I asked if I might enter: he opened the door civilly to me and I saw him about such work as for the curiosity of handling, drawing and studious exactness, I never had before seen in all my travels". Asked why he worked in such an "obscure and lonesome place" Gibbons replied that there he might work in peace. Evelyn spoke to the King about this new-found genius and Gibbons was introduced at court. He started carving in marble and was soon put to work decorating the royal palaces, St Paul's Cathedral and the chapel at Windsor Castle. It is thought that the reredos screen at St Nicholas' Church, and possibly the wood carving of *Ezekiel in the Valley of the Dry Bones*, which once guarded the St Nicholas' Charnel House, are the work of this famous carver.

Now we must leave the lord of the manor and begin to reconstruct the everyday Deptford of the early modern period. A rather sarcastic view of Deptford is provided by a pamphlet of 1700 called *A Frolick to Horn Fair (Charlton)*. It describes the houses as wooden dens "all of one form, as if they were obliged by Act of Parliament to all build after the same model". There were many shops but the stores were limited to "a few apples in a cabbage net, a peelfull of Deptford cheesecakes, an old waste-coat, a thrum cap and a pair of yarn mittings". The conclusion was harsh: "The town's without necessaries, they've butchers without meat, ale houses without drink, houses without furniture, and shops without trade, captains without commission...a church without religion."

Although work on the docks and auxillary trades provided for a great deal of Deptford's employment, other industries included brickmaking, leather and metal-working and brewing. Of all the industries away from the Thames, farming and market gardening were the most important. Deptford was famous for its onions, celery and asparagus. At Brockley, Myatt's Manor Farm grew the first rhubarb ever to appear at Covent Garden and the achievement was commemorated centuries later when a railway siding in Trundleys Lane was known as Rhubarb Siding. Kent was becoming the 'Garden of England' and the riverside gravels were manured and intensely cultivated. Many gardeners worked rented plots and imported "dunge and noysommes" by river from London. These 'gardeners' were really small farmers growing parsnips, turnips and carrots. Their success relied on easy access to markets, cheap London labour and pumped Thames water. The potato was introduced into Thames-side gardens at the end of the 16th century though it was nearly a hundred years before it caught on further afield.

For many years there was a flower called the Deptford Pink, but its story is not easy to discover and in 1993 a row was brewing between two local gardeners. After a 14-year search John Dolding had found some of the precious five-petalled flowers in Holland and shipped home some seeds. Rival gardener Roy Ramsey called this stubby little plant "a weedy imposter", insisting that the real Deptford Pink is a large pink carnation, perfect for a buttonhole. Sources supporting both arguments are available. The LCC Souvenir Guide for the opening of Deptford Park in 1897 describes the Deptford Pink as a meadow flower, the *caryophyllus pratensis*, named because it grew so abundantly in the area's fields. The *Official Borough Guide* for 1951 asserts that when Deptford Council created the Municipal Playing Fields on three acres near Deptford Bridge in 1931 no less than 150,000 of the flowers were growing there. The *Guide* explains that the land by the bridge was used until the 1920s as a nursery which gave the name 'Deptford' or 'Simpson's Pink' to a type of carnation. Further research, please...

Poor chalkland sheep were fattened on drained marshland at Deptford for the 'cutting butchers'. Hay was sent by water from Deptford to the cow-keeping areas of inner South London. Birds, fishponds and pigsties added to the agricultural mix in the area. When Arthur Young, the Secretary for Agriculture, toured the south east counties in the 1770s he chided Deptford's common farmers as "very great slovens" and was disgusted by the weeds in the fields but small farming remained an important occupation, maintaining both self-sufficiency and a good reputation at the London markets. In 1800 there were still 500 acres of market gardens in the area.

View of Deptford from New Cross Rd with Mr Emmett's market garden in the foreground. The London & Greenwich railway and the two churches of St Nicholas and St Paul can also be seen.

Some seasonal employment was available in carting crops to the city markets, transporting dung to Deptford Creek and harvesting greens. Sea-fishing was one of the most dangerous occupations in the area and many pauper boys were apprenticed into this business, never to be seen again.

One of the best ways to reconstruct the everyday lives of 17th century Deptfordians is through the study of crime and punishment. This is not because Deptford was a town full of crooks but because these records can give us an outline of community life. Studying crime takes us close to the core of some fundamental aspects of our ancestors' lives.

In 1688 the Justices of the Peace (JPs) at the West Kent Quarter

Sessions ordered a Ducking Stool to be provided at Deptford "for the correcting and well governing of idle, lewd and disorderly scolding women and others". The parishes of Deptford and Greenwich were said to contain "contentious and brawling women...that are very vexatious and troublesome to the rest of their honest and quiet and peaceable neighbours". The Stool was to be set up at Deptford Bridge and both parishes were to pay equally for it.

Here we have dropped right into the complex web of community relations. The first thing to remember is that the 'honest, quiet neighbours' are simply a figment of legal writing: these 'contentious and brawling' women were not the only people causing trouble in Deptford. The second point is that 'scolding' is a minor offence, but a very important one in terms of community life. Scolding was stereo-typically a woman's crime: physical violence was thought of as masculine, verbal violence as feminine, though there were plenty of women who disproved that distinction. The 17th century has been seen as a time of rising anti-feminism and increasing concern with the idea of 'masterlessness'. Unmarried women were like vagrants, a danger to the Great Chain of Being which preserved divine and natural order through a series of deferential power relations modelled on the domestic unit in which a man controlled his wife, his children and his servants/apprentices. If man could not control woman how was the social order itself to be maintained?

Like witchcraft, scolding is a crime of its period but it is comparable to the kinds of 'nuisance neighbour' offences we are familiar with today. Deptford would certainly be a different kind of place if the Ducking Stool remained on the bridge now. If this seems an attractive idea to those troubled by local 'nuisance' of one kind or another, we should bear in mind that such punishments require a shared sense of what neighbourliness and good behaviour actually mean. Such 'community sanctions' depend on a local willingness to mind each other's business which goes against our modern desire for privacy.

Scolding is linked to another offence which deserves attention: defamation. When we think of libel cases today they seem mainly to centre on famous celebrities and the newspapers and the huge sums of money involved distance such cases from the lives of ordinary people. In the 17th century, by contrast, most defamation cases were brought to court by ordinary women who felt that their reputations had been damaged by harsh words, usually in a public quarrel with another woman. This is an indication of one of the main changes in attitudes to the law over the past 300 years. Nowadays we try to avoid the law as much as possible: in the 17th century, though the penalties for many crimes were far greater, the lesser courts could be and were used much more readily by ordinary people. Indeed some took this to extremes and persistent legal action over trivial matters could be as disruptive to community life as the wilful spreading of rumour.

The Ducking Stool, along with the stocks, cage and whipping post, was part of a range of more or less informal sanctions available in the early modern period. The colourful medieval custom of Rough Ridings or *charivari*, which continued into this period, allowed locals to express their contempt for hen-pecked husbands or unruly wives with a complicated performance in which the victim (or a model of them) was placed backwards on a donkey, dressed as the opposite sex, and

The site of the old stocks and cage. Norfolk and Sons Brewery, 1890s. In earlier times the Ducking Stool was off to the left on Deptford Bridge. The building with the bay front faced Gardiners store at the east end of the Broadway on the junction with Mill Lane. The Brewery occupied a large area on this corner. It was also known as Norfolk House, after Thomas Norfolk the last brewer before 1909 when the brewery was replaced by shops. The Deptford Distillery, which can be seen in the background, survived for decades in the hands of the gin firm Seagers but has now been converted to light industrial units.

paraded through the streets accompanied by 'rough music' and much jeering.

Pepys described an example of this in 1667: "took boat and down to Greenwich where I find the stairs full of people, there being a great Riding there today for a man, the constable to the town, whose wife beat him". So busy were the spectators humiliating their local officer that Pepys had great trouble finding a waterman to take him down to Woolwich on important Navy business.

The option of such community-based methods of control allowed the parish to display a fair amount of tolerance before setting in motion the actual processes of law against a local person. Even in cases of theft, witchcraft or persistent nuisance, attempts would be made by the parish priest, an employer or the local constables to persuade the offenders to change their ways, before they were finally irritated into prosecution at the Quarter Sessions. The situation was quite different for outsiders. One study has shown that not only were locals less likely to get to court at all, but that once there only 68% of them were convicted, compared to 93% of outsiders. The reaction against the vagrant thief was swift and merciless throughout England. Deptford's large size and its position on the Dover Road made it an inevitable target for the opportunist thief, the begging traveller or the soldier returning unpaid and hungry from foreign wars.

It is the petty offences which furnish best our historical reconstruction. Their range is enormous: from infringing the customs and bye-laws of the manor to theft and violence. Presentments to the local courts were concerned with breaking pinfolds (animal pens) to rescue impounded livestock, failing to keep hedges in repair or allowing swine to stray into a neighbour's garden. Others dealt with affrays and bloodsheds, theft of firewood, keeping disorderly houses, harbouring vagrants and other undesirables, scolding, defamation and poaching. Many of these offences against neighbourhood standards would result in a fine. Some had more specific punishments like the Ducking Stool.

The Quarter Sessions courts were used to crack down on disorderly or anti-social behaviour. In 1703 forty-one Deptford people, ranging from carpenters to gentlemen, were presented at the Maidstone Quarter Sessions for 'not watching', that is for failing to take up their duty in keeping the night guard from the watch-house on the Broadway. Other Deptford offenders included Mary Adams 'for a common whore', William Vince and John Hocketshaw as 'common drunkards' and four presentments of 'common disturbers'. Six people were presented for keeping disorderly houses and one for having 'inmates' (illegal lodgers). Four women, two of them sailors' wives, were presented for assault and John Kither, one of the sheriff's bailiffs, found trouble at the Allen household when he was assaulted by four of the men. A couple of Deptford men were involved in a 'ryott and forcible entry' at Otford but most of the presentments were much more low-key. Thomas Fleming, a local cow-keeper, was presented for not clearing the ditch from Deptford to Counterhill (the northern part of Lewisham Way). William Chapman was a 'profaner of the Sabbath'.

Throughout the 17th century there was much concern about disorderly alehouses. The tradition of hospitality which inns provided to travellers had been extended to feed workers who could not get home for dinner (hence ploughman's lunches), but many law-enforcers were aware that alehouses had become an important part of popular culture. Alcohol played many roles. Beer was a staple nutritional necessity for "poore labouring people, without which they cannot well subsist, their food being for the most part of such things as afford little or bad nourishment". Not only did alehouse keepers serve the poor, they were frequently poor themselves. Many were widows and an alehouse licence could serve as a pension. Occasional ale-selling could form a kind of aid system blending economics, mutual assistance and festivity. Drinkings were sometimes held to raise money for a needy neighbour, although these could result in a prosecution for unlicensed ale-selling if the local officers were hostile.

Drink was a vital part of social life. It warmed the blood, dulled hunger and fatigue and contributed to good-fellowship. Drunkenness was generally tolerated not only at specific occasions like fairs, baptisms or funerals but also on informal occasions such as when an argument had been settled. Given the low standards of comfort in domestic houses and the gradual loss of other recreations (see below), the alehouse was a central meeting place.

A ballad called *The Deptford Plumb Cake* or *The Four Merry Wives*, dating from around 1700 begins:
  Come all you sweet lips, round me stand
  With each some Plumb Cake in her hand
  and Cup of good napping Ale.
It describes, with much innuendo, how four wives took a fancy to a young mealman's servant and planned to bake him a good plumb cake for which he sent them 11 pounds of plumbs, a peck and a half of flour, seven pounds of butter and plenty of sugar. When it was made one of the wives asked:
  Come Neighbours where shall we it take
  and have our young Ned today?
One suggestion was a local pub on the south side of the Broadway, still standing today:

What if we to the Fountain go,
and there have our merry bout?
Fie, fie, one of the Wives did cry,
Our Husbands will find us out.

They decide to avoid the pubs and get some take-out liquor instead. The end of the story, which has the thunder-god Vulcan smiting the Cake with his Hammer, is a little confused but it concludes:

Yet Ned did all the Wives command,
and play'd Boys at up tails all.

The anxiety among the 'middling sort' about alehouses was part of a larger change in this period which is usually known as 'stratification'. Village life had previously involved the whole community from the squire to the pauper. Increasingly during the 17th century a gulf was opening up between the 'well-affected' and the ordinary commoners. The upper levels of village and town society were becoming more identified with the gentry and ultimately the State.

This growing gulf can be seen in the changing attitudes to communal festivities which had previously been important moments of solidarity within the village or town. As the 'higher sort' began to take on the ideals of Puritanism, such customs were seen as demeaning to their dignity and morally harmful (especially when they involved large quantities of beer and revelry or took place on a Sunday). Attacks on customs like the 'church ale' (for which the churchwardens provided barrels of beer in the churchyard) meant that the alehouses were bound to take on a greater not lesser role. The fate of another very old custom during this period is a prime example of the changes underway. Rogation-tide had been a time when every parishioner old enough to walk had made a circuit of their parish led by the parish priest. In an age when even ordinary houses were known by names and had picture signs like pubs, with few signposts and fewer people who could read them, Rogation was a way of getting to know the local landmarks. Yet during the 17th century the procession became limited to property owners and became a confirmation not of community but of property (although it was later revived in a more jovial manner, (Ch.8).

It was not only communal festivals which came under attack. As early as 1541 a statute prohibited "tables, tennis, dice, cards, bowls" except for the élite. Puritans denounced such games along with other popular recreations such as "bull-baiting and bear-baiting, dancing, drunkenness and whoredom". Their success in eradicating such entertainments was limited. Deptford police were shocked to find cock-fighting and bare–knuckle boxing on the greens of Crossfield Estate in the early 1970s.

Parliamentary legislation was giving JPs far wider powers as well as turning customary behaviour into crime. Alehouse keepers came under attack on all sides for petty offences like failing to attend church, sexual misdemeanors or allowing gatherings on Sunday. Other statutes laid down punishments for hedge-breaking (for firewood), gleaning (picking up leftover corn after the harvest) and scrumping (collecting fallen apples from orchards) which had all been ways the poor managed to eke out a living. In earlier times landowners had budgeted as much as £40 per year for such losses and seen them as normal. Now the offender could be whipped and placed in the stocks. Some laws simply did not have the respect of local people. This was a bitter struggle over alternative definitions of property and the rights of central authorities to interfere with the careful balance of order maintained on the local level. The crucial importance of popular participation in the capture of criminals and the workings of the legal system (Ch.6), gave such struggles over the definition of 'crime' a very practical aspect alongside their ideological force. For example, many smugglers even in the 18th century did not see any harm in their work. Smuggling in Deptford and elsewhere was well organised and enjoyed widespread popular support.

Smugglers' wares ranged from tea and coffee to brandy and lace. In 1772 a milkman with a pair of pails was stopped by a Custom House officer on Deptford Rd. On investigation, the pails turned out to have false bottoms hiding more than £200 worth of French lace. These early customs officers faced great dangers in their work. One was murdered in 1776 by four Deptford labourers and a few years earlier two were seriously wounded in a fight with a gang of smugglers in Deptford Rd. Three of the smugglers and two horses were killed.

The ultimate social effect of the Reformation and the establishment of the Protestant religion was divisive, reinforcing the latent notion of poverty as sin. The Civil War, with its breakdown of censorship and social control, made religion a political issue on the local level. Meanwhile, though the quality of the clergy was improving, the more 'professional' they became the further they moved from that familiarity with local custom and tradition which had been the strength of the medieval priesthood and would only return with some of the 19th century city missions.

At the very top of the social order and among old-fashioned conservatives there were different priorities. They believed that such divisions within localities increased tensions in the parish and alienated the lower orders. With this in mind, the King issued a proclamation called the *Book of Sports* (1618 and 1633) laying down that such customary sports should be allowed since they provided recreation which kept up the nation's strength and an opportunity for the relief of discord between neighbours.

Although historians have shown that pre-industrial societies were far more mobile than was once thought, the problem of 'settlement' was crucial to community welfare. Whatever the reality, there was an ideology of stability which meant that the parish where you were born was the only place in which you could officially receive poor relief. It was where you had the rights of 'settlement'. An Act of Parliament of 1662 gave parishes the power to remove newcomers. Elderly or single women, and men with large families, were often singled out. In 1719 the St Nicholas' vestry noted that "sundry persons intrude themselves into diverse parishes as inmates or as renting houses under £10 pa... To prevent this growing evil such persons who harbour them will be liable to prosecution". Particularly troublesome to the parish were "young women who live with their friends, who take alms and do nothing to maintain themselves".

The settlement certificate had become a guarantee of security and astute methods were sometimes used to obtain one. For example

Sarah Brown, who was lodging with a Deptford lady, Elizabeth Martin, pretended to be married to her lover Michael Gamball. Gamball's wife testified at court that her husband went often to Elizabeth's house to 'live incontinently' with Sarah Brown who had no legal settlement. The court were doubly concerned by this case because if Sarah had become pregnant any child born in the parish would have had legal rights of settlement there.

Illegitimate children were likely to become a charge on the poor-rate. This economic motive, combined with a religious ideology with strict notions about 'orderly sex', lay behind some very cruel behaviour. In 1727 the parish of St Nicholas paid a waterman to "carry out of town...a big-bellied woman almost ready to lye in, she having two children with her". If an unmarried local woman fell pregnant her neighbours would do their utmost to discover the father's identity since he could be forced to pay maintenance, keeping the single-parent family off the poor-rate. This explains the willingness of neighbours to mind each other's business, including sexual activities, as well as the disapproval and harsh treatment of 'fornicators'.

The new social world created by these gradual changes will be explored further in the section on Expansion. Both of Deptford's workhouses were built in the 18th century but it is the Victorian version of the institution which remains in the modern mind. Although an increasing gulf between the poor and the 'middling sort' can be traced over this period, new forms of social control took many decades to develop.

Ghosts of Deptford – past and present

The first record of ghostly happenings in Deptford comes from an anonymous pamphlet published in 1673 titled *A True Relation of a Ghost at Deptford*. The author begins by advising "let us not, for a little transitory pleasure here on earth...give ourselves over to such sensual, libidinous and vicious living here" or we will become woeful fellows of this ghost. It is an old idea, found in Dickens' *Christmas Carol,* that the soul cannot rest because of its earthly misbehaviour, but nowadays we tend to think of ghosts as more sinned against than sinning. The ghost of a handsome woman appeared first at the Three Mariners near the King's Yard. Appropriately enough it was seen by three sailors from "the good ship call'd the Monk". On the next night the woman appeared again causing great confusion, especially when her icy fingers touched the face of one of the sailors and he was "flung off the Bed, Heels over Head the length of two Yards". A doctor was called but his blood-letting remedy cannot have done much to help the poor man who "looks very ghastly". Soon the ghostly woman began to appear to the rest of the household, once in a black hood, again in a white sheet, once causing the dog to cower at her feet, another time leaning against a post looking grim. The pamphlet ends unable to explain "whom she represents, nor the cause of it" but leaving her as "your real Example to moderate your Deeds and Actions in this life".

In 1809 there was a new ghost at Deptford which appeared under the Quaker Meeting House in Butt Lane. The watchman whose duties took him near the spot had seen "a certain Gentleman, who had recently been buried, rise from his tomb and heard him, with the good humoured tone for which he was distinguished, call for a pot of beer and invite the watchman to share it with him". The next night two colleagues joined the watch and all three saw and heard the same thing. The story was told to the magistrate and created "no small bustle and apprehension throughout the neighbourhood". Unfortunately I have not been able to discover the identity of the 'certain Gentleman'. He sounds a very amiable ghost!

Later Deptford ghost haunts include the transport cafe between the Odeon and the Lady Florence Institute on Deptford Broadway. Phyllis Lennard, who worked at the cafe in the 1970s, remembers one room at the very top that was "always icy cold, summer or winter. I used to make the beds up there for overnight drivers. This driver was coming up the stairs in front of me. He walked into the room and then all of a sudden he came flying out backwards and all the colour just drained out of his face. He said, 'somebody just pushed me'. He was terrified. He collected his luggage and he left."

Just as frightened was Mary Amanze who lived next door to an empty house in Albury St in the mid-1970s. She had been told that the house next door had been used by Nelson for his affair with Lady Hamilton. Sadly, there is no evidence to support this or any other story relating Nelson to Deptford. However, for Mrs Amanze that was little consolation. Lying in bed she would hear people talking in the attic and walking up and down the stairs. The handle of a door connecting the two houses would turn from the other side and there was a spooky gravestone embedded in the garden wall, so old that the inscription was worn away. Mrs Amanze's three Alsatian dogs refused to go anywhere near the basement of the 250 year old house and her eldest daughter left home after hearing a horse galloping on a cobbled street outside.

5

A Pearl in the Biscuit Bin

"an ornament to ye town and a credit to ye nation"
– Sir John Vanbrugh

Back at the river things were going well. Long-established as a major port town and so close to London, Deptford was now to become the centre for the provision of the Royal Navy and many private ships. This role would continue long after shipbuilding itself became impossible in the area. The Victualling Yard on the site of the old Red House warehouses by Grove St did not close until 1961.

There were storehouses at Deptford from the 15th century onwards and it was an early centre for naval storage. The original date of the Red House is not known but a building of this name was burnt down in July 1639. It was rebuilt in 1665, on land from the Sayes Court estate, by Sir Henry Cranden who was the private contractor responsible for victualling the Fleet. The silting up of the Thames near London Bridge and the increasing size of merchant ships made moorings near the naval dockyard at Deptford the most economic point for transfer of goods. Now that the new Red House could act as a central warehouse, Deptford had everything a merchant or sea captain could need.

View near the Red House, Deptford, 1770. These old Thames-side storehouses were rebuilt by Sir Henry Cranden in 1665 and became the navy's official Victualling Yard in 1742 giving their name to the hard Red House Biscuits which formed the staple diet of sailors.

The dockyards, both royal and merchant, were a magnet for men seeking work. Deptford's population increased rapidly between the 1660s and 1710 when the churchwardens of St Nicholas estimated it at 12,000 people (2,300 families). Most of the immigrants were dockworkers and their families and apprentices.

In 1724 Daniel Defoe, author of *Robinson Crusoe*, noted that "several villages formerly standing as it were in the country" had begun to be swamped and "the docks and building yards on the riverside between the town of Deptford and the streets of Redriff or Rotherhithe are effectually joined and the buildings daily increasing".

The official victualling depot was established by the Navy Board just upstream from the Royal Dockyard in 1742. At this stage biscuit baking was the primary occupation though it would later expand into providing the fleet with pickled meat, rum, clothing and other supplies. By 1756 it had 60 employees ranging from Measurer of Bran & Small Coal to Senior Pastryman.

Biscuit Baking.

The dough, just flour and water, was worked by a large machine until it was handed over to a worker who sliced it with a large knife ready for the five bakers.

The *moulder* formed the biscuits, two at a time.

The *marker* stamped them and threw them to the splitter.

The *splitter* separated the two pieces.

The *chucker* supplied the oven by throwing the bread onto a flat wooden board with a long handle called the peel. His work was so precise that he must not look away for a moment.

The *depositer* received the peel full of biscuits and arranged them in the ovens, each tended by teams of five men.

70 biscuits a minute were deposited in the oven and there were 12 ovens at the yard. Every day this process produced enough biscuit for nearly 25,000 men. 'Red House Biscuit' became a common naval term.

"All the men work with the greatest exactness and are, in truth, like parts of the same machine." (*Book of Trades*, 1811) This was probably the first assembly-line in the country. The Victualling Yard also hosted the world's first monorail, built in 1826 for transporting stores between the warehouses and the ships waiting in the river.

The Biscuit Bakers received an allowance of bread and beer but there was only beer for the Pastrymen and Millers. The mill was powered by two horses and the millwright worked on a contract basis alongside two or three women who mended and washed the 'bolting cloths' used to sift the flour. Other employees included coopers and their assistants. There were rarely vacancies in the work-teams and there must have been a pool of labourers awaiting employment.

Security at the Victualling Yard was in the hands of a Warder with a team of four Watchmen and two dogs, whose handler had a daily allowance for their keep. One of the major problems was rats and the officers were always searching out more efficient ways to kill them. Crowds of cats lived in the barns and the yard's own Rat Catcher, George Inkpen, killed around 40 a month. In 1813 a new experimental method resulted in the capture of 82 rats in just 10 days.

The yard's activities were expanded over the 18th century and new work included a Pea Loft and Bread Lofts. Soon biscuit baking was joined on site by the manufacture of chocolate and mustard as well as a meat salting complex and vast supplies of clothing, food, tobacco, rum and medical stores. One rum vat alone held over 32,000 gallons. The rum stores can still be seen fronting the river, now occupied by the Pepys Resource Centre and dwarfed by the 24-storey Aragon Tower of the Pepys Estate. Thames frontage has been very valuable throughout most of London's history and only a 1960s architect would build these towerblocks so that the main river view is from the stairwells.

Innovation was not exclusive to the Victualling Yard with its modern processes and guard dogs. In 1743 an experiment for destroying vermin on board ship was first tried on the *Squirrel* man-of-war in Deptford Dock with a crowd of interested merchants and shipowners looking on. The vessel was empty except for ballast and on top of this was laid all sorts of inflammable materials including brimstone and straw. This was set alight and the airholes immediately stopped up. In the hold they found more than 2,000 rats suffocated in a few minutes. In the previous year another well-publicised experiment had demonstrated methods for moving ships in a calm. In 1765 a new invention for raising water out of ships was tried on board the *Surprize* at Deptford, watched closely by a Committee of Mechanics. It threw out more than two tons of water in a very short time and was "esteemed by all present as a very curious and useful invention". Another experiment aimed to show that pitch extracted cheaply from sea-coal could be just as good as common pitch from the north. In a forerunner to the 20th century *Head & Shoulders* adverts, a sloop was painted on one side with this new extract and on the other with common pitch before setting off on a long journey. The *Lady Nelson*, launched from Deadman's Dock in 1798, was one of the new 'reversible' ships. Innovation at Deptford ranged from a yacht of new design launched in 1774 and said to sail faster than any vessel ever built, to a gentleman who imported Spanish sheep to the Deptford fields to improve the quality of English wool through interbreeding.

Back in 1665 when Cranden was rebuilding the Red House, the nearby wharves were being used for embarking soldiers to join the British army in Flanders. For over a century after 1694 England and France were at war more often than not and war work became a major industry in the Thames-side areas. One Sunday evening in July 1721 300 men and boys worked flat out to get the *Royal Anne* galley fitted up and out of Deptford Dock by the next morning. The work was not perfect and the ship was sent back for re-rigging. A decade later more than 100 men were daily employed just to keep the Wet Dock clean. In 1744 men were working "double Tides, Sundays not excepted" to finish the rebuilding and provisioning of war-damaged ships and in 1798, at the height of the revolutionary wars in Europe, a London newspaper reported: "The River Thames exhibits at this time an aspect of as much warlike preparation as of commerce." Soldiers marching through the streets of Deptford down to the docks became a familiar scene. Regiments passing through included the Blue Guards, Ligonier's Dragoons and Colonel Cholmondley's Regiment of Foot. In 1742 no less than 30 transport ships were lying off Deptford. The town was the last possible option for deserters: in 1776 four Irishmen from the 40th Regiment went to ground there.

Although war brought prosperity to Deptford, it could be dangerous for local workers. The Military Academy in Church St worked throughout the holidays to move lads quickly into the services but there were never enough. The old tradition of press-ganging, the forcible conscription of sailors, fishermen and shipyard workers of all trades into the navy, became more systematic in the 18th century. The crew of the *Royal George* privateer put up a fight in 1758 when a press-gang arrived to conscript them. The navy was lucky to lose in this case since it was later discovered that the crew had been looting plague-ridden vessels near Gibraltar. In 1775 whole fleets of private ships and barges lay deserted on the Thames, their crews bundled into the navy ships. Twenty years later there was a massive strike all along the Thames until one of the shipwrights had been freed by the press-gangs. Families of press-ganged workers had to depend on parish relief. Unlike the cost of raising local militia, which was spread evenly throughout the country in wartime, support for naval families fell heavily on towns like Deptford.

Being bundled into the navy gangs was not the only danger facing Thames workers. In 1731 a ship bound for Virginia caught fire in the river. The press report expressed admiration for the speed with which King's Yard workers put out the blaze but there was some damage to the ship "and a Boy about 10 or 12 years old was burnt so that he died soon after". Some years later a 15 year old lad was working at the top of the mast-head on a West India ship when he was blown into the river by a sudden squall of wind and drowned. The watchman of the private Bronsden & Wells shipyard was found dead in their west dock after being missing over a week and on another occasion "the Body of a Man well dress'd rose up suddenly at the Head of the *Hardwick* Privateer, and hung some Time on her Cable, from whence it was towed to Shore". Drownings were a regular feature of Deptford life: Mr Dudman's Dock to the north of the Victualling Yard was known for centuries as Deadman's Dock.

Other dangers included both ice and fire. A riverside blaze in 1667 caused a panic in London, where it was thought the Dutch had come stealthily up the river and taken Deptford Dockyard, the prize of the Thames. A fishing boat was discovered in the hard winter of 1768 iced up near Deptford Creek with its dead crew sitting stark upright, frozen solid. Five years earlier gunpowder on board the *Hermione* frigate being repaired for the King of Sardinia took fire and killed a man. 'Loose powder' was also the cause of a fire on an East Indiaman (ie. a ship built for the East India Company) at the end of the century when two men were shockingly burnt. A waterman crossing the Thames near Deptford was jammed into the ice in 1771 and all his hundreds of colleagues could do nothing but watch him struggle. Watermen's boats were supposed to take only eight passengers but many took more and when one overturned near Deptford five people were killed and six more managed to keep above water till they could be rescued. In general the watermen themselves seem to have survived these accidents either by swimming or catching hold of nearby ropes, but there were other dangers for them as when an oyster-woman refused to pay the 3 pence fare and "words arising, she immediately stabbed the waterman in the Belly with her Oyster knife".

One did not have to be a river worker to get into trouble with the mighty Thames. In 1744 a Mr Lanburn "who went to visit an Aquaintance on board a ship at Depford, had the Misfortune to fall overboard, and was drowned in sight of several Persons". On another occasion a young mother and her child slipped when stepping into a boat at Red House Wharf and both were drowned. Even the son of a boatbuilder was not sure-footed enough: he drowned when his foot slipped on the side of a corn barge under repair. It seems that strand-lopers, who checked the shoreline for useful or unusual flotsam and jetsam, were paid more for drowned corpses in Deptford than in Rotherhithe, which may account for the high numbers of these 'findings' in our area.

The ships themselves could be dangerous as when the 'Tyger'

escaped from an East India ship (Ch.3). In 1803 sailors received a similar shock as they unloaded huge bags of sugar from the *Admiral Aplin* which had arrived a fortnight earlier from Madras. They discovered in the hold a green snake and, "it being well known that its bite was instantaneous death", a general alarm was sounded. Quick-thinking and brave, the dockworkers tied a spade to one of the oars, caught the snake by the neck and severed the head from the body. According to the press report, "it was as green as grass, 15 feet long and 18 inches in circumference". People could also bring trouble on board ship. At Christmas 1796 a crew of Lascars (Indian sailors) lay sickening in a ship off Deptford. They were put into the sick quarters at the Gravel Pits workhouse behind Church St but six of them were dead by April. The winter of 1801-2 saw more Lascars dying on a ship near Grove St and these men were buried in Deptford, though their names were never known.

There were other problems in the shipyards for local people. Wages were always in arrears, causing great hardship. In 1775, when dockyard workers had not been paid for six months, a shipwright wrote to the local paper asking why the Commissioners and Clerks of the Navy were being paid but the shipwrights and labourers were left to rely on expensive credit dealers or embezzlement. Other disputes centred on the erosion of the traditional 'perks' of the jobs such as taking wood chips from the yard for use as fuel. In October 1786 this came to a head when "a meeting of a very alarming nature took place at Deptford among the shipwrights". The tension rose to such a pitch that the whole town was in a general panic and it took all available troops to regain control. With the community struggling to survive through such hard times a thriving black economy grew in Deptford. Edward Curry, vestry clerk of St Nicholas and steward of the Wickham Estates which owned much of the land near the dockyard, was sympathetic to poor tenants. He noted that some were "so much in arrears but impossible to evict them in these hard times when all kinds of provision is so dear that poor working people can hardly buy bread for their families...Samuel Jones and wife, dead, in Church Street – poor honest folk". Curry was angry that even when wages were paid there had been no rise for many years despite large increases in the "cost of every necessary of life". Such problems may have been at the root of arson attacks on the Victualling Yard. Certainly there were frequent fires: in 1749 fire swept through the storehouses causing more than £200,000 worth of damage. Since the tide was out firemen used several barrels of beer to quell the flames. Nine years later another fire was thought to have been started maliciously and the government offered a £500 reward to catch the arsonist.

The sailors' uprising, 1774

A newly built warship manned by sailors from Portsmouth and Chatham had been brought to Deptford for fitting out. Unpaid and unfed, some 50 sailors came ashore foraging for food. In the market gardens they filled their sacks with cabbages; from the farmers' yards they took pigs and ducks and carried their booty back on board. Someone complained to the JPs at Greenwich and by Monday five of the sailors were captured and placed in the watch-houses at Deptford Broadway and Greenwich. The King was conducting a review of troops on Blackheath that morning and the sailors waited till the guards were gone and the roads clear. Then "about 300 sailors came ashore...armed with handspikes, hatchets, iron bolts, staves and cutlasses and immediately broke down the watch-house at Deptford". The sailors had found a ready sympathy among the inhabitants of Lower Deptford and by 7 o'clock there were 2,000 menacing people marching towards Greenwich to release the other sailors, "swearing most bitter oaths they would hang in the market place at Greenwich every magistrate and constable they could find".

At Greenwich they attacked the watch-house but it was strong and they had to rob a butcher for meat cleavers and a blacksmith for hammers before they could demolish it. Meanwhile the people of Greenwich barricaded their shops and houses. Around 10 o'clock a report was spread by a young druggist's apprentice that Justice Russell was coming at the head of a company of Guards from the Tower. The crowd fled, threatening to return and set the town on fire. The Greenwich people kept watch all night and some of the ladies were apparently in fits of fear. There had been no hangings but it was a dramatic sign of the power of hungry sailors and the volatility of Deptford's underpaid workers.

By the mid-18th century Deptford had the highest output of navy ships in the country. Ships were built at private yards throughout the century for the East India Company. This was the period of greatest expansion and 1,265 men were employed at the Royal Dockyard alone. In the 17 months up to August 1757 three large ships were built at Deptford. Such rapid work was unheard of in the naval dockyards. Many launches were attended by royalty and the river would be covered with innumerable small boats filled to the brim with spectators. There was special interest in 1732 when the *Ann* galley sailed from Deptford for the new colony of Georgia with 35 families aboard, providing a meagre 116 people for the first settlement. While waiting at Gravesend a child was born and five couples had decided to marry which led a journalist to remark with approval "they begin already to increase".

In May 1768 Captain James Cook took charge of the *Endeavour* at Deptford, getting it fitted out for his trip to the Pacific. Determined to fight against scurvy, the dreaded sailors' disease, Cook arranged for huge numbers of limes to be included along with the ship's biscuits, rum and other more usual stores from the Deptford Victualling Yard. Without much knowledge of the role of vitamin C deficiency in causing scurvy, Cook had made the right decision and, to his credit, not one of the men died of the disease in the whole long trip.

The *Endeavour* charted the coast of New Zealand and then in 1770 sailed west. Contrary winds drove the ship northwards to make the famous landing at Botany Bay, so called because of the wealth of new plants which delighted the botanists on board. By the time of his return in 1771 Cook had charted 5,000 miles of coastline. He continued his voyages and it was great testimony to his international prestige that despite the outbreak of war between England, France, Spain and America all countries gave orders that Cook's ships should proceed unmolested.

One of Cook's ships, the *Discovery*, later became a notorious convict hulk moored off the wharf at Deptford Dockyard for a decade after 1824. A 20 year old lad from Carmarthen who gave evidence to the House of Lords Inquiry into the State of the Gaols in England and Wales described his stay on the *Discovery*: "He was in the upper deck, where there were a great many prisoners, probably not less than one hundred; they all slept together in the same division, in hammocks, as close as they could be stowed; there were old prisoners appointed as watchmen, who sat up, had a light burning, and relieved each other every 2 hours; the watch was not set until 10 o'clock; from dark until that hour they did as they pleased; there was singing, but not in a loud voice, cursing and swearing, and obscene talk; thinks it is impossible for anyone to be on board the hulks even for a few days without contamination."

The *Discovery* was broken up in the 1830s and replaced by the *Thames* frigate. On being moved to its new place the *Thames* ran aground and laid on its end for a couple of days. The 300 convicts on board were "alarmed but not hurt".

The Discovery convict ship, 1826. The Discovery sailed with Cook on his last voyage (1778-9) and was laid up at Deptford as a convict hulk by 1824. It was broken up in 1833 and replaced by the Thames frigate.

Meanwhile, in Deptford Town behind the waterfront, accommodation had to be found for all these workers, and this meant spiritual as well as domestic homes. St Nicholas' parish in 1710 had a population of around 12,000. The church itself could hold only a fraction of these and the vestry petitioned the government for help in rebuilding since "...we have reason to fear that many wholly neglecting all Public Worship and due Observation of ye Lord's Day may be abandoned to ignorance and irreligion and that many who would gladly join with ye established Church do resort to ye Assemblies of Separatists three whereof are constantly held within our Parish". This petition, along with other pressures and political motives, led the Tory party to set up a Commission to build 50 new churches in London. Their purpose is made very clear in the minutes of the Commission's meetings where it is noted that "the buildings should stand free on open sites – for their political propaganda value". After the death of Queen Anne in 1714 the Tory government fell and it was left to the new Whig Commission to administer the scheme. Less determined than their predecessors, the Commission was wound up in 1733 having built only 12 new churches.

One of these was the glorious St Paul's, described by Sir John Betjeman as "a Pearl in the Heart of Deptford". Designed by Thomas Archer, this Baroque-style church is in the tradition of the Italian architect, Bernini, who insisted that every line has a meaning and of

Sir Christopher Wren who was one of the original Commissioners, and the first Englishman to apply scientific thinking to architecture. Sir John Vanbrugh said of the new church that it would "become an ornament to ye town and a credit to ye nation".

St Paul's church and rectory 1739. One of the Fifty New Churches planned in Queen Anne's reign (only 12 were built), St Paul's was described by Sir John Betjeman as "a Pearl in the Heart of Deptford".

Thomas Archer was a well-to-do country gentleman but a serious gambler who managed to land the post of Groomporter at Queen Anne's court, giving him control of gaming tables in the royal palaces. Unlike the other Baroque architects he had been to Rome and brought its grandeur home in a most uncompromising style. He seems to have designed buildings more as a hobby than a career. There is an inscription at his country estate (which he probably wrote himself) saying that he had been exceptionally handsome as a young man! Archer came back into the news in the 1990s through the story of Peter Wayne, a prisoner at Long Lartin high security prison serving 10 years for armed robbery. On the run in 1989 Wayne stumbled upon St Paul's on a wet, dark December night. "There was something slightly mesmerising about it – I went up and touched it." He even went to a service to get a glimpse of the interior; next day he was back in prison. He has been researching Archer ever since and has been offered a place at the prestigious Courtauld Institute of Art, parole board willing.

The site chosen for the new church was a market garden between the High St and Church St, owned by Richard Wise, a Master Caulker in the Royal Dockyard. In 1713 Wise sold the three acres of land with their five tiny houses to the Commission for £640. The gardener, Samuel Priestman, was growing asparagus, gooseberries and fruit trees and was paid £80 compensation for the loss of his crop and £4 for dung. He was recommended by Wise for appointment as first sexton but the inhabitants of the five houses were not so lucky, becoming dependent on the parish for relief when their homes were pulled down.

Building started in 1713 but slowed down as difficulties began to appear with the high level of water which had made the site so good for gardening. The water had to be pumped away while the foundations were excavated and the pump was always breaking down. Thomas Lucas, a local bricklayer who had already begun to lay out and build the lovely houses of Union Street (later Albury St), was responsible for the brick pillars and vaulted roof of the crypt. The portico took 10 years to complete after frost damaged the work in 1718 and it had to be redone. The painting contractor, Henry Turner, painted "a large curtain, Cherub Heads and a Glory in the Spherical Arch". Photographs of the interior before modernisation in the 1850s show that several of these cherubs have moustaches. Turner may have used the building site workers as models!

The three-decker pulpit was made and carved by Joseph Wade "after the design of Mr Archer, very difficult and troublesome to execute" and the original pews were of the old box style but deliberately made low enough so that the preacher could be seen. The well-off sat in the centre front with their servants behind. Free seating for ordinary people was provided at the back and in the galleries. Outside at the east end of the church was the 'best burial ground' enclosed by a stone wall with iron entrance gates to keep out grave-robbers. In the 50 years after consecration there were over 13,000 burials. The ground continued to rise, making the great stairs progressively less imposing, until 1857 when burials were stopped. (See Ch. 15 for the one man for whom this rule was broken).

In October 1801 a suspicious-looking youth was caught removing some items, including part of a lead coffin, from St Paul's porch. He was taken into custody and on the way to the watch-house at the Broadway another lad betrayed himself as an accomplice. Both were lodged in the cage prison. In the churchyard eight burrows were found, large enough for a slim person to crawl through into the vaults. Several family vaults had been broken into and the lead removed from the old coffins leaving "the remains of the bodies scattered about in a manner very shocking to humanity". It turned out that more than 20 lads were involved "led on by a hoary receiver of stolen goods in the neighbourhood" who bought the plunder at 20 shillings per hundredweight. In the evenings they would go to the pub and were sometimes so late in beginning their grave-robbing that they had to hide in the tombs when daylight came. The prisoners, tried before the magistrate at Greenwich, faced extra charges of highway robbery, housebreaking and 'borrowing' all the loose copper, iron and lead they could find from employers and neighbours. The case was said to explain why so many apprentices were better dressed than their masters.

It was local bricklayer Thomas Lucas who struggled to decipher Archer's slightly crazy plans for the Rectory. This was a three-pointed building with octagonal rooms costing £1,412. A large triangular staircase rose in the centre. The first floor windows matched those of the church but the rooms were panelled and very dark. The Rectory was dark and damp and needed frequent repairs. It was demolished in 1885, to be replaced by the Rectory Buildings tenement blocks and St Paul's Terrace of cottages along Crossfield St. These lasted until slum clearance in the early 1970s. A new rectory had been purchased in Lewisham Way but by 1914 it was agreed to be too far from the centre of the parish and St Paul's House was built in Deptford High St. In 1949 this huge building was sold to the LCC and the Rector spent some time in Albury St until the new houses near the church were finished in 1963. This area was redeveloped in the late 1980s to form a set of small flats and workshops. The *Architects' Journal* called the style of the new development "stripped Classicism". Sadly the "mighty gabled pediment" facing the High St, with its graffiti-proof glazed tiles, tends to look more like a set of public toilets, but the side facing St Paul's has an attractive terrace with balusters inspired by those on the staircases around the church.

St Paul's became at once a magnificent centre for Deptford, though the role of the Church of England changed and steadily diminished over the following centuries. Lovingly restored to physical splendour and community relevance by Father Diamond from 1969 until his untimely death in 1992, the High St church now lives up to its name as the Pearl of Deptford. The 'biscuit bin' at the Victualling Yard lasted nearly as long.

Main gate of the Victualling Yard at knocking-off time, circa 1900. A bell mounted on this wall summoned employees to work and beneath it was a lighted gas point where they could light their cigarettes since they were forbidden to carry matches because of the fire risk. The Yard was established in 1742 and renamed the Royal Victoria Victualling Yard after Queen Victoria visited in 1858. The Yard closed in 1961 and these gates now grace the Grove St entrance to Pepys Estate.

EXPANSION AND THE END OF AN ERA

6

Keeping Control

*"Strange and Dreadful News from the Town
of Deptford" – the story of Anne Arthur*

This chapter covers a wide range of topics from highwaymen and drunkards to gypsies and spies. It describes the poor relief system, the short life of the House of Correction and the founding of the Deptford workhouses. Linking all these issues is the notion of control. Population expansion over the 18th and 19th centuries was to change Deptford completely and, as it changed, the forces of law and order were faced with a combination of old and new problems. Their reactions were novel and represent the culmination of the slow change since the days when the Ducking Stool was thought to be sufficient for keeping order.

Newspapers always give a sensational picture of the world and peaceful, everyday life is rarely news. However, looking back over the detailed press reports of Deptford held in the British Library we can begin to understand the dangers facing the people of 18th century Deptford at every turning.

The traditional myth of the highwayman is of a brave and daring professional criminal but most were quite low-grade crooks and the crime was more akin to mugging than to Dick Turpin. Concentrated on the roads out of London, highway robbers would stop gentlemen travellers, journeymen workers or just about anyone. Although there are plenty of reports of them taking large bank-notes and jewellery, one Deptford example shows that you did not have to be rich to face such dangers. John Morris, a poor knife-grinder coming with his barrow from Deptford one February evening in 1765 was "attack'd near the Peckham-gap by two shabby young Fellows who robbed him of 19 pence which was all he had". Oddly enough, they then took him to an alehouse and treated him to beer, bread and cheese telling him to keep quiet about the robbery or they would cut his throat.

The attack could be a violent one, especially if the assailant was a footpad rather than a mounted highwayman. In 1729 Mr Lathbury was set upon by a footpad who "presented a Pistol to his Breast and bid him stand". A fight broke out but the attacker was joined by his 'Confederates' who knocked Mr Lathbury down, dragged him into the fields and stripped him down to breeches and stockings before they "beat him in a most barbarous Manner" and left him tied to a gate. Highway robbery was a particularly sensitive subject since the roads were officially the responsibility of the monarch so crimes on the King's Highway were a direct affront to his ability to keep the peace. The arrest of a gang of seven footpads near Deptford in the 1790s was a great coup for the local constables.

There were travellers more frightening than highwaymen on the Lower Road as shown in a 17th century pamphlet *Strange and Dreadful News from the Town of Deptford*. This is the story of one Anne Arthur who, according to her own confession, in 1684 "had divers Discourses with the Devil". Anne Arthur lived near Flagon Row (later Wellington St, now McMillan St), making ends meet by selling Deptford Cheesecakes in the street. Coming home from London one day she had passed the Half-Way House between Redriff (Rotherhithe) and Deptford when she was approached by a human shape in a dark habit. She would have turned back but a sudden wind pushed her onwards. The gloomy apparition demanded where she was going and where she had been. She stammered out her business and "after some horrid Mutterings, a Hand was held forth full of Silver". She refused, praying to herself. The spirit told her many things about herself and how she had suffered from poverty, and held out a pile of gold. She refused again. Then he told her of her straw-bed and named her utensils which were poor and mean. Yet still she prayed for deliverance and kept walking till she could see the lights of her home town. Before she could reach them another devillish wind arose "and she was taken up, together with her Basket, a considerable Height, and carried, pitiously crying out for Help for the space of a Furlong; and there, with great Violence, thrown amongst the Bushes". Her cries were heard by some people who thought someone had been robbed and bound. They carried her to a nearby house and later to her own lodgings, but she was "in a manner bereaved of her senses...often starting, and appearing fearful, as if she saw some dreadful Shape before her eyes". Poor Anne Arthur continued to suffer from nerves and began to confess her sins: notorious living, swearing, breaking the Sabbath and saying she would "go to the Civil Old Gentleman in the Black at last".

You did not have to be travelling on the road to lose your valuables. Mrs Manywell, a Deptford gardener who had been saving for years for a poor child she looked after, left her house safe when she went to market at 4am but on her return £100 in gold had been stolen. Two local women were detained for this crime and for robbing a Mrs Grace of linen and other goods worth £50.

Deptford also figured in crimes elsewhere. In 1730 a gentleman of Rochester was told he would have his house burnt down unless he put 10 guineas "in a Hollow Tree in the Road near Deptford". The threatening letter was passed to the JPs at Greenwich who ordered the High Constable to make a rota of Petty Constables to keep watch near the tree. They saw no one but found hand-prints and believed the tree had already been visited.

Deptford's waterfront position was sometimes a problem: many crimes seem to have been committed by sailors. When the butcher shop on Deptford Broadway was robbed by "three fellows in sailors habits" it was probably to stave off hunger but there was no excuse for the treatment of 21 year old Ann Scrimshaw who died after a sailor robbed her and "used her in a most cruel Manner" in 1765.

Being 'much in liquor' could produce some terrible results as when Mr Dawson, a Deptford miller, staggered too close to the sails of the windmill and was killed instantly when one struck him on the head. Even drunken driving appears in the reports: an over-the-limit servant riding full speed near the New Cross turnpike collided with a one-horse chaise so that the shafts speared his horse and it bled to death beneath him. Less gruesome effects of alcohol are found in the story of three Kentish graziers passing through Deptford on the Lower Road on their way home from Smithfield market. One of them, very drunk after a successful day, foolishly put his lighted pipe into his waistcoat pocket and was only kept from burning to death by his more alert companions.

Other dramatic moments were linked to crimes. In May 1774 four armed men landed at Deadman's Wharf. Two kept watch while the others broke into a house in Grove St and stripped the lower floor of valuables. As they forced their way upstairs they set off a bell tied to the door and the mistress of the house rapped on the thin wall to alert the gentleman next door. Her neighbour threw up his window and shot at the man on watch outside, bringing the others hurtling down the stairs. They tried to shoot the neighbour but missed. Meanwhile the woman of the house fired her own gun at them but aimed too high and nearly shot a woman in the house opposite who was opening her shutters to see what was going on. The thieves ran off with their booty, leapt in the boat and got away. The proliferation of guns shows that offensive weaponry is no novelty in the area.

People often tried to help each other in this way. After all, you never knew who would be next and your home patch had to be defended. A gentleman robbed by a footpad in the lane leading from the Lower Road to New Cross met some helpful bricklayers who went in pursuit. They found the robber lying in a ditch but he pulled out a pair of pistols so they threw stones and dirt at him till he ran again. Trying to leap over a muddy ditch he fell short and stuck in the mud. They tied him up and carried him off to a magistrate.

Participation was a key part of the law and locals would often be involved in helping the constable to make arrests (though, of course, they just as frequently hindered him if they thought it was unjust). Other local ways of dealing with crime included printing up handbills with details of stolen goods and offering rewards for their recovery. These rewards could sometimes backfire, however, as in this story of the London thief-catchers.

Macdaniel and Berry were professional thief-takers. Egan was a salesman at fairs and Salmon a breeches-maker. All four were 'persons of infamous characters'. Berry and Salmon's sons were London pickpockets and belonged to several gangs out of which the fathers would select some for the gallows when they wanted money, which they did regularly.

On this occasion they used a friend, Blee, to lay the trap. They chose Deptford for their latest trickery because catching a thief there would entitle them to the £20 reward offered by the inhabitants of the area on top of the statutory rewards. Plotting an artificial robbery, they selected two lads who were used to picking pockets, one a chimney-sweep. Blee treated them with gin and told them a parcel of linen was to be had near Deptford if they made the attempt. The plotters carefully marked the items to be stolen and began to set the trap.

Blee got the boys drunk in Kent-street (Old Kent Rd) and they went to sleep in the fields to pass the time before dark. At Deptford he took them to the sign of the Ship near the Tide Mill where they overheard Salmon talking drunkenly of his intention to go to London that night. The boys knew Salmon by sight, having picked pockets with his son. They followed him with Blee's encouragement and robbed him by the four-mile stone, unwittingly taking all the marked items.

The conspiracy went well with plenty of play-acting. Macdaniel arrested the lads and took them by boat to a magistrate at Greenwich. They were condemned to die at the next Kent assizes and the four plotters turned up to claim their reward, but Mr Cox, the sharp-witted High Constable of Deptford was suspicious. He had heard about Blee from the boys and sent officers to capture him. Meanwhile Cox himself travelled as far as Tottenham to investigate the gang's earlier crimes. Once caught Blee confessed and the lads were reprieved. It was legally difficult to try the 'corrupters' for attempted murder, but they were sentenced to the pillories where Egan and Salmon were killed by sharp stones in among the rotten vegetables. Cox continued his research and discovered earlier cases where the duped 'robbers' were actually executed, but the same legal trouble appeared and poor Cox spent large sums of his own money to no avail. He was satisfied, however, that he had done the right thing: "The duty of my office first led me into this tedious and intricate enquiry and as an honest man I could not afterwards decline it – Whatever labours I have undergone I shall never think my time misspent in the service of the Public."

Other dramatic moments in Deptford at this time were often connected with national politics. The whole of the 18th century was a time of constant rivalry and warfare between England and France. Early in the century 50 French seamen had the insolence to hoist up the French colours on the rigging of the new ship *Mississippian* at Deptford. One day in 1756 two well-dressed Frenchmen were stopped crossing Deptford Bridge and found to have suspicious letters hidden in their wigs. The letters were sent at once to the Secretary of State's office, presumably because no one could work out what they were about. In March 1779 a conspiracy to set fire to His Majesty's dockyards around the country was uncovered when a sail-maker in the Deptford Yard turned King's Evidence.

More local dramas included the fire at St Nicholas' workhouse when several of the paupers were badly hurt as they tried to save the furniture. When Ambrose Old was imprisoned in the 'round-house' at Deptford charged with forging sailors' wills, he took a dose of poison while still in the cage and died within a few hours. We can get an idea of the scale of this ancient local prison from the auction of its materials held in 1839. The stone building had a strong oak ceiling and floor, four windows with iron bars and shutters and three iron-bound doors. The round interior was reinforced with iron and the whole building was surrounded by 50 feet of stout oak fencing held by 12 strong posts. The auctioneers specified that purchasers were to take the building apart from top to bottom and clear it all away within three days – a cheap and easy method of demolition!

Attitudes to the poor had been hardening for many centuries and they were always most harsh towards travelling groups who seemed to threaten the very fabric of the social order. In 1765 a gang of around 20 gypsies was said to have 'infested' Deptford and the surrounding areas "to the great Terror of the inhabitants". William Burrell, an active JP based in Beckenham, sent orders to the constables of St Paul's parish "to take those wretches, who have long been a nuisance to society, into custody". Other undesirables were given assistance to remove them from the parish and in 1819 a parish officer was paid expenses to Paddington to find out the cost of sending the Higgins family back to Ireland. The vestry kept a close eye on legislation relating to Irish immigration, particularly because children of married Catholic parents were considered bastards and therefore chargeable to the parish.

At the start of the 18th century rapidly increasing population made social control a pressing problem, especially because of the heavy costs involved in transporting prisoners to the county gaols.

Houses of Correction, or Bridewells (after the name of the first one built in London), were an early form of prison which concentrated originally on vagrants and idle paupers. After 1650 they became more mixed, general dumping grounds for lunatics, prisoners of war, disobedient children, disorderly servants, women with bastard children and so on.

The Deptford Bridewell, on the gravel pits near Church St (the site of the present Crossfield Estate) was opened in 1707 after a request from magistrates anxious about the expanding population of migrant workers. By 1717 complaints were being made against the keeper as he "doth keep a disorderly house...doth not give offenders due punishment...he has not kept some prisoners there but hath suffered them from time to time to go at large". To cap it all he was charging the prisoners exorbitant fees. Later that year a grim list of necessities was drawn up, including bars for the windows and chains with shackles, but in 1721 the Bridewell closed. Maidstone Gaol was again used for Deptford criminals and indeed the area provided some of the gaol's staff. When Jonathon Heate of Deptford was appointed head keeper in 1765, he cannot have been encouraged to know that he was to replace "the unfortunate Mr Stephens, who was lately cruelly murdered by the prisoners".

St Paul's workhouse, Deptford Church St, 1840. The old Deptford Bridewell at the Gravel Pits near Deptford Creek opened in 1707, was converted into a workhouse in 1726, enlarged in 1781 and had further additions in 1827. It closed in the late 1830s and the inmates were tranferred to the East Greenwich workhouse.

The old Bridewell building soon became a workhouse, opening in 1726 and filled with the poor who had been staying in the temporary workhouse built on the site, and using the materials, of Evelyn's old manor house at Sayes Court. It was agreed that the Church St workhouse, with its schoolroom, workshops and separate space for the more respectable or the infirm, would cover both St Nicholas' and St Paul's parishes. In the 1740s, however, disagreements began to erupt between the parishes. The St Nicholas' vestry decided to remove its poor, taking utensils, material and furnishings with them. In 1759 the Sayes Court building was beyond repair and an advert was placed in the *Daily Advertiser* asking for tenders, though the new workhouse was not ready for another 20 years.

St Paul's workhouse was enlarged in 1781 and 1827 but was closed in the late 1830s with the advent of the new Greenwich Union. John Wade, one of the workhouse Guardians told a vestry meeting that "the poor of Deptford were very much injured by being compelled to go as far as Greenwich to make their application for relief and instances had occurred of poor persons going over at 11 o'clock in the morning and continuing in attendance until 9 o'clock at night, and then being sent away unrelieved and told their case could not be gone into".

Sayes Court workhouse, 1841. Built around 1725 with materials from the old Sayes Court manor house. By 1852 the building was being used as an emigration depot and in the following year it became a factory for emigrants' clothing using what was said to be the first sewing machine in England

The workhouses were not the only form of parish relief. Indeed, the Bridewell had marked an important turning point on the road from outdoor relief to institutional 'care'. For over a hundred years the Deptford vestries had managed a relatively consistent pattern of cash grants and pensions, although the Trinity House almshouses had remained as a back-up indoor service. One group who were helped by these 'outdoor' cash allowances were single mothers who could often keep their children with the aid of a few shillings a week from the parish. In 1817 St Paul's vestry began to keep records of illegitimate children born in the parish and the *Bastard Book* would be brought out at every committee meeting to provide information on each case so that the children could be removed from the parish charge when they reached a certain age.

Such records not only show the attitudes and work of the Overseers of the Poor, but also give an opportunity to reconstruct some picture of the people involved. Two-thirds of these children took their mothers' surnames. It seems that each case was different and there are as many forms of family life depicted here as there are in our society today.

Some Deptford Families

Elizabeth Sedgwick had an affair with Lieutenant Brown of the 14th Regiment. They had two children who lived with Elizabeth but took their father's surname. Brown had paid the parish £40 for their keep. George Bowing's illegitimate children were in a similar position and he had given the parish £35. Some of the children took both names, as many middle class couples do today, but there was no particular ordering of the mother's and father's surnames in these working class double-barrels.

Tobias Burk and Alice Flagon lived happily unmarried with their three children but Maria Ody's child lived with its grandmother, not its father, after "the Mother was found drowned in the Canal" in 1824. Cornelius and Joanna Murphy may have been siblings since both lived in Five Bells Lane and each had illegitimate children in the 1820s. It is interesting that both sets of children took the name Murphy. Perhaps they were from a more respected family than their lovers?

When Louisa Vaughan had two children by John Lake, a navigator, their father gave nothing, but Louisa's husband, a labourer at the Victualling Yard, agreed to take the children in if the parish would stump up nine shillings a month.

Some names appear in more than one combination. Elizabeth Moore was married to a foreman in the Victualling Yard but she had children by James Gosling and Thomas Limes. James Maslin fathered a girl with Rebecca Mace and, five years later, a boy with Ann Sedgewick.

The Residence column was left blank in half the entries but of those where details were given, 27 lived with mother, eight with grandmother, and three with other relatives. 16 of the children lived with other carers given by name and address but with no other detail. Some of the women would probably have been wet-nurses for children without mothers or left on doorsteps. In 1766 a male child was found tied to the knocker of a gentlewoman's door in Union Street (later Albury St) with a note pinned to its breast: "Pray, Madam, send this Child to the Workhouse, it is a Month old, and not christened; I am very poor and in Distress." It is possible that this lady would have taken the child in herself and become one of the unofficial fosterparents.

Management of the workhouses aimed to be self-sufficient. At Sayes Court the able-bodied worked the parish field growing vegetables, and in both houses inmates catered for themselves. St Paul's provisions included tobacco as well as "good well-browned small beer and best bread". Towards the end of the 18th century there

pauper's diet at St Paul's workhouse in 1831. Each person also received some bread and a pint of beer.

	For rea ast.	For inner.	For Supper.
Sunday	One quart of good Milk Pottage.	Six ounces (when cooked and free from bone) of beef, with 1-lb. of Potatoes.	Two ounces of Cheese, or 1 oz. of butter.
Monday	One quart of rice Milk.	One quart of Peas Soup.	Ditto
Tuesday	One quart of Milk Pottage.	Six ounces of Beef, and 1-lb. of Potatoes.	Ditto
Wednesday	One quart of Rice Milk.	One quart of Peas Soup.	Ditto
Thursday	One quart of Milk Pottage.	Six ounces of Beef or Mutton, and 1-lb. of Potatoes.	Ditto
Friday	One quart of Rice Milk.	One quart of Peas Soup or Broth.	Ditto
Saturday	One quart of Milk	Twelve ounces of Suet Pudding.	Ditto

were radical changes in management and a tendency for the parish vestries to contract out the large social work role that had developed. Tenders for the workhouse master show that he was to provide low-cost diets, care for insane paupers, pay for pauper burials, provide a schoolmaster and mistress for the children's education and sub-contract medical provision. In this new scheme of things it was very tempting for the master to use short measures or diluted milk to cut his costs once the contract was agreed.

High costs for the workhouses and outdoor relief had convinced public opinion that the problem was the settled poor and that they should be discouraged from burdening the parish. Paupers were treated by the Poor Law authorities with the same contempt 'idle state scroungers' have received more recently. Workhouse inmates were forced to wear distinctive (and rough) blue clothing and, after 1789, they had special badges to mark them out from others.

The first years of the 19th century saw rising food prices and an intensification of the wars with France. The national crisis was reflected in Deptford and poor-rates rose steeply. With the sea routes full of fighting ships and merchant vessels pressed into naval service, food prices rose and corn was being imported in 1813 at the impossible price of 80 shillings a quarter. Caught in a perpetual double bind, in which war brought both employment and hardship and peace was always a mixed blessing, Deptford was blighted by the ending of the Napoleonic Wars. All new shipbuilding at the Royal Dockyard ceased in 1816 and large numbers of families joined those lightermen and merchant dock labourers who had already lost their livelihoods.

In 1817 typhus fever struck Lower Deptford, festering in the badly drained area around the Sayes Court workhouse. The workhouse was placed under strict quarantine. No non-medical persons were allowed in, no pauper was allowed to leave. The meagre supplies were dropped off outside the kitchen and the fever raged for two months. When the mistress of the house became seriously ill the vestry asked for help from a London fever hospital. A surgeon visited, accompanied by the workhouse doctor, and his report gives an unpleasant picture. He recommended cleanliness and frequent washing of the body with "proper people to superintend the washing of the knees, feet and legs of the inmates as...every patient I attended stood much in need of soap and warm water, the dirt on the knees and feet appearing literally to form a component part of the party". The walls, ceiling and wooden floors were filthy and windows were rarely opened to ventilate the place. Chamber pots were left with their contents under the bed and a heap of kitchen slops formed quickly in the yard.

Fever struck again in 1832 when cholera raged throughout the country. By this time the Deptford Board of Health had been established and health notices were distributed to every house. "Fellow Parishioners – For your own sakes, use the utmost care to remove from your Houses every kind of Rubbish and Filth, and Lime-white the Walls and Ceilings as often as they become discoloured. Keep your drains clear, and destroy all unpleasant smells by opening the Windows of your Bed Rooms as much as possible but not after dark; and remove all Slops the first thing in the Morning. Wash the Floor daily, but dry it well. Keep yourselves and your Children as clean and as warm as you can. Abstain from Spirits. Boil your Vegetables well and abstain from Raw Salads and Fruits." Advice was also given on remedies including mustard powder or common salt dissolved in warm water, warm poultices of mustard, linseed and hot vinegar to the stomach, and heated plates, bricks or tiles to the feet.

A report on the workhouse in 1836 showed that not much had changed and it remained "in a condition so truly deplorable and with such a total absence of good order, cleanliness and management". By this time the ancient parish of St Nicholas, which had lost most of its land to St Paul's a century before, had become a truly depressed area of poverty and unemployment and its poor-rate was seldom less than 5s.6d in the pound compared with 2s.4d in St Paul's. In the 30 years up to the new Poor Law of 1834 parishes all over the country tried to hold down the poor-rates, to chip away at outdoor relief and to pioneer the new managed workhouses. The Act of 1834 took these policies much further with the doctrine of 'less eligibility' which meant conditions in the workhouses were deliberately designed to be worse than those of the poorest labourers outside. This could be difficult to achieve given the squalor and poverty of some casual or sweated labour but discipline and restraint were explicitly used to make workhouses "so severe and repulsive as to make them a terror to the poor and prevent them from entering".

Routines were laid down to the last detail. Silence was required during meals and hard work at other times. Every possession the pauper had managed not to sell or pawn was removed. The sexes were separated and families were split up, leaving the welfare and discipline of children to the Master and Mistress.

St Nicholas workhouse rules

All paupers to have "their hair cut short at least once a month, compelled to wash twice in any week and their face and hands washed and their hair combed every morning, change their body linen once in every week. That the bed linen be changed once in every month. Rising bell at a quarter before six, at six prayers and afterwards employment, retiring to bed at nine, chidren at eight. Breakfast shall be at eight, the dinner hour at one, and supper at seven. All other hours shall be considered working hours. No person to be permitted to leave the House. All inmates to attend Divine Service – both morning and evening. The time allotted for a child to attend the teacher not less than an hour each day. That all articles of wearing apparel be marked with a proper mark. Paupers capable of employment shall be employed, allowed a fifth of what would be the wages outside. Grown persons who shall refuse to work shall be confined and kept on bread and water." These were the rules before the new Act. Afterwards conditions were stricter, just as the town outside was sliding into despair.

To end on a more cheerful note, not all the poor stayed that way. John 'Lord' Greenleaf was a local fiddler who played country dances at fairs. By the time he died at Deptford he had amassed a fortune of £3,000. Not all the workhouse inmates could be cowed. Bridget Bonner, who was found cavorting naked in the gravel pits at Blackheath, was sent to the workhouse simply because no one knew what else to do with her. Everyone was talking about her, speculating over the mysterious circumstance, and then one day she simply left Deptford for Aberdeen to join her rather respectable family and was never heard of again!

7

Roads, Railways and Riverwork

"It seems that this world is full of trains." – *George Glazebrook*

The Directory of 1823-4 describes Deptford as "a large town three miles from London...remarkable for its noble docks, in which a large number of hands are employed". It goes on to describe the merchant and trade docks which would be "in any other country, sufficient for the navy of a Kingdom". Despite the slow-down of shipbuilding after the long wars with France, Deptford was still dominated by its Thames frontage.

Soon, though, it would be home to the first station of the first urban railway in the world. In February 1836 the London & Greenwich Railway Company opened a line from Spa Road Bermondsey to Deptford. On 14th December that year London Bridge became the first South London terminus. Before describing the coming of 'railway mania' to London, we should take a look at the forms of transport to be found in pre-railway Deptford.

The roads around Deptford were very dangerous indeed and not just because of highwaymen and footpads. The road over Deptford Bridge was dangerously uneven and in 1770 it was ordered to be repaired with pebbles of a regular shape because of damage to carriages. Further west, coaches would compete to be first through the turnpike gate at New Cross and on one occasion the race was so fierce that one overturned causing many injuries. When a crowded coach broke down by the Half-Way House in Deptford Road two men were thrown from the top and fractured their skulls. The newspaper editorial noted that "it is a Matter of Reproach that some legal Restraint is not put to the Avarice of the Owners of Stages". Greed, as ever, was getting in the way of safety. Another man fell from the box of an omnibus when it collided with a gardener's cart and a dramatic moment occurred when a coachman, who had left the horses to drink by the Five Bells Tavern and gone in for some swift refreshment, found they had bolted with the coach and all its passengers. By 1823 at least 10 coaches set out from Deptford every day, making their way by slightly different routes to Fleet Street and the City.

Travellers paying their toll at the old New Cross turnpike at Turnpike Hill (Clifton Rise), 1783. This gate, established in 1718 by the New Cross Turnpike Trust remained on the site until 1813 when the main turnpike was moved to New Cross Gate.

Turnpikes and toll-gates have been mentioned several times and they were very important in this area. The Turnpike Acts allowed 'local worthies' to take responsibility for certain lengths of the highway and to levy tolls for maintenance. The New Cross Turnpike Trust had been formed in 1718 and a turnpike gate erected at the top of the present Clifton Rise. At first the Trust was responsible for the highway from Southwark to the Lime Kilns at Blackheath. Eventually it gathered more than 40 miles of road under its protection and became one of the largest and most efficient turnpike trusts in the London area, renting out the lucrative toll-gates to the highest bidder. In 1813 the decrepit old turnpike building was demolished and the main turnpike was moved to the junction of Kent Road and Peckham Lane (Queens Rd). Soon the fame of the Trust overtook the quiet hamlet of Hatcham and the district became known as New Cross Gate. Its important role as a stop-off place for travellers provided continuous trade for local inns like the Five Bells Tavern.

Despite such hustle-bustle Hatcham remained a rural area for many years. The poet Robert Browning, who lived with his parents in Telegraph Cottage (near the site of Aske's Girls School), gave these directions to a friend: "...if in a week or two you will conquer the interminable Kent Road, and on passing the turnpike at New Cross, you will take the first lane with a quickset hedge to the right you will descry a house resembling a goose pie...We have a garden and trees and little hills of a sort to go out on."

As traffic on the roads increased and the toll-gates became an unpopular hindrance, travellers became cunning at avoiding the tolls. In 1848 the Trust had to place a new toll-bar on the corner of one of the tiny paths leading to Five Bells Lane, since its west exit could be used to avoid the New Cross Gate turnpike.

Five Bells Lane, bridge over the Croydon Canal, 1837. Five Bells Lane ran from Clifton Hill to the Five Bells Tavern in New Cross. The lane was blocked in the centre by the London & Brighton Railway which opened in 1841. Parts of the lane survive at each end, now called Hatcham Park Rd and Batavia Rd.

Five Bells Lane was one of the areas most affected by the coming of the railways. Once a useful back lane joining Kent Road to Coney Hall Lane (Clifton Rise) with a footbridge across the Croydon Canal, it was cut in half by the London, Brighton and South Coast Railway. All that now remains of this old lane is the one-way Hatcham Park Rd, cut short at its east end by massive railway sidings, and the virtually unused Batavia Rd with its depressing blocks around Clifton Rise. Thankfull Sturdee, Deptford's famous 19th century photographer, described the Cage which once stood at the eastern end of Five Bells Lane, known as Sweeps' Alley. The Cage was "generally tenanted by some of the rough characters who frequented this lonely thoroughfare".

There were other gates, including the Gibraltar Toll-gate which stood at the junction of Evelyn St and Princes St beside the Brandy Ball Shop kept by Mrs Haylock and another on the Greenwich side of Deptford Bridge. By the 1860s, however, turnpikes were seen as outmoded and their days were over. At midnight on 31st October 1865 the toll-gates at New Cross were removed under the eyes of a lively crowd until a sudden downpour of rain drove them away. The Gibraltar was removed that same year.

New Cross Gate turnpike, circa 1850. These were the main toll-gates in the area from 1813 to 1865 when the were removed due to pressure of traffic. The Whi Hart pub in the backgroun is still standing. The toll-house area is now occupied by a set of elegan but sadly derelict public toilets.

The other pre-railway form of transport, the canals, were not for travellers but for commercial traffic. Around 3,000 miles of canal still survive in Britain but today they are used mainly for leisure purposes and their quaint appearance signals their irrelevance to industry. Though boat outings to nearby woods were common in the southern reaches of the Croydon Canal (1809), the Grand Surrey Canal (1807) near Deptford lacked such scenic attractions. Nevertheless, in the early years of the 19th century pleasure boats were to be found in the dock basin of the Grand Surrey and locals got into trouble for bathing and duck-hunting or for lending out small boats to the 'low rabble' to muck about in. As the area became more industrial the Canal Company was adamant that it could not allow bathers to mix with commercial traffic. Even so Charles Buckley remembered the 'dubious luxury' of bathing in the Surrey Canal near Braby's ironworks in the 1870s. Angling had been encouraged at the start with tickets being issued to individuals in 1812, but it was soon turned into a commercial operation and the fishing rights were leased out. One activity the canals certainly came in handy for was suicide. Around this time the newspapers were full of reports of bodies being fished out with suicide notes soggy in their pockets.

View of Deptford and the London & Greenwich Railway from the Surrey Canal, circa 1840. The windmill in Blackhorse Fields was owned by Mr Martin until 1854 when it was burnt down while grinding corn for the troops during the Crimean War. Horses towed barges along this canal until the Second World War.

The main canal trade was timber and the banks became one long timber yard set in the market gardens which provided the other early commodities. By 1844 the transport and dock access had attracted more varied industries including the gas works north east of the Old Kent Rd, the Mazawattee Tea Company on the road now called Juno Way and the Coldblow Pepper Mill near Senegal Fields.

By the 1830s there was trouble with the banks of the Croydon Canal and the lack of financial return meant the proprietors were losing interest. Developments in railway technology led to plans for a London & Croydon Railway and it was decided to purchase the old canal which was "almost if not quite moribund". A good price was paid for the canal and all the working barge-owners in the area, indeed anyone who could find a barge at all, claimed compensation. Six months after the sale the canal overflowed its banks and flooded over 200 houses in Deptford, for which the new owners were liable.

The Grand Surrey Canal survived way into the 20th century but its doom was written long before when a Thames guide-book of the early 19th century noted that "the docks are sliding down the River to the ships instead of the ships coming up the River to the docks". In the 20th century, with the demands of containerisation, the docks would move even further downriver. By 1945 the Camberwell section of the canal was disused and decayed. In another decade it had been closed. Too many people lived beside this dirty backwater and children had died. Although the rest of the canal continued, busy up to the end with the timber trade, the closure of Surrey Docks in 1970 was the final death-knell. Hopes to keep the canal as a leisure amenity were crushed by official arguments over expense, leakage and narrowness. Yet the commercial value of the land was never realised (nearly half ended up as grass), all canals leak, and most recreational canals are only half the width.

Deptford Railway Station is the oldest surviving passenger train station in London. In the commuter age when too many of us shuffle about, uncomfortably squashed, aggrieved by a five-minute delay, we inevitably forget what the engines of the London & Greenwich Railway meant when they first came puffing over the viaduct in February 1836.

Thirteen years before the opening of Deptford station an Act of Parliament had authorised the use of steam locomotives on the Stockton & Darlington Railway. In just one month 49 separate companies were formed planning to raise £23m capital to build 3,000 miles of railway. 'Railway mania' had arrived, though experience could only come with time. Questioned in the House of Lords about his railway knowledge, George Walter, Director of the London & Greenwich, answered only "I have seen the Liverpool and Manchester Railway and passed over it several times". It did not sound hopeful, especially considering the enormous feat of engineering represented by those hundreds of arches. Luckily Colonel Landmann, the engineer responsible, had some military experience which apparently came in useful.

Two years before the opening a letter appeared in the *Greenwich Gazette* describing a walk down by the railway works. The scene around the Lower Road was very rural and there were nightingales singing. The writer explained: "Deptford being considered 'a low neighbourhood', no building speculators have thrown down its hedges and built upon its meadows. A canal, for commerce and fishing, cuts through and gives a picturesque effect to its green plain."

The new railway sliced through some of the most dismal areas of Southwark – Frying Pan Alley and Foot's Folly, the Maze, Oatmeal Yard and Crucifix Lane. Alongside the viaduct a road followed the line for those who could not afford to travel on trains and for access to the arches which the company hoped to let out as dwelling-houses. Nothing like it had ever been seen before in London and, of course, it cost a great deal more than anybody had expected, nearly a million pounds in the end (£270,000 per mile), but it cut the journey time to London Bridge from one hour to 18 minutes and was taken up by both commuters and pleasure-seekers. During the first month the railway could boast of over 20,000 passengers and the figure had doubled by the end of April.

Reactions to this novel form of transport were mixed. Kitty Sharp of Greenwich had "fondly cherished the most exhilarating anticipation of taking frequent rides by steam" to take her mother shopping in London, but was shocked by "the cattle and pigs (not to say a word of the innocent sheep)" carried by the railway in the early years.

This letter was probably invented by a creative London & Greenwich copywriter as an advert for the railway. It supposedly comes from 'Greenwich Osspital'.

Mister Edittur- I no youre verry parshal to this countery and Wont see the place Cutt Up by these Raileway roads, its a imposishun and deservs exposur – besydes – what do you think Sir? – The Greenige Homtribusses and Stagis will giv you a ryde for half an nour or three quatters, for six pense,

but thes ralerode peopl dont give you no more than ten minnits of it – You jist git into there carridges and wwiz gos the steme and teir you are at Deptfurd in 10 minnites – i like the ould fashened way sir and plente of ridin for my monny not to bee wisked along in sutch a fluster that you cant enjoi nothin at all. youer umbel st.
betty Cringle
My husbend as lost his rite flipper and so i do all his riting.

On the opening day in February 1836, according to a song of the time, Deptford wore "a universal grin". The Lord Mayor came and flags waved at London Bridge as five trains took the 300 guests down to Deptford at around 16 miles an hour. All along the line the bells of parish churches rang out and the housetops teemed with cheering spectators. At Deptford some of the guests were keen to visit the local inns but the Lord Mayor was in a hurry to get to the lunch waiting for them at Southwark. His short speech welcomed the contribution that the railway would make "by promoting the wealth and the domestic comfort of that large class of the citizens of London whose villas adorn the picturesque scenes which abound in the neighbourhood".

Deborah Wybrow of 'Crossfield-lane near the New Church' (St Paul's was still called this a century after it opened) had lived in Deptford for 102 years. The old lady, who continued to make a meagre living by her needle, had been chosen to be the London & Greenwich's first passenger. Sadly, she died after a fall in April 1835 and never saw the new age which would change her home town so much.

The touch of fantasy present in this amazing venture from the start was epitomised by the endless viaduct snaking its way on 878 brick arches across the market garden landscape and by the classical design of Deptford station (rebuilt in 1842 with a domed turret modelled on the tomb of Lysicrates in Athens). The novelty of train travel was further increased by bands playing the trains in and out of the station, a practice which local groups are hoping to resurrect.

The London & Greenwich railway viaduct was lit by gas with over 200 lamp standards spaced at 22-yard intervals. Since streetlighting was unknown outside major towns, the viaduct must have provided quite a spectacle at night. Gas was also used for cooking and heating in the houses built into the arches. A gas works was built between Creek Rd and Deptford Creek, approached through what became known as Gas Arch. There were immediate problems with the houses in the arches: they were cramped, they leaked and the trains caused vibration. Above all, the supply of gas would have been dangerous and unreliable since its use in cooking and heating was not taken seriously until the competition from electricity in the 1880s. Along with these earliest 'all gas' dwellings, gas lighting on the viaduct was abandoned in 1838.

The railway rapidly became a commuter service and sold London's first season tickets, known as 'free tickets'. There was even a 'free ticket' valid for life! People descended on Deptford station from all around, stabling horses and leaving carriages in Mechanics Passage, or taking the omnibuses from Lewisham and Blackheath. At London Bridge a rush hour quickly developed as people arrived from the City in cabs. "When the whistle blows for an approaching train, drivers of carriages and Hackney cabs whip up their horses and a kind of chariot race in Duke Street and up the inclined planes takes place". Duke

The viaduct of the London Greenwich Railway from Mechanics Passage, circa 1840. A pedestrian footpa[th] with a penny toll ran all t[he] way alongside the railwa[y] from London Bridge to Greenwich. The railway u[as] lit by gas and the lamps c[ould] be seen at 22-yard interva[ls] On the right was the St Paul's parish yard.

Street Hill still runs along the north side of London Bridge station.

The railway was also used for pleasure. On Whit Monday 1836 13,000 people took the train to Deptford to visit Greenwich Park. Also very popular were the footpaths which charged a penny toll and ran alongside the railway all the way from the Maze near London Bridge to Blue Stile, the site of the original Greenwich terminus.

The next station to open in the area was the one we know as New Cross Gate on the London & Croydon line along the old Croydon Canal. Trains started from a newly built section of London Bridge station, sharing tracks with the London & Greenwich before separating to take their different routes to Deptford and New Cross. New Cross Gate was a bustling but peaceful little bit of road in the ancient hamlet of Hatcham. It would not remain so. In July 1841 a member of the Hardcastle family who lived in the mansion at Hatcham Park, wrote "we have been wellnigh stunned this morning by the tremendous noise which the Brighton trains have made whizzing by. The line has been opened this morning and all the directors of the railway have been amusing themselves at our expense by flying up and down at an astonishing rate in trains of 16 carriages and 2 engines, adorned with flags etc. A spark from one of the engines set fire to the hay in Bacon's field and caused a great conflagration."

Joseph Hardcastle was a successful merchant who leased Hatcham Park House in 1788 and devoted himself to religious and philanthropic work. He was closely associated with the movement to abolish the slave trade and Thomas Clarkson wrote part of his *History of the Abolition of the Slave Trade* at Hatcham. Hardcastle was also an active member of the Church Missionary Society and Hatcham Park House became a centre of hospitality for all involved in such work.

Having these iron monsters so close destroyed the privacy and seclusion of Hatcham Park House. The Hardcastles spent less and less time there and finally sold the remainder of their lease to the

Haberdashers' Company in 1868. The site was soon covered by artisans' dwellings, railway goods yards and industrial sites, though the church built on the corner of the estate was named All Saints to commemorate Joseph Hardcastle and 'all the saints of Hatcham Park'.

In October 1844 a terrible fire broke out at the works attached to New Cross (Gate) station causing enormous damage. It was nearly an hour before any engines arrived and by then the fire had spread to a carriage factory. It also ruined a rather grand octagonal building attached to the site, but most dramatic of all, as the flames leapt higher, King Louis-Phillippe of France appeared at the station on a State Visit.

A terrible fire at New Cross Gate which coincided with the arrival of the French King Louis-Phillippe on a state visit, October 1844.

In 1846 the London & Croydon amalgamated with three other companies to form the London, Brighton & South Coast Railway. By 1854 the main line had been widened to four tracks. Freight traffic was dealt with at New Cross Gate because of the link with the Grand Surrey Canal. This required fairly extensive sidings, as well as an engine house, a carriage shed and coke ovens. The Railway Company owned nearly three acres of land around the station.

For the railway companies South London had obvious appeal. Access to central stations and to the waterfront was better than north of the river since the land was not yet so built up. Like pioneers viewing the inhabited but open land of some new and alien territory, the railway directors began the fierce battle for the south. The decisions made in railway boardrooms created the particular pattern of the new suburbs. H G Wells described it as "a mindless, wasteful, anarchy which was suburbia...roads that led nowhere, that ended in tarred fences studded with nails and in trespass boards that used vehement language. It was a multitude of unco-ordinated fresh starts, each more sweeping and destructive than the last."

The competition to bring 'civilisation' and the joys of commuting to lands long protected from the turmoil of the city resulted even by the 1860s in the New Cross Railway Tangle. This spaghetti field of criss-crossing lines and the confusion of embankments, viaducts, goods yards, stations and approach roads, colonised the land west of old Deptford and north of New Cross Rd. It had a profound influence on the life of the whole area which lasts even now that many of the lines and stations are dead and forgotten.

Such schemes brought overcrowding and distress in the wake of demolition. The railway companies still insisted that those made homeless could move into the new districts opened up by the line but cheaper workmen's trains were not common for some decades. Most casual workers needed to be at work very early each day and suburban rents were often far too expensive. *The Times* commented in March 1861: "The poor are displaced but they are not removed. They are shovelled out of one side of the parish, only to render more overcrowded the stifling apartments in another part...But the dock and wharf labourer, the porter and the costermonger cannot remove. You may pull down their wretched homes; they must find others, and make their new dwellings more crowded and wretched than their old ones. The tailor, shoemaker and other workmen are in much the same position. It is a mockery to speak of the suburbs to them."

However terrible the social effects of the railways there is no denying that they provided work at an crucial time. Between 1830 and 1870 an entirely new occupation opened up for working men and grew at an incredible rate to become one of the largest industrial groups in the country. The progression from building the lines to staffing the trains and stations was far from smooth for workers. Navvies, whose reputation was one of the lowest among 'unskilled' workers, did not easily find work as guards, signalmen or porters. A complex hierarchy of command and status evolved among these 'railway servants' and the tradition of railway work passing from father to son often reinforced the distinctions.

Deptford was lucky, in some ways, to get its railway so soon. Gliding on its arches like a Roman aqueduct, the London & Greenwich Railway cast shadows on market gardens but few houses stood in its way and the town suffered far less in these early years than the slums of neighbouring Southwark and Lambeth. However, the influence of the railways began immediately to change old ways of life in Deptford. It represented, after all, a direct threat to the watermen whose long dominion on the Thames was drawing to a close.

Small boats carrying passengers up and down and across the Thames had been a familiar sight for many centuries. The records of the Watermen's Company stretch back even before the terrible winter of 1281 when people crossed the Thames on foot between Lambeth and Westminster and the watermen were "very much distressed for want of their usual employment". Most watermen wore a kind of uniform and there was a strong solidarity between them despite the stiff competition. Theirs was a dangerous job but they were proud of the risk. In all the hundreds of drownings it is amazing to see how often the waterman himself manages to survive. Indeed, when an old waterman was accused in 1809 of getting a 17 year old girl pregnant he "tried to drown himself several times on Friday afternoon". Perhaps his long years on the water had made him immune to it!

In 1807 a Grand Regatta was held under the sponsorship of the General Steam Navigation Company. Six Deptford watermen dressed in different colours raced from St George's Stairs to the mouth of the Creek. The first prize was a new wherry and there were cash prizes for the rest. The race became an annual custom and there are still old Deptford families whose forefathers staggered proudly to the pub, heralded as kings of the Thames.

Long hailed as the Cradle of the Navy, Deptford could also be described as the birthplace of steam navigation. It was here that Mr Thomas Brocklebank built his first steam vessel. Its success encouraged him to form the General Steam Navigation Company which bought land at the Stowage in 1825, described as "neat as a drawing-room". The Company's ship-repairing yard remained beside the Power Station at Deptford Creek until the 1940s.

River transport enjoyed a last boom in the 1840s and fares were temporarily reduced by competition. There was always the winter to contend with, however, and the Thames was regularly choked by ice. Accidents were common, scaring off potential customers who were being offered speedy alternatives by the railways. When the Bill for the London & Greenwich Railway went before Parliament it carried with it 18 separate counter-petitions from local landowners, riverside wharfingers and watermen, stagecoach owners and carriers, the turnpike trustees, the vestries and the Commissioners of Sewers. The Bill was passed and the understandable fears of all these other interests went unheeded.

The watermen had fought a long war to protect their trade. In 1803 a company had been formed to build a bridge across the River Ravensbourne near to its mouth at the Thames. Many watermen made their living ferrying people over the Creek at this point and they petitioned against it. The Act was passed and, though the watermen received some small compensation, they were forbidden to carry passengers over the water near to the new wooden footbridge. In 1815 a permanent bridge suitable for carriages was built and the watermen had lost the battle.

Around 1818 the watermen were kept busy taking visitors to inspect the vessels being fitted out at Deptford for Captain Parry's Arctic voyages and in 1824 the Watermen's Company was presented with a model of an Eskimo and his canoe by Thomas Long, a Woolwich waterman who had served in the expedition.

Another battle was fought over the Deptford Pier in 1835. The pier was built to embark passengers, cattle, carriages, goods and merchandise. The watermen lost the fight but at least this time their voices were heard and the company was ordered to construct stairs and a causeway and keep them in good repair for free use by the local watermen. In 1842 new stairs were erected at Lower Watergate by the Deptford Pier & Improvement Company to serve the watermen. This company regularly came into conflict in the town. It had grand plans for Deptford and must have raised many hopes with the slogan 'Making Deptford Herself Again'. The committee included local magistrates, solicitors and the conservative shopkeeper Samuel Gardiner. After his success with the London & Greenwich Railway, the company appointed George Landmann as engineer. Within weeks of the brochure being released they had received £140,000 worth of applications for shares of £20 each. Had the company succeeded in its spectacular redesign of Deptford, there is no doubt it would have been a transformation to match the 20th century building of the estates.

Gradually the main business of the river became summer excursions as regular travel by river ceased to be competitive. Things were changing at the docks as well. For centuries it had seemed that shipwrights and dockers were a part of Deptford, as fundamental and inevitable as the river itself. Their hardships struck at the heart of the town and all Deptford cheered at their triumphs. We will see more about their political activism in Chapter 10 but neither old tradition nor their budding union strength could save the docks from the march of 'progress' and the hard bite of recession.

The silting up of the Thames had been noted even in the 17th century and in 1680 the Navy Board had purchased a 'dredging machine'. They spent £1,950 on deepening the river in 1702 but by the end of the 18th century ships could only leave Deptford with the wind in five of the 32 compass directions and may wait up to two months for such a wind. In 1800 engineers reported that any money spent on Deptford would be wasted because of its distance from the sea, the difficulty of navigation and the shallowness of the Thames.

The old abuses in the dockyards had further increased with the opportunities offered by the long wars with France and this time they prompted a Parliamentary Inquiry which led to the impeachment of Captain Henry Dundas, Treasurer of the Navy. In 1801 the shipwrights took advantage of the situation to push for a pay rise. They were proud and well organised and delegates from all the yards rejected the concessions offered by the Admiralty, insisting on double pay. The delegates were immediately dismissed and other workers were threatened. Shocked and scared, the remainder went back to work at once but 21 men were discharged from Deptford.

In 1827 massive reductions were being considered in the Navy and Victualling Departments and there were rumours that the Deptford Dockyard would be left to rot. Forty clerks were laid off at the Navy Board and hundreds of Deptford families waited in apprehension. For more than a decade the dockyard was closed down and used only for breaking up old vessels. The age of the iron ship had arrived, replacing the 'wooden walls' of the old navy, and Deptford was unsuitable for such work. The yard reopened in 1844 to build ships of the 'composite' type (wood covered with iron plates), until the launch of the *Druid* in October 1869, the last Royal Navy ship to come out of Deptford. The yards at Deptford and Woolwich both closed that very month and the area descended into a despairing poverty.

These changes were affecting all the private Deptford yards as well. In 1834 local feeling was strong against Edward George Barnard, MP for Greenwich (which had included Deptford since the 1832 Reform Act) for non-payment of poor-rates for his shipyard at Deptford. He pleaded that the yard had been very little used recently and referred to himself as "a poor broken-down shipbuilder". John Dudman had been forced to sell his shipyard in 1813 and by 1834 it had been taken over by the Thames Ironworks & Shipbuilding Company. A serious fire four years later prompted their move to Blackwall and another private yard was lost.

So little had the future been anticipated that 1856-9 had seen more than 20 acres of ground acquired by the Royal Yard. By the time of closure it covered over 27 acres and held 2,000 feet of river frontage. The land was bought by Mr T P Austin who sold it to the Corporation of the City of London for a foreign cattle market.

At the time of closure the yard employed 800 people. Some of the dockyard labourers obtained work in the new cattle sheds, others moved to the Victualling Yard, but many drifted out of Deptford hoping to find work at other yards. The hardest-hit went to the workhouse or to sea. In 1870 the Admiralty provided three troop-ships for the emigration of discharged labourers at Deptford, Woolwich and other 'Government towns'. Emigrants had to pay only for food (£2 and 5 shillings per head) and many Deptford families joined the queue for registration held two nights a week at the dockyard.

A great age was over and Deptford would never do so well again but Britain was still 'the workshop of the world' and over the next few decades new industries grew up providing identity and employment for new generations of Deptford people.

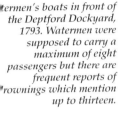

Watermen's boats in front of the Deptford Dockyard, 1793. Watermen were supposed to carry a maximum of eight passengers but there are frequent reports of drownings which mention up to thirteen.

PART TWO

MAKING MODERN DEPTFORD

INTRODUCTION

A Deptford Tour

"Here, then, is Deptford..."

South London's strange mixture of villages, slums, palaces and dockyards was gradually submerged from the 1830s in a tide of new housing which poured outwards, filling in the fields and market gardens with bricks and mortar. Often this reinforced early patterns of social class. In Deptford comfortable working class areas grew up around the railways and the southern area was developed with large middle class houses, leaving the oldest part of the town to fall further into poverty. These patterns had a long-lasting effect: class has a logic of its own which interacts with social and political change to shape and reshape our local areas over time.

Deptford can be fitted into a general description of South London. By the 1880s an inner poor working class zone had formed, reaching out as far as Southwark and Lambeth. Rents here were expensive due to competition with industry and tenements were overcrowded since so much land had been lost to the railways. Food at the old markets was poor quality but cheap and employment for all the family could be had nearby. A second inner ring, which included Deptford, formed among the older, more socially mixed communities as the land between the villages was built over for 'respectable' working class families moving out from central London. Prosperous London tradesmen brought their families to live out in the southern villages of Stockwell, Brixton, Herne Hill and Lewisham. Wealthier residents moved still further south to an outer zone of country villages like Wimbledon and Bromley.

Another pattern visible in South London as a whole mirrored the east-west distinction north of the river. The docks and the 'noxious' industries, the crowded streets and poor housing of South East London compared unfavourably with the attractive areas to the west where Lambeth Palace marked the beginning of open fields, ornamental gardens and the 'handsome houses' of Wandsworth and Battersea.

Meanwhile railway development encouraged suburban spread and, once workmen's fares became compulsory with the Cheap Trains Act of 1883, the railways played a major role in opening up surburbia to the working classes. However, the process of decentralisation from inner London took many decades and left us with a pattern of inner city poverty compounded by the feeling of being left behind.

But these sketches are too general to give us a true picture of Deptford and its surroundings. It is obvious, for example, that the east-west division was not complete: the upper classes never left Blackheath and Greenwich remained a fashionable area, attracting businessmen and naval officers. The railway had come very early to Deptford and its effects were different from elsewhere. Most crucial of all, Deptford was not some new suburb taking its character from the fortunes of the later-19th century. It was one of England's oldest settlements, a town that had come to prominence in the 16th century and had built itself up independent of the metropolis. Even after the closure of the dockyard and the trade depression of the 1880s, Deptford, Greenwich and Woolwich can be seen as "separate, identifiable communities, self-sufficient in their social relations, and more complete in their social composition than most parts of London" (Crossick, 1971).

Though Deptford began to lose some 'old and respected inhabitants' from the 1850s there was no mass exodus of the prosperous until the end of the 19th century. Unlike the inner zone, Deptford remained an independent community with its own middle class, its own industries and a complicated web of internal social relationships. It was separated from London by acres of docks, railways and market gardens and offered its own version of urban life. To Ellen Chase in the 1880s it was "uncommonly like a small country community in some ways".

It was also quite clearly divided from its nearest neighbours. The Ha'penny Hatch toll-gate over the Creek was a strong barrier to the mixing of the towns of Greenwich and Deptford. When men crossed the bridge into Greenwich for work their wives would bring lunch to the barrier and pass it across to save the toll. The fertile farmland around the borders of the town enclosed Deptford, giving it a self-containment that disappeared only very slowly. "Despite its trim neighbours, Deptford made no attempt to become suburban. It was a town in its own right." (Willis, 1953).

Ha'penny Hatch, 1890s. The pedestrian toll-bridge over Deptford Creek was attached to the south face of the railway bridge. The Ha'penny Hatch could be negotiated free of charge if the toll-keeper's attention could be diverted. The footbridge was removed at the beginning of the 20th century, cutting the link along the railway between Deptford and Greenwich.

Separate from London and from Greenwich, Deptford was also internally divided and each area had its own character formed by a complex mix of social forces. The areas changed over time and were further cut up by more railway lines and road extensions, but their characters were built on older traditions and centred on the physical features which had always moulded Deptford – the London Road, the Lower Road, the Thames and the Creek.

So, with the help of Charles Booth and his social researchers (1900), let us begin our late 19th century Town Trail in the most ancient part of Deptford along the Thames frontage. The narrow, crowded streets around St Nicholas' Church and Deptford Green still housed riverside workers but they had been badly hit by the closure of the dockyard. The new Foreign Cattle Market which opened on the site in 1871 was an important employer but its better-paid workers chose to live further away from the overwhelming smells of the riverfront. The Stowage in 1900 was "a stinking unpaved lane" occupied by a rough waterside population. Near the ancient parish church the houses were older and more respectable. The old Green itself was a very mixed area both in style of houses and character of occupants. Some were comfortable three-storey houses with red-tiled roofs. Others were wooden and distinctly slummish with many

South side of the Stowage, 1932. In 1900 the Stowage s described as "a stinking paved lane". By the 1930s it was still a poor area, except for those lucky enough to work at 'The Light' as Deptford Power tation was affectionately nown. The power station chimney is visible behind the houses.

families in each. Hughes Fields was similar and the London County Council (formed 1899) prioritised this area for clearance. At the northern end of the Green was Hood & Co's Ironworks and the Dry Dock, both employing many men. Further west along the riverfront were Humphrey & Tennants and Penn's large engineering works, both pioneers in ships' engines. Humphrey & Tennants closed before the First World War and was replaced by Lloyds who manufactured wood and tin containers. Edward Buckmaster, who worked there as a young man in the 1920s, remembers the tea-boy bringing tea in cans strung on a pole.

St Nicholas church from Deptford Green, circa 1900. The houses on the left made way for Deptford Power Station at the end of the 1880s. This was the heart of old Deptford but was split from the rest by the London Government Act 1963.

Chislehurst District Times, 1/7/1898
"It is a well-known fact...that there is a tendency on the part of the lowest classes to congregate around particular places, where they form communities...and it is a remarkable fact that the nearer you get to the streets, the courts and the alleys which are nearest the riverside, the more the poverty of the people and their insanitary conditions increase...This kind of thing seems to have accentuated itself at Deptford."

The northernmost part of Church St had some large old-fashioned houses where the people kept servants and such comforts extended to old Flagon Row. One of Deptford's oldest roads, it was renamed Wellington St just before the major changes in this area caused by the extension of Creek Rd to meet Evelyn St in 1895. What is left of it is now called McMillan St. By 1900 most of the dilapidated old houses of Armada St (running northwards parallel with Hughes Fields) had been cleared for LCC tenements. They were well built, although the small windows gave them a heavy appearance. The whole area, which had contained some of the worst slums, is a surviving example of the potential for good quality clearance. The LCC blocks retain a municipal elegance which puts 1960s planners to shame.

Watergate St (formerly Old King St) was another ancient Deptford thoroughfare and the main access to the river. Old red-roofed houses faced west towards the cattle market wall. Along the wall ran Orchard

Northern end of Deptford ⸜*h St before the Evelyn St-* ⸜*reek Rd extension of 1895* ⸜*which demolished most of* *this old shopping area.* *the left: New King St had* ⸜*been known as Back Lane* ⸜*ntil the mid-19th century.* ⸜*n the centre: Old King St,* *which led to the ancient* ⸜*per Watergate marked on* *maps as early as 1623,* *was renamed as* *Watergate St by 1894.* *To the right: Flagon Row* ⸜*hich joined the High St to* ⸜*urch St had been renamed* *Wellington St by 1868.* *What is left of it is now* *McMillan St.*

Place, a narrow, unpaved roadway which was once part of the Wickham Estate (Ch.5) and can be clearly seen on a dockyard plan of 1753. After the dockyard closure the area had become very dangerous and people were often lured there to be robbed. Two old wooden houses occupied by costers were still standing in 1900. The place was filthy but it had become less used and soon after this the land was taken to extend the cattle market.

Old Joe's clothes shop, ⸜*atergate St. This building* ⸜*as demolished in the 1895* ⸜*nsion. Opposite the shop* ⸜*d the Fishing Smack pub* ⸜*and Fishing Smack Alley,* *reminding us that the* *Watergate was built for* *fishing boats long before* *the Navy took an* *interest in Deptford.*

Back in Watergate St the character deteriorated further south. Old three-storey houses, once high-quality family residences, were let out in tenements to costermongers or cattle market 'gut cleaners'. A faint fetid smell prevailed, overpowered in places by a truly disgusting stench. The women in this area bore the brunt of their men's poverty – black eyes and bandaged heads were common. Shoeless children skulked around; older women slumped on doorsteps; rough girls with coarse fish-aprons shouted to each other. The police sergeant who accompanied a researcher working for Charles Booth around the area in 1900 said of these people: "wherever there is beer, there they are." The place was certainly full of pubs, ranging from large gin palaces to small but fully licensed establishments. The researcher felt that "in their decadence [the old houses] retain much of their quaint picturesque appearance...but the LCC buildings in the centre show that the old order is passing away". The 'careless hand-to-mouth class' described by such social commentators would in fact have had to be very careful simply in order to survive.

The old Deptford Road, scene of so many highway robberies, had been renamed Evelyn St in the middle of the 19th century. It remained a very mixed area of old houses interspersed with shops and small-scale businesses. Tucked between the street and the cattle market were the old grounds of Sayes Court, converted into a pleasant open space around a large meeting hall where the Irish National League held a public meeting in 1893. Further north west Grove St followed the line of the Victualling Yard and housed many of its workers as well as coal porters and dockers. In 1856, when it was known as Victory Rd, a petition complained that barges were depositing large quantities of river mud on the houses. Grove St is an old name in the area but its present form dates from around 1880. At this time many of the houses were empty and the street had a rough character but it had improved greatly by 1900.

Grove St, circa 1915. Par the Deptford Wharf bran railway ran down Grove to the Foreign Cattle Ma Such trains were rare in early years of the 20th century but became a common sight in Grove S during the First World W when the market became Supply Department. Edw Buckmaster remembered trains carrying rum jars marked SRD (Supply Reserve Depot)

The building of Pepys Estate in the early 1960s has left us with little of the old Victualling Yard area. Windmill Lane, at the north end of Grove St, cut across the Grand Surrey Canal to join the Lower Road. Nearby Hanlon St was being built up for engineers employed in the nearby works. The Scott & Co factory at the end of the street also provided employment for many young women of the area.

Before Deptford Park was formed and the northern streets (Scawen Rd, Alloa Rd) were developed, the Ida Wharf area was largely wasteland hemmed in by railways and the canal. Nevertheless it housed one of Deptford's most important firms. The ironworks of Frederick Braby & Co flourished here from 1869 until just after the Second World War. Sophie Lake, whose father worked there for many years, has vivid memories of timber-laden barges bound for the wood-yard opposite being pulled along the canal by horses on the towpath. Braby's was well known as a good employer and they ran a library and classrooms in Sarah's Place for their workers. Below Blackhorse Bridge was a crowded area of small labourers' houses and tiny pathways joining up with Grove St.

Looking north west over Blackhorse Bridge, 1881. This bridge over the Surrey Canal, forming part of Evelyn St, had just been widened by the Greenwich Board of Works. The building on the left is ederick Braby's ironworks.

Blackhorse Rd, running parallel with the canal, was fronted along one side with the many industrial works that used the canal, from the timber-yard to the asphalt and chemical works to the oil refinery by the railway. The houses on the other side were poor and narrow with many broken windows. The men were mainly dock labourers but there was wood-chopping work for women in the timber-yards and employment for younger girls in the tin factory or the cattle market. According to Rev. Pring of St Luke's this was an area of "lax morality" inhabited by prostitutes. At the end of the street a footpath led under the railway to Oareboro Rd. In the 1890s a large area of vacant land here had been used for games of 'pitch and toss' and the occasional kick-around or improvised boxing match. The police had raided the spot several times, putting a stop to these activities, and by 1900 the place was empty except for a few women collecting wood for fuel. By 1914 the land had been cleared to make way for the tenement buildings of Folkestone Gardens.

George Glazebrook remembers Folkestone Gardens as the place 'where no flowers grow'. It was one of those strange islands formed so often by the unplanned mess of the New Cross Railway Tangle. "Sometimes you pretend to be a train as you stare through the panes. You know all about trains, of course. You feel you could almost touch them as they scream across the viaduct above the arches and belch smoke against your window. You make puffing noises spit from your mouth...It seems that this world is full of trains. All day long they rattle by. At night the railway follows you to bed. You hear shunting, metallic noises and the sound of hammering on iron. 'They are mending the rails' your father explains as you call out to him in the darkness. But for a long time you are haunted by hammers beating on iron."

Another footpath led back under the railway to the new neighbourhood along James St (Childers St). Before the mid-19th century the single street between Loving Edwards Lane and the canal had long been known as Coney Hall Lane. By 1868 this had changed to Rolt St and the new neighbourhood was built up around it. Charles Buckley, born in 1877, remembered bird-catching in the area on Sunday mornings before Etta St was built. Buckley's parents were the first tenants of 29 Etta St in 1884 and he says "it took my breath away to think that enough people could be found to occupy this area, and when Trundleys Rd was built we were most surprised".

The old varnish works, Trundleys Rd, 1890s. The road was commonly known as Knackers' Lane and wa full of small factories like this one adjoining the London & Greenwich Railway arches.

Of the three streets remaining today, Etta St was the most up-market, Gosterwood St was clean and eminently respectable and Rolt St was slightly poorer. The houses were mainly fitted out for two families with three rooms and a scullery on each floor. Some residents owned their homes in this neighbourhood and they enjoyed the broad streets with their tidy forecourts and the clean, tiled pavements. To the south east were the older streets, Dorking Rd and Shere Rd, where families were long established but not so respectable. These roads were taken up in the 1970s for extensions to the Evelyn Estate. The last street of the block was Abinger Rd which was extended in the 1870s to cross under the railway arches. The islands between the railways, which had remained market garden or waste for years, began to be colonised by industry. In this triangle Stone & Co bought up three acres and the well-kept houses of Arklow Rd were tenanted by mechanics. There was a large Coffee Tavern and Institute on the corner of Arklow Rd and Kerry Rd used mainly by Stone's workers. The building was later taken over by Lady Florence Pelham-Clinton after her breakaway from the Deptford Fund (Ch.11 and Epilogue).

Josiah Stone was born in Deptford in 1800, the son of a Royal Dockyard shipwright. He worked for the shipbuilders Gordon & Co at Deptford Green before setting up a small workshop in 1831 to produce copper nails and rivets for shipbuilding. From these small beginnings Stone & Co became an international business, famous for their ships' propellers and watertight ships' doors.

In 1842 the works moved to four arches near Deptford Station. Josiah died in 1867 but his partners kept the name and by 1871 there were 280 employees. Ten years later they moved to Arklow Rd. In 1894 Stone's branched out to produce the first successful electric lighting for trains which had previously been dimly and dangerously lit by oil-gas. By the turn of the century they were making baths and toilets, pans, kettles, coal scuttles, fire hydrants, water pumps, steel drainage and complete sewerage systems for urban areas. Some of Stone's manhole covers are still to be found in Lewisham today. Turnover reached £1 million by 1911, with 1500 employees by 1927 and during the Second World War over 2,200 propellers were produced for naval vessels. They were expanding all the time, taking on new factories, in Charlton, New Cross and also in the north east of England. In 1950, when the Deptford site covered six acres, J Stone & Co was a large international firm. The business moved to Crawley in 1966 and the Deptford factory finally closed in 1969.

Loving Edwards Lane was an 18th century road linking Turnpike Hill (Clifton Rise) with Butt Lane (Deptford High St). By 1900 the picturesque name had been reduced to Edward St but many old houses remained including a timber cottage on the north side occupied by the Cushion family. Mrs Cushion was born and died in the same room where she lived for over 70 years. The old White Swan coaching-inn (now Mamie O'Leary's) on the corner of the High St, once a bustling centre for news from London, was still a large and important pub.

Church St had been the 18th century shopping centre of middle Deptford while Butt Lane had developed as residential but the large High St houses adapted better to the expansion of Victorian retailing than the tiny shops of Church St. By 1900 the High St was a wide market street with "almost as many styles of building as houses, the only agreement being that all have shop fronts".

Deptford High St had been called Butt Lane up until 1825 when a public notice was posted around the area informing 'the Publick' that 'by the general Consent of the Inhabitants' the name was to be changed.

At the northern end, below the railway, trade was not so brisk and the shops not so good. The streets off to the west had been developed in the mid-19th century. By 1900 they were old-fashioned and were occupied by poor families, though Hamilton St maintained an older dignity with flowers in the windows and clean white curtains. The railway arches were used as stables and carts stood on the ground in front. Those at the bottom of Ffinch St (named after the Rev. B S Ffinch, Rector of St Paul's 1834-73) housed a growing colony of Italians who took their carts around the area hawking ice-cream in summer and hot potatoes in winter.

The Creek Rd extension of 1895 caused havoc in the old block at the northern end of High St and Church St, destroying the old wooden houses of Flagon Row and much of Queen St (Lamerton St) as well as the old Harp of Erin beerhouse and the Three Compasses on the corner of Church St. Albury St was now the first full road joining High St and Church St, and a rather special road it was too. Built by local cook-turned-bricklayer, Thomas Lucas, it was originally named Union St in commemoration of the Union of England and Scotland in 1707. By 1717 Lucas had built 40 houses in the elegant metropolitan style rarely found outside central London. He managed to enforce a striking regularity of appearance whether the houses were built by him or the plots let out to other builders. Each porchway was carved by local craftsmen with unique detail of flowers and cherubs, many resembling the ships' figureheads carved by an earlier generation of

Albury St, circa 1900. Built as Union St by local bricklayer Thomas Lucas in the early 18th century, it ha become a poor and crowdec street by this time. The doo carvings were renovated by the GLC but many were los in a major burglary at County Hall in the early 1980s.

Deptford craftworkers. Behind his own house at the corner of Union St and Butt Lane, Lucas had built a malt-house which linked up with the King of Prussia pub at No.6. It is likely that beer loomed large in payments in kind to his labourers. Originally inhabited by wealthy sea-captains and skilled shipwrights, with one or two larger houses for the very affluent, the riverside link continued with the dockyard until it closed in 1869. From then on the street declined with some houses in multiple occupation and a striking growth of small private schools. In 1882 Union St was renumbered as part of Creek Rd. By 1898, when it became Albury St, three or more labouring families were crowded into each house.

LCC policy in the 1920s had *both* condemned the houses as unfit *and* had them listed as of special architectural or historic interest. This completed the ruin of the south side. Lucas' own house (and the malt-house) had been demolished before the beginning of the century, probably as part of the Evelyn St-Creek Rd extension of 1895. They had been replaced by the Deptford Medical Mission.

In 1950 the north side of Albury St was still more or less complete and the GLC promised to renovate those buildings in disrepair. The houses were emptied and the doorcases removed. By 1973 only four had been repaired and some terrible bureaucratic cock-up led to the demolition of some of the others. To complete the sad tale, in 1982 the carved brackets remaining in storage with the GLC were stolen.

From Church St a winding passage led westwards to Mary Ann Buildings, passing a tiny cottage with a vegetable garden and a sign saying "new laid eggs for sale". Two steps led down to the old two-storey cottages and the Salvation Army Hall by the High St. Further south the splendour of St Paul's Church was offset by the squalor of Crossfield Lane. Old boots and stockings were strung up to advertise the wares of one of the lane's tiny shops and costers' barrows blocked the passageway. At the east end were the Rectory Buildings, three blocks of five-storey tenements built by the Industrial Dwellings Company. In 1890 a whole block lay empty and although it was full by 1900 the area was declining. In the small lane joining up to Church St dirty ragged children played among the litter.

Church St, now a noisy and dangerous dual carriageway, had once been a narrow old road straggling southwards from St Nicholas' Church to Deptford Bridge. The three-storey houses and shops had been good but 19th century neglect had made the peeling bricks, rotten woodwork and broken flagstones an appropriate backdrop for the rough men and women who hung around the doorways. The old Baptist chapel behind St Paul's was said to date from the reign of Charles II and had been attended by the young Disraeli during his time at boarding school in Blackheath. Facing the chapel until 1871 stood the Trinity Corporation's almhouses, known as Trinity Hospital.

The area east of Church St was once known as 'the city'. Self-consciously separate from the rest of Deptford this was a small Creekside world with its own rules and customs, fiercely defensive of its boundaries. Around 1780, according to Dews, a bricklayer named Elder became the first 'Lord Mayor of Deptford' and started the yearly festivities known as Lord Mayor's Day. Passing through the streets of 'the city', he was saluted as 'My Lord Elder'. For many years he was accompanied by the Lady Mayoress, Bet Sedgewick, "whose character will not bear too close a scrutiny". Always overfond of a tipple, the Lady Mayoress was found one day dead in the street from drink. Elder's successor was a wit named Epsom, elected because he was "wise enough to puzzle the parson" and well known for giving impromptu pub speeches on subjects of international importance.

Lord Mayor's Day saw a great procession of sweeps, tinkers, dustmen and coal-heavers followed by the Lord and Lady on their donkeys and a long train of attendants in masks and tinsel. They passed through Church St and to Copperas Dock where they took boats out in front of the old town before returning to their favourite pub, the Crispin and Crispiana, to finish the day. Dews tells how one time when the procession met the state barge of the Lord Mayor of London they managed to persuade him to pay homage of 7 shillings to his local equivalent.

The construction of the London & Greenwich Railway demolished old Russell Square, the very centre of 'the city', and this proud and secluded area was opened up to the public gaze. For the social researchers of the late-19th century it was not a pretty sight. Poor Creekside workers were crowded into three-room cottages flush with the pavement. Nevertheless in some of the streets there were signs of an older dignity in the clean doorsteps and fresh paint.

South of the railway the area of poverty covered most of the side streets down to Reginald Rd. Addey St, parallel with Church St, was considered the worst in all Deptford. It was an area of criminals and prostitutes. On going to arrest a man there in the 1890s Inspector Gummer had found father, mother and five children all living in one room. In the block between Giffin St and Hales St people were poor and rough. Even in the 1850s the Giffin St houses were said to be "very filthy" and by 1900 many of the dilapidated houses were boarded up. Some of the women were well-known prostitutes and they moved off quickly when the police came through. On another visit the researcher found them "sitting in groups on the footpath, one on a chair, more on the edge of the kerbstones whilst one woman completed a small circle by sitting in the road with her feet towards the kerb". The men were mainly costermongers and evening saw them driving home on their pony carts. One such cart stood in the road outside the Oxford Arms pub (now the Birds Nest) chalked FOR SALE while the men sat about in the July sun of 1899 with their feet stretched complacently across the pavement. In Stanhope St the roadway was blocked with barrows and two men were breaking up some gas fittings, putting the metal in an old sack.

The area just north of the Broadway was much quieter and the 'nice little houses' were taken by those with regular work. Amelia Terrace, in Reginald Square, was a row of old cottages with flower gardens in front. The centre house sported a full-sized figure of a sailor holding a Union Jack. The Broadway itself was a large, cobbled open space in a rough triangle. Once home to the stocks and the watch-house, it was the meeting place of the area and there were always men standing about while respectable Deptford did its shopping at Peppercorn's or Gardiner's General Stores. In the 1880s the road from the Broadway towards Blackheath was widened "forming a noble avenue".

ptford Broadway looking west, 1898. Peppercorn's tores stretch all along the right hand side of the photograph, including uildings now occupied by e Antique Warehouse. The rse-drawn trams were on their last legs. The LCC electrified the lines and opened them for public use around 1904.

Joseph Peppercorn opened a small grocery on the north of the Broadway in 1822. The shop gradually expanded in both directions until it came to dominate one side of the Broadway's triangle. By the 1890s there was a Peppercorn's branch in the High St and another at Greenwich. The Broadway shop closed in 1916. While the Peppercorn family had a tradition of liberalism, the Broadway's other main shopkeeper Samuel Gardiner was the Treasurer of the Deptford Conservative Association which first met in 1835 at the Red Cow in the High St. The distinctive Scotch House, built for Gardiner & Co at the Broadway around 1882, required the demolition of many old buildings, including the Mitre pub known as the Clockhouse on Deptford Bridge. Gardiners traded from the Scotch House until the late 1950s.

eptford Broadway looking east, circa 1910. The Scotch ouse in the centre was built for Gardiner & Co in 1882 and they traded from there until the late 1950s.

Before the dawn of the 19th century the area immediately south of the Broadway was market garden and pasture. Butt Lane extended right up to Lewisham High Rd (Lewisham Way) as the present Tanners Hill. Mill Lane ended abruptly at the entrance to the Kent Waterworks on the Ravensbourne. Dog Kennel Row, known sometimes as Dark Lane, lay between them. In 1829 it was called George St but by the end of the century it had been obliterated in the development of New Town Deptford. Friendly St runs the closest to the line of the old road.

The main landowner who profited from the development of New Town Deptford was the Lucas family (apparently no connection with Thomas Lucas, the builder of Albury St). The family was divided between Deptford and the United States. On his return to London in 1823, Jonathan Lucas built Lucas Villa on Lewisham High Rd which is now used by the Welsh Presbyterian Church.

A massive increase in population early in the 19th century put pressure on housing everywhere and the railways were also encouraging suburban development. However, St John's station, in the heart of New Town, did not open until 1873, by which time much of the area had been built up: development here was related to the economic activity of Deptford itself rather than general trends in the capital. Lucas was a good estate manager, building sewers and paving streets in preparation for development and maintaining the streets himself before they came under public control in 1833. The quality of housing was high, despite its piecemeal construction by a large number of small firms. Slum building would have easily reaped equal profits and Lucas' responsible attitude helped to stave off some of the most horrific features of 19th century working class housing.

In 1868 a stone coffin was found in Nelson Street behind Mill Lane. It contained a well-preserved skeleton thought to be at least 200 years old.

In Mill Lane, the focus of one of Deptford's worst slums, the buildings were older and the cramped lodging-houses were filled with beggars and wandering labourers, with a concentration of poor Irish. While Mill Lane itself was described by the Booth researcher in 1899 as 'vicious' and its inhabitants as 'prostitutes and bullies', many of the streets behind New Cross Rd were also poor and the usual costers, flower sellers and Italian organ-grinders and ice-cream vendors are found. Rose Champion remembered how the Irish and Italians of the area "used to hold their wakes just inside the door with the corpse propped up in his coffin, a rather gruesome affair".

Miserable death of a lady.
In September 1830 an inquest was held at the Fountain Tavern on the Broadway into the death of Elizabeth Guillot, the 30 year old daughter of a wealthy East India merchant and heir to £500,000 in property. Elizabeth had left her parents' home in Blackheath Hill on Friday morning "to take an airing on the heath" and never returned. She had wandered down to Deptford and taken a room at the Fountain before going on Monday to "a miserable lodging house in Mill Lane, occupied by a man and his wife, named Hetherington, who let out beds to poor weary travellers". She paid 4 pence for a filthy bed in a room with a wretched old man and "a poor

famishing woman in the last stage of existence from the small pox". That evening she called at a chemist in Deptford and bought an ounce and a half of laudanum. The chemist knew her as an habitual laudanum taker and opium eater. Handing it over he said "You take a great deal of laudanum, Miss". "Yes", she said and immediately swallowed nearly half an ounce with the greatest unconcern. Back at Mill Lane she emptied the rest into a glass and drank it off. She was dead within the hour.

The jury visited the body "in that mansion of wretchedness" and hastily returned to the congenial Fountain. The Coroner deplored that a lady should die this miserable death and blamed the Hetheringtons for taking her into their "infectious hovel". With some dignity Hetherington replied that he was not aware of the lady's rank or he would certainly not have allowed her to enter his house. She had asked if she could have a bed, and he had said 'yes'. He was sorry that she should have died in his house.

West of Tanners Hill the Lady Florence influence was strong (Florence St, Rd, Grove, Cottages) and there were signs of respectability: "fancy flower pots and clean white curtains". The decline of Heston St, where fights were common at night, was attributed to "people from Mill Lane" coming in. In 1896 Tanners Hill residents signed a petition against the nuisance caused by crowds of boys and girls who gathered in the street. Their conduct and language was apparently "so indecent that no respectable person could pass up or down Tanners Hill". At the northern end of Heston St were eight tiny cottages below street-level known as Fishers' Rents. These remained until they were described in 1933 as "very old and thoroughly decayed" and were placed under a Deptford Borough Council clearance order. The old labourers' houses off Tanners Hill had broken windows stuffed with rags. Kentford Place in Summer St was a collection of six small cottages with wash-houses and two WCs on the ground in front. The people were rough and lived in crowded rooms but one woman pointed out that most tenement blocks, far from the nearest water pump, had "not half the Convenience you have here!"

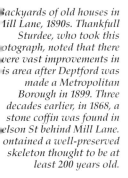

Backyards of old houses in Mill Lane, 1890s. Thankfull Sturdee, who took this photograph, noted that there were vast improvements in this area after Deptford was made a Metropolitan Borough in 1899. Three decades earlier, in 1868, a stone coffin was found in Nelson St behind Mill Lane. It contained a well-preserved skeleton thought to be at least 200 years old.

There were plenty of deaths associated with Mill Lane. Opposite the entrance to Friendly St was the house of the Stratton brothers who were executed for the murder of an elderly couple, Mr and Mrs Farrow, who were looking after Chapman's oil shop at 34 High St in May 1905. When 14 year old Cissy Bartlett of Armada St landed herself a job at Chapman's in 1922, her mother was still squeamish about it. The case was especially celebrated because it was the first time that fingerprint evidence was used in a murder case.

Skilled workers who lived in the Ship St area in the north of New Town in the 1840s had moved southwards into more recently built streets by the 1870s. Most of the population who came from old Deptford were semi-skilled: few of the poorer could afford the high rents and those that could chose to go further south. The New Town area as a whole was declining. Despite some clearance schemes, its fortunes would not improve significantly until after the First World War.

Chapman's oil and colour shop in Deptford High St soon after the notorious murder of Mr & Mrs Farro⟨ by the Stratton brothers of Friendly St in May 1905.

The Greenwich Board of Works addressed some of the problems of New Town in the 1860s and 1870s by repaving, laying sewers and ensuring systematic rubbish collection. The key area of need in Mill Lane continued to deteriorate and there were major outbreaks of disease in 1875 and 1892. Medical Officers' reports betray the attitude of the authorities. Noting that the people were "of the lowest class...dirty...and irregular", they implied that the inhabitants were to blame not the conditions. Of course, condemning insanitary buildings did little for the inhabitants and in many cases simply intensified overcrowding in neighbouring lodging-houses. Only with the Housing of the Working Classes Act 1890 were authorities given the power to build on land after demolition and mandated to rehouse at least half of those made homeless. When the Greenwich Board of Works reported the conditions to the newly-formed London County Council, prompt action resulted in the demolition of eight Mill Lane lodging-houses. It took five years to decide on the redevelopment but when Carrington House opened in 1903 it had a capacity of 670 men. In the same year Sylva Cottages further along Mill Lane were opened with accommodation for 144. The scheme eventually provided housing for more than had been made homeless and the LCC took an obvious pride in it.

On the other side of New Cross Rd between Deptford High St and New Cross Station the houses were well kept and occupied by railwaymen and tradesmen of various sorts. In Amersham Vale a dairyman sold "milk, butter and eggs of the very best quality". A double-fronted house in Amersham Grove was occupied by an old sailor who built a small museum in his garden for the curiosities he had collected on his travels. Douglas St was a wide, airy roadway with quite large houses. To the north the streets were regularly laid out and the houses were smaller but comfortable, with the occasional live-in servant. To the south Stanley St was a quiet, respectable road but the cottages were small. The east side of Glenville Grove was taken up by the engineering works of Clarke, Burnett & Co which employed over 100 men and separated these blocks from the disreputable area around Watson St.

At the top end of Watson St the New Cross Empire Theatre of Varieties was opened in 1899 after long squabbles about licensing with Dr Hodson, the Rector of St Paul's. The irregular little cottages further down the street were "built when every man did what was right in his own eyes". At the other end was the Coroner's Court, which represented the demise of the local pub as the HQ of state administration. Baildon St was one of Deptford's worst. The first sight was three old wooden cottages, one resembling a converted stable. Further round were two large lodging-houses and a terrace of small dirty houses where women stood watching the research party curiously. "Frowsy and half-dressed...one asked the sergeant whether he had come for her this time." Ragged, shoeless children played in the street, in and out of the open doors, dodging the costers' barrows and ice-cream carts, overturning the knife-grinder's wheel as it stood in their way. The street was nicknamed 'Tug-of-War Street' because there were so many fights though the police believed it was better than it had been. They had been used to sending 20 men out to make arrests. Now it was hardly criminal at all, discounting the violence within and between families which the police had no orders or inclination to confront. Still, in the eyes of the Victorian researcher, the people "bore the criminal brand on their faces".

In the area wedged between the two New Cross stations the railway influence was very strong. The land had remained entirely market garden until the mid-19th century. By 1900 all that was not taken by the railway companies was built upon.

The stark contrast of opportunities in railway work was graphically represented in Railway Grove. Running alongside the tracks near New Cross Station and reached by a narrow footpath from New Cross Rd, the first section was inhabited by the navvies and common labourers who had sweated to build the railways and now faced unemployment of over 40%. Further north the street was cleaner and the flowers in the windows marked the prosperity and aspirations of the new servants of the completed service: signalmen, guards and porters with an unemployment rate of less than 3%.

Increasing demand for houses from those in regular work slowly drove out the 'more undesirable people'. East of Woodpecker Rd the streets were wide and there were large gardens. To the west the houses were more diverse and the gardens smaller but the open ground by the railways meant that they received plenty of air and light.

West of New Cross Gate Station the land was owned by the Haberdashers' Company who gradually let it out for building. To the north of New Cross Rd there was a general appearance of comfort and respectability among the railwaymen and clerks who lived in the area. The women were well dressed and the doorsteps spotless. The houses were quite large and many were fitted out for two families. Larger families took in a gentleman lodger and used the whole house. Once let or sold the houses rarely came back on the market and generations followed each other down the decades, reinforcing the old traditions (such as never giving Deptford as their address!).

The poorer triangle of land between New Cross Rd and Queens Rd was 'compact and monotonous'. The inhabitants were described by their local vicar as "rough and squalid labourers". East of Kender St, as the triangle closed up, there were half a dozen tiny slummish courts including the low-class 'Cook's Folly' of 1843. With no less than five pubs and a brewery, the reputation of Pomeroy St was low but the roughest populations were further west towards Southwark. There were some very large works here including the old Hatcham Ironworks in Pomeroy St which had been taken over by Eno's Fruit Salts. Other local employers were the South Metropolitan Gas Works north of Old Kent Rd and the South Eastern Hospital, established in the 1870s as a smallpox hospital to the horror of the Haberdashers. In general the main roads tended to be lined with large gentry houses. The crowded streets hidden behind them were inhabited by ordinary Deptford folk. This pattern was to be found throughout the country until the take-over of the motor car. The decline of major roads in Deptford did not become obvious until after the Second World War. The constant traffic on the A2 has covered the grand old houses and apartment blocks with soot but the small terraces, now mainly hidden from general view by shopfronts, offer some inkling of an older tradition. Staffordshire Place on the south side of New Cross Rd beyond the White Hart pub was built in 1838 when the turnpike gates still cut it off from the rest of Deptford. Nearby, the unusual shape of the Clutch Clinic dates from the beginning of the 19th century when it belonged to a horse dealer named Bacon.

If the main roads had a tradition of gentry houses, the developments around Lewisham High Rd and the hilly southern part of the Haberdashers' Estate were to create a new south western area which few residents would dream of labelling 'Deptford'.

The Haberdashers completed their plans for the estate in 1875, the year the Hatcham Aske's schools were established. It was hoped that these middle class schools would make the estate more attractive to potential house buyers and the plan was for "nothing but buildings of a superior class, including villas and high class mansions". By 1900 the building development was complete, leaving space for a recreational park. St Catherine's Church, built by the Haberdashers in 1894, was magnificently placed on the summit of the hill to reinforce the feeling of being 'above it all'. Even by 1900, however, the area was showing some signs of deterioration. Houses began to be let instead of sold and there were two patches of poverty. One was Foxwell St, near Brockley Station, where a block of buildings were so vile and filthy that the parish visitors had given up on them. They belonged to a local builder and were occupied by his workers. The other area was a crowded slum known as Mud Island, around Rutt's Terrace to the south of Queens Rd. Another local Mud Island was replaced in the 1960s by Silwood Estate and Senegal Fields park.

Once known as Plow Garlic Hill, the name Telegraph Hill came from the Old Admiralty semaphore station established on the top of the hill in 1795. News of Wellington's victory at Waterloo had been sent via such telegraph stations and this one was the last in a long line from the coast to London.

On the other side of the London & Brighton Railway, which followed the route of the old Croydon Canal, another gentry area was developing on the Tyrwhitt-Drake Estate. A walk along Wickham Rd, even in the 1990s, gives an idea of the grand scale of these houses. Less uniform than the Haberdashers' villas, these mansions are magnificent statements of the Victorian upper middle class desire for privacy and grandeur, country life close to town. Servants in this area were paid 50% more than their equivalents in New Cross.

In the smaller houses surrounding these broad boulevards of wealth, some of the respectability rubbed off. There was a saying that Brockley people were "all on the way to Chislehurst". Most of the residents were salaried clerks, independent people 'above' the need for Sunday Schools or church visitors. Instead, St Peter's Church gave £300 a year to the poorer parishes of Deptford and charitable members of the congregation were encouraged to help out at the Deptford Ragged School in Giffin St.

The first part of Lewisham High Rd had once been known as Counter Hill, a corruption of County Hill since it sloped off into the county of Kent. The tall houses further south were built around the middle of the 19th century, along with the Royal Naval School which was purchased by the Goldsmiths' Company in 1891 and handed over to the University of London in 1904. At this time the area between Sandrock Rd and Algernon Rd, which had been a brickfield for many centuries, was not yet built on and stretched up as far as Hilly Fields. Deptford was a large town and its population was increasing every year. In 1831 there were a mere 13,759 inhabitants. By 1891 the figure was a staggering 101,286. The narrow, crowded streets of St Nicholas' parish by the river began to stagnate into poverty from the first closure of the dockyard in the 1830s. Although the old shipyards were eventually replaced by engineering works and the Foreign Cattle Market provided work for many, unemployment was rife. In 1887 the northern part of Deptford was selected for a Parliamentary inquiry into the conditions of the working class in London. Unemployment was found to be 32.6% and the table below shows the clear movement away from shipbuilding, navvying and housebuilding towards railway work of all kinds. In fact unemployment was even worse: these figures represent those out of work at the moment of the questionnaire. When asked if they had been unemployed at all in the previous six months the numbers rose still higher.

Unemployment in Deptford. March 1887

OVER 40%

Rough labour, navvies, roadmen, coal-heavers	**43.3%**
Dock labourers and stevedores	**64.6%**
Masons, bricklayers, plasters, roofers etc	**44.7%**
Shipwrights, boat and barge builders	**48.9%**

UNDER 10%

Railway guards, signalmen etc.	**1.6%**
Railway porters	**4.3%**
Printers, compositors, bookbinders	**7.4%**
Policemen	**7.1%**
Messengers, watchmen, timekeepers	**9.8%**
DEPTFORD AS A WHOLE	**32.6%**

'DIRTY DEPTFORD'

8

Sights, Sounds and Smells

"although at first it was not pleasant,
the girls quickly got used to it..."
– *Vornberger, owner of the Foreign Cattle Market*

The Stench at Greenwich
To the Editor of the *KENTISH MERCURY*

Sir – Possibly some of your readers can give an explanation of the abominable stench in Greenwich Town on Monday, which was worse than any continental town and perfectly unbearable. There is always a disagreeable smell, more or less, at Deptford, of what appears to be sewage, and now it seems we are to have it extended to Greenwich. If private residents are not to be driven away, it is time the local authorities bestirred themselves. It would seem, on the face of it, that they are exceedingly apathetic, as the smell referred to at Deptford has been going on for a long time. If it arises from the pumping station there...steps should be taken to stop it. It certainly shows great carelessness somewhere.

– I am, Sir, &c.
E DUDLEY WARD,
Northumberland House, Greenwich, 2 April 1889

The "stench at Greenwich" was a temporary problem. At Deptford it was a fact of life. There were only two main sewers south of the Thames – one from Putney to Deptford, the other from Balham to Deptford. Both carried their flow by gravity and the Deptford pumping station raised the contents by 18 feet from where it made its foul way nearly eight miles to a large reservoir on the Erith marshes before being discharged, totally untreated, into the river at high tide. The main drainage system was an amazing feat of engineering: 82 miles of brick tunnelling through densely populated areas, channelling away around 420 million gallons of sewage and rainwater daily. In the 1860s there were still more than 13,000 feet of sewers to be constructed in the district, especially on the undrained heights of Brockley and Telegraph Hill which were about to be built up. This would have been an opportunity to improve conditions for the sewer flushers. Crawling through the 3ft by 2ft pipes was so hard that chambers had to be made to allow them to unbend occasionally from their cramped position. The engineer suggested larger tunnels but the brickwork would have to twice as thick and the cost was considered too high. It would be interesting to have the flushers' views on this matter.

It was not only sewage which gave Deptford its water problems. In 1856 Henry Pink the Medical Officer wrote to the local press about the impurities picked up by the Ravensbourne even before it reached the reservoirs of the Kent Waterworks near Mill Lane. The problems included "a large number of persons bathing in its waters...horses, wagons, carts and other vehicles constantly washed and cleansed in its stream...the practice of destroying cats and dogs...and the river is exposed to every contamination that mischievous or filthy persons may throw into it".

Such complaints convinced the Kent Company in 1861 to abandon the Ravensbourne in favour of purer well-water but elsewhere other pollution was increasing. Industrial output on the Surrey Canal, from such as the Phoenix Chemical Works and the asphalt works, prompted reports of "offensive liquids and other effluvia". On the Creek huge tar tanks gave off an acrid burning smell and further south a large chemical factory faced a tannery on the other shore. As early as 1852 the *Kentish Mercury* listed the chemical works, breweries, bleach, dye and glue works, tar distilleries and manure manufactories which made the Creek area "one great stinking abomination". Gas works near the Canal and on the Greenwich bank at the mouth of the Creek let out their sulphurous pong and on Deptford Bridge Norfolk's Brewery and Holland's Distillery sent forth the sickly smell of hops and fermentation. In the very centre of Deptford the soap and candle factory in Regent St (Frankham St) filled the air with "evil smells". The soapmaking tradition in the Deptford area dated back at least to the 1740s but it was a nasty business: the main ingredient was animal fat. Not until the late 1950s did the stink finally cause the closure of the Frankham St works when the LCC decided it did not conform to their development plans. The Managing Director, Arthur Wigner, asked prophetically: "Is the LCC going too far? The face of Deptford changes almost daily. Already it houses countless LCC estates...Soon this factory, once a Deptford landmark, will be demolished. Another mother will be given a fifth-floor flat and will worry over the safety of her children. Is this progress?"

Even with all these competing whiffs, nothing in 'Dirty Deptford' could compare with the Thames waterfront. Once, the strong fresh smell of the sawpits had mingled with the background odour of the rotting woodpiles. The huge baking ovens of the Victualling Yard gave off their warm bread welcome and fishermen landed the day's catch at the Upper Watergate stairs. Already by 1805 there was slaughtering of oxen at the Victualling Yard and a series of experiments were organised to decide the relative virtues of the traditional method of 'pole-axing' (knocking down with an axe to the forehead) and the new mode of 'pithing' (thrusting a six inch knife into the spinal marrow at the nape of the neck). Certainly you cannot butcher cattle without causing a stink but with the opening of the Foreign Cattle Market in 1871 the smell around Watergate St and Butcher Row became constant and overwhelming. Before the 1890s there was little refrigeration and it is difficult to imagine what was worse on a summer's day – the river itself or the streams of blood flowing down to it from the cattle sheds.

The 23-acre Deptford cattle market was established by the Corporation of London to replace Smithfield after a century of mutterings that central London was no place for the sale of live animals or their mass slaughter, especially with the dangers of foot-and-mouth disease. The move to Deptford, despite the horrors of the smell, was crucial for local employment prospects. Ellen Chase described how prospective tenants would hope to make a good impression by announcing "with an air that their husbands worked at the cattle trade". The most controversial aspect of the market was the employment of women in the offal sheds to clean out the innards of the slaughtered animals. Known locally as the Gut Girls, these were independent working women ranging in age from 14 to 40 and earning a good wage of 10 or 13 shillings a week. When a local journalist paid a visit to the gut merchants he was told that "although at first it was not pleasant, the girls quickly got used to it and never objected to it". He described the sheds as well ventilated and insisted that one got used to the offensive smell after a while. The girls told him they would rather do this work than be general servants. At least they had their evenings to themselves.

The central shed of the new Foreign Cattle Market on the site of Deptford Dockyard, 1872. Many of the old launching slips were converted into cattle pens when the market opened in 1871. Animals were slaughtered here and meat was prepared but it was never very financially successful. The market closed in 1913 and the site became a war supply depot.

The vicar of St Luke's thought the slaughtermen were "a brutal, drunken and degraded lot" and his colleague from St Paul's believed they asked only for "a good drink and a woman". It was felt that the roughness and bad language of the slaughtermen rubbed off on the girls with "a horribly degrading effect". The Foreign Cattle Market had other moral enemies in the form of the Humanitarian League who called Deptford one of "the dark places of the world". A League pamphlet of 1902 described a visit to the market with all the detailed horror of a modern battery farming or vivisection video. The cattle were flogged and prodded into the pens before each in turn was hooked up by a chain around the horns to a windlass which pulled the animal to its doom, while the others in the pen outside looked on as silent spectators of the pole-axing. The visitor did not accuse the slaughtermen themselves of cruelty but denounced the "habit of flesh eating" which set aside "a large class of men to carry out the sickening and unjust work of which society is ashamed to know the details". The League also published figures on how many foreign cattle died during exportation. In 1897 the losses in the South American trade were 81 dead per 1,000.

In 1898 the Corporation's new restrictions on live imports in favour of the frozen meat trade led to many redundancies at the Foreign

Cattle Market, among them the forewoman who lost her job after working there for 20 years. The market finally closed in 1913. It became a war supply depot and was not reopened after the war despite strong local pressure.

"Deptford was industry and industry was Deptford...No economist would despise Deptford although many preferred to say they lived anywhere but in Deptford." Charles Buckley, who wrote this, was proud of his town but sad to see so many local people give up agricultural work and "many with little regard or respect for farm work streamed into the neighbourhood". Short-cutting across the fields to get to work became so common that a constable was placed on the corner of wheat fields to scare people off. An 1893 *Guide to Greenwich and Deptford* boasted that "almost every industry of importance is represented in the busy district, and the admirable facilities it offers for manufacturing purposes cause the rents in the neighbourhood to stand abnormally high". At high tide the Creek was full of heavily laden barges bringing the cargoes of ocean-going vessels lying in the river. On each Creek bank were "vast industrial establishments" making marine engines and other ships' fittings. The closure of the dockyard had not completely killed Deptford's fame as a shipbuilding centre.

Other workers, neither farm nor factory, provided services of one kind or another. The potman delivered cans of beer, carried on a long pole, "to save mother going out and sometimes saving her from being seen in that despicable place, the pub!" The muffin-man's approach was announced by a handbell and a band of children straggling along behind but if they chanced to see one of the Italians the children would abandon the muffin-man. Deptford's Italian families were poor and lived in the worst areas. Some worked on the roads and were black-faced with the tar and asphalt, but many worked the ice-cream rounds in summer and sold hot potatoes or chestnuts in winter. Others played the barrel-organ, a huge 'piano on wheels' with a handle to grind out the tunes. Some had a monkey and it was said the mad monkey's dance was due to the hot brick the organ-grinder carried. Later some of these families became established local fixtures, like the well-known Rossi family who owned provision shops around the area.

Other things, from vegetables to old clothes, were sold from the streets and the costers' barrows and donkey carts were piled high in the mornings as they made their way to markets all over London. Sometimes they had to pawn their Sunday suit in order to buy stock for the day (Ch.12). There were a hundred different ways of making a few pennies, from selling flowers to telling fortunes, from chimney-sweeping to the dust-cart round. Ellen Chase described the High St in the 1880s: "rough, hearty sailors from the cattle-steamers...women selling jumping-jacks from trays hanging about their necks...men hawking primrose roots from baskets, or rabbits dangling from the end of a stick. Here would be a vendor of whirligigs, there a mender of old umbrellas, or perhaps a blind bugler...Italian women with cages of fortune-telling canaries..." As is still true today, many of those with poorly-paid or casual work lived always on the thin line between enterprise and crime in their struggle to feed themselves and their children.

The streets of 19th century Deptford were full of bustle: people on business and pleasure, shopkeepers competing for custom by shouting their wares at the top of their lungs, children playing hopscotch or using the gas lamp posts as cricket stumps, the clatter of the cart wheels, the sales patter of the born coster, and the rise and fall of everyday life. Sometimes a fight would break out, especially as the evening wore on but just as common was a burst of music and singing from a pub. Someone was doing the rounds with an accordian or a mouth organ. During the week a trio of men with blackened faces would do a working pub-crawl; a beer, a song and the hat went round.

Sometimes a major entertainment came up, such as the visit of Samuel Scott, the celebrated American Leaper and Diver. Adverts appeared all over Deptford in 1840 urging people to come down to Lower Watergate where Scott would dive into the Thames from a mast of 167 feet with a cat on either side of his body. If this sounds odd, the advert also states that Scott had previously leapt down Niagara Falls "without sustaining the slightest personal inconvenience".

Scott and his wife settled down in Deptford while he did the London rounds. He had a trick of placing a noose attached to a cross-beam around his neck and hanging from it until the crowd went wild when he would kick at the lower cross-beam to regain his position. At Deptford the noose slipped tight. While the spectators clapped and cheered Scott's face began to go black but at the last moment he flung himself desperately upwards into the air. His feet were caught by a brother tar on the rigging and Sam managed to loosen the rope. The crowd called out "are you injured?". "Not at all," he replied, "the hemp that is to hang me is not grown yet." That day he raised double his usual reward. Foolish words, though, because in January 1841 the dangerous stunt went wrong again on special scaffolding at Waterloo Bridge. This time no-one could even get to him and the poor man swung from the scaffold being strangled to death for 15 minutes. Even when he was finally cut down and taken with a team of doctors to a local pub, the 'treatment' was horrific. "Everything was done for him. We inflated his lungs. I opened the jugular vein without success. Stimulating embrocations were applied to various parts of his body. He was placed in a warm bath and electrified, and our efforts were kept up for an hour and a half. The veins of both arms had been previoulsy opened, as also the temporal artery. He lost about a pint of blood after he came in."

Then there were the fairs. Deptford Fair was held every Trinity Monday. Over the years it included theatre shows, waxworks, wild beasts, popular dancing, balloon ascents, 'rural sports' and weight-lifting. Sometimes there were 'freak shows' and the 1838 fair featured 'Arabs'. Some decades earlier the Surprising Irish Giant and the Learned Pig had been the star entertainments all over London (see cover). There were also boxing booths, fortune-tellers, scores of minor stalls and gallons upon gallons of beer. In 1839 the Deptford Fair was particularly well attended, "the Cockneys having availed themselves of the railway to an unprecedented extent". That year Thomas Abbott of Bethnal Green ran donkey rides at the Deptford Fair and was surprised to find himself hauled up in court by an officer of the new Society for the Prevention of Cruelty to Animals. The donkey was in a terrible condition with a large raw area on its back. As it buckled under the weight of a huge woman, Abbott beat it with a long ash stick, seeming "particularly pleased whenever he struck it on the raw". He was fined 20 shillings.

Samuel Scott, "the unfortunate American Diver" who leapt from a high mast at Lower Watergate with a cat on either side of his body. Afte[r] his death through an accident at Waterloo, Scot[t's] widow settled in Deptford.

The huge Bank Holiday Fair at Blackheath was a great entertainment for the whole area. In the early-20th century it often featured a stall with a wax-cylinder gramophone where customers paid a penny to listen with earphones for a minute or so. Smaller fairs in the area included the respectable Hatcham Park Fair on grounds hired from the Hardcastles and, later in the 19th century, the small fairground in Giffin St which was described by the vestry in 1891 as a nuisance to the neighbourhood but managed to survive right up to 1961. Charles and Thomas Cain, the last owners of the fair, had been there since they were youngsters. Before World War II hundreds of people flocked to the fair every evening, especially for the tombola where winning tickets gave credit at the local shops.

For most of the year cheap entertainment was more limited. There was the brass band of the Salvation Army or the Bands of Hope attached to local churches. Sometimes amateur performances were put on by churches and chapels and there were free concerts as well as temperance meetings at the People's Hall in Tanners Hill, established by Rev. McIntosh of Brockley in 1889 as a mission centre "to help and bless and save the working classes". Such respectable entertainments could rarely compete with the more populist versions available in the pubs and streets.

Salvation Army bandsmen playing a Sunday morning open-air in Lamerton St, 1920s

The history of gambling must be as old as money and its range of applications is very broad. In 18th century Deptford they include a race between two local horses over the 21 miles from Deptford to Dartford on which it was said £2,000 worth of bets were placed; a nine-mile running match between two tanners on Deptford Road; and four Welsh women who walked from Westminster to Deptford Bridge and back for a wager of £20. Other forms of chancing your luck were also available: in 1743 Mr Eldridge, the draughtsman to the Royal Dockyard, had won £10,000 on lottery ticket No. 52,802.

Fighting could be organised as a form of entertainment, either at fairs or in pubs. There was holiday wrestling at Mr Bull's Railway Tavern in New Cross in the 1840s with the grounds "splendidly fitted up, and capable of containing one thousand persons". Between the wars the Deptford Arena off Giffin St featured all-in wrestling, boxing between locals and outsiders and a boxing booth where lasting three rounds with the house champion could win you a few shillings.

Less formally, an unresolved quarrel could lead to a pitched battle in a field. Everyone knew the rules: each fighter would appoint a second and give his stake to the stakeholder who may take a few other bets from the crowd. Someone would keep time with a watch and the rounds would continue until one of the fighters did not get up.

In 1822 two young men with an old grudge met at the turnpike on Deptford Bridge and agreed to fight it out. They went into the toll-house and handed over their 5 shilling stakes before going into a nearby field where a ring formed round them. They stripped, shook hands and began the fight. By the fourth round Higgins was badly hurt but continued to fight until the ninth round when he gasped "I'll fight no more" and Jones was declared the conqueror. Higgins was carried off to the Bricklayers Arms on Lewisham High Rd but died within a few hours. The Coroner reminded the jury that pitched battles were unlawful and that everyone concerned was liable to be tried for murder if they stood by aiding and abetting while one of the parties was beaten to death. The jury returned a verdict of manslaughter and Jones was sent to Maidstone Gaol.

In 1835 trouble had flared up by the Navy Arms pub outside the dockyard gates when a drunken Royal Marine started leering and pawing at a local woman, Sophia White. Sophia's companions got angry and a row broke out. Another marine came up saying "I am your man – that man's drunk, but I am sober; I am a Lancashire man and will fight his battles". He was punched in the head and fell to the ground, whereupon Sophia started to kick him, swearing she would spill his guts. He died soon after and Sophia and her friend, Thomas Carter, were committed to Newgate for manslaughter.

The old Deptford Theatre in Creek St (Creekside) had originally been a school, then a china warehouse and then a chapel where, according to Thankfull Sturdee, the fanatical Johanna Southcott had preached. There are references to the theatre dating back to 1747 when the main attraction was a Turk on a tightrope. The theatre was very successful when it reopened in 1835 after extensive refurbishment. By 1840 it was under the sole management of a Mrs Yates. The entertainment often involved live animals and on one occasion *The Trial of the Deserter* was performed almost entirely by a troupe of dogs. Polly showed off her skipping rope dance and Tiger hammed up his role as the invalid! Another show, entitled *The Revolt of the Basket Women or the Amazons of Deptford,* included the song 'On the Banks of the Creek's Dirty Waters' and ended with a farce called 'A Lesson for Husbands.' The theatre was greeted with approval by the middle class press in the 1840s but within a decade it had "terribly degenerated, as a private box could be had for sixpence and a seat in the pit for twopence" (Sturdee, 1895). Having lost its licence and become a nuisance it was finally closed in the 1860s.

Just before the theatre closed, two clowns were running a little show there, playing a harlequinade where Clown chases the leaping Harlequin around the stage. On this occasion the poor Harlequin leaped not only through the backdrop but also through a window at the back of the stage and belly-flopped straight into the Creek. He was saved by his agile brother, Tom Lamb, who was playing the Clown.

Deptford Theatre, 1840. ...n more like a circus, live ...nals featured strongly in ...any of the theatre's early ...vs. Edmund Kean, Henry ...ll, Miss Lydia Foote and other famous actors appeared here but it degenerated after the mid-19th century, later ...ming a coal depot called ...eatre Wharf. The Oxford ...ns on the corner of Creek ...(Creekside) was renamed ...ie Birds Nest in the early ...0s and keeps up tradition ...y having a small theatre ...space. The Creek is sadly ...h less accessible and less desirable than it looks in this picture.

In 1897 the flamboyant Broadway Theatre opened on the corner of Tanners Hill with a majestic safety curtain showing Peter the Great as a carpenter at Deptford Dockyard. The reception and auditorium were decorated in Italian renaissance style with the Deptford connection brought home in portraits of Drake, Benbow, Pepys and Evelyn and a reproduction of Drake's *Pelican* at the top of the central arch. The theatre opened with the pantomime *Cinderella* making further local connections: it was set in the village of Louis Scham with characters Sir Brokele Jak, Lord Mihl Waul, Sir Negh Kross Rhode and the villain of the piece, King Blaykethe. The theatre held occasional film shows but it was not very suitable. One time the projector had to be placed in the ladies' lavatory with an opening made in the wall to project the pictures through. The LCC inspector pointed out that the ladies were being inconvenienced and the projector was moved again. A friendly rivalry existed between the Broadway Theatre and the New Cross Empire Music Hall which opened in 1899. Teams from the two leading entertainment centres would meet to play cricket on Blackheath.

For wealthy residents the social round was quite separate, although members of all classes would sometimes meet in time-honoured tradition in the theatres. There were select balls and masques held regularly at the Lord Duncan Tavern and other large pubs and many public dinners for a variety of local dignitaries. The Goldsmiths' Company provided Saturday evening entertainment in the college on Lewisham High Rd. It was not very expensive but Sophie Lake of Hamilton St remembers it only as a very special annual treat.

Deptford was divided socially along the line of New Cross Rd. Mr Hall, Secretary of the Working Men's Club and Institute Union, who lived in Deptford for many years believed that functions held on one side of this gulf could never attract an audience from the other side. He gave the examples of Goldsmiths' whose many free lectures and 'social amusements' were not taken up by the poorer people north of the road and

Broadway Theatre, circa 1900. The Theatre opened in 1897 on the corner of Tanner Hill and the Broadway. It became a cinema in 1916 and was renamed the Century Cinema in 1955 but closed just five years later.

an art exhibition held at Sayes Court unattended by any of the southern art-lovers. Laurie Grove baths were erected at the very centre of the parish but northsiders complained "why didn't you build them in Deptford – not right out there?"

These were the days of pubs, not of off-licenses, but we have seen how the potman would deliver on order and, in fact, there were wine and beer shops. One, near the dockyard gates, had the odd name of Sheer Hulk. At the clockhouse on Deptford Bridge, Passmore wine and spirit merchants sold a range of booze from sparkling champagne at 6 shillings a bottle to double brown stout at 3 pence.

As early as 1730 the Vine & Still Distillery (later Holland's) near Deptford Bridge was improving poor British brandies with foreign grapes to make a new brandy as good as the French and far cheaper.

Although horizons were limited by our standards, excursions were becoming increasingly popular at the end of the 19th century. Families might go to Woolwich to see the Church Parade or to Greenwich Hospital to hear the Boys' Band play and going up to Blackheath was a best-clothes family outing. On Sundays children would often be packed off to Sunday School while their fathers "loaf about in their shirt-sleeves" but in the evening many dads would "buck up and go for a walk". The vicar of All Saints found that late rising and Sunday bicycling were very prevalent.

Some of the earlier customs were kept up during the 19th century. The old tradition of Rogation-tide became a Perambulation of the Parish, more commonly known as 'Beating the Bounds'. The St Paul's version of 1834 shows the scale of such an operation. The vestry decided it must not exceed £20 in total expenditure although they worried that if refreshments were stinted the officers would get severely 'bumped'. On the previous Perambulation, which cost more than twice that amount (one wit asked whether any champagne or rose water had been included), the drunken revellers had broken into the refreshment booth and assaulted the officers.

The programme was advertised in the local papers but the occasion did not quite live up to expectations. There were no banners and no music was allowed, the local MPs were needed in the House of Commons and "the tail [of the procession] was too long for the body". Nevertheless it was a grand entertainment with all sorts of local officials being bumped against gates, posts and trees. The route had to follow the parish boundaries exactly. Ladders were used to clamber over the rooves of the Trinity Almshouses and the leader had to swim the exact boundary line in the Quaggy while the rest crossed by a plank bridge. Near the lane to Hilly Fields some 'buxom lasses' lay in wait, eyeing the young rector (the newly-appointed Rev. B S Ffinch) longingly. It was 78 degrees in the shade by the time they arrived at the Crown & Anchor on the Kent Road around 2 o'clock. After plenty of cold water and a lunch of ham, beef, ale and biscuits, they continued down White Post Lane by Hatcham Park House, giving three cheers to the navvies working on the new London & Greenwich Railway. The procession finally arrived, exhausted, in Deptford High St at 7 o'clock and the parish officers crawled their way to the White Swan for dinner. That very night Richard Porter the Beadle dropped dead 'by the Visitation of God'. In a state of great heat he had downed a pint of cold water at the White Swan and been taken ill immediately.

Another local custom, obscure in origin, was known as Jack in the Green or Fowler's Troop of Mayday Revellers. This was a chimney-sweeps' May Day event dating back to around 1800. The Jack would be hidden in a wickerwork frame covered with leaves and flowers while the party of men dressed as women danced around to the 'rough music' of tin whistles and drums, collecting pennies which were later

Jack in the Green, Deptford, circa 1910. A chimney-sweeps' May-y custom dating back to around 1800 but with precedents in the rough music and charivari of medieval times.

spent in the pub. The custom died out in the early years of the 20th century when, as Thankfull Sturdee noted, "the police stopped all such customs".

After 1910 Deptford had a new form of entertainment which was to prove the most popular of all. Millwall Football Club crossed the river and moved into its grounds at the Den behind the western end of New Cross Rd. The first game against Brighton attracted 20,000 spectators and the following year the ground hosted its only full international match when England beat Wales 3-0.

Football's popularity had expanded enormously in the second half of the 19th century. By 1889 thousands of matches were being played all over the country and the press had begun to report the scores. In that year the *Times* was the centre of a debate over the morality of the game (it was said to encourage "intemperance and gambling") and its dangers both on and off pitch. Two Midland teams and their supporters had recently met at a railway station after the game and "engaged in a free fight...the result of the angry feelings evoked during the game". The long list of injuries of that season was attributed to the extension of the game to "factory operatives, miners and artisans" who "cannot be expected to play in the friendly and generous spirit with which gentlemen are imbued from their youth".

In 1937 Millwall became the first Third Division side to reach the FA Cup Semi-finals when nearly 50,000 watched the Lions beat Derby 2-1 in the Quarter-final at the Den. Wartime bomb damage at the Den matched the poor playing of the time: in the 1944-5 season 18 matches went by without a win and Millwall finished second from botttom in the League. The rest of the 1940s were dismal and, although the 1950s opened with three new players and a great start to the season, by the end of the decade Millwall were founder members of Division Four and finished in ninth place. Financial problems made it difficult to sign new players and in 1962 Peter Burridge was sold off to neighbours Crystal Palace for a meagre £8,000, much to the disgust of the fans. Nevertheless, Millwall crept back up the ladder to Division Two and in 1972 the team narrowly missed further promotion. The later 1970s saw the team fall through the ranks to be 14th in Division Three by 1980, but during the 1980s they were promoted again and two years after the club's 1985 centenary they won the Division Two championship and landed in the First Division for the first time in the club's history. The triumphant glow faded when they were relegated once more in 1990 and it was a sad day in May 1993 when the last game at the Den was lost to Bristol Rovers.

Millwall fans are famous, and not just for the hooliganism of the 1980s. Lions player Johnny Johnson who joined in 1945 remembers the enormous loyalty and appreciation of the fans and Jim Constantine whose two hat-tricks against Millwall persuaded them to sign him up in 1948, received many letters from fans when his wife died recently. Charlie Hurley loved the support of the regular 20,000 in attendance and most of the old players describe how the crowd used to intimidate the opposition, who hated to play Millwall at home. Barry Kitchener, who made nearly 600 appearances for the Lions says the biggest buzz he got was making the fans happy and hearing the 'Millwall Roar'. Nicky Chatterton, who joined in 1978, had previously hated playing at the Den for Crystal Palace because "the fans were so passionate, and so close to the pitch". For George Graham (manager 1982-1986) Millwall fans' passion for the game brought back memories from his days in Glasgow. When John Docherty, who managed the team through the promotion to Division One, walked into the Royal Archer pub with the championship trophy, the fans couldn't believe their luck.

Early trams and buses were not numbered but were painted all over in a certain colour. The lower deck was reserved for ladies. Men rode on the open top whatever the weather. Along the main roads many of the horse-drawn buses belonged to Thomas Tilling of Peckham who kept up business by hiring out carriages and horses for weddings. At the turn of the century horse-drawn trams were a common sight throughout Deptford but by 1906 the LCC had laid the lines for motor trams on most of the main routes. The tram depot at New Cross Gate which opened that year was the largest in London with 326 tramcars, providing work for many local men.

New Cross tram crews outside the depot on New Cross Road. The prevalence of medals dates this photo around 1919. This was the largest of London's tram depots. It opened in 1906 on the site of Fairlawn, an 18th century house occupied by a prominent market-gardening family. To the left of the depot was the South Eastern District Synagogue which opened in 1904 but became a Kingdom Hall for the Jehovah's Witnesses in the 1980s.

One of the great sights of early 20th century Deptford was the new Power Station. Designed and built by the genius of electric power, Sebastian de Ferranti, Deptford Power Station was the first large-scale power generator in the world. For most people lighting was provided by candles and paraffin lamps. The Blackpool illuminations had begun in 1879 but the technique used made them very intense and gas companies their reassured shareholders that "the electric light can nver be applied indoors without the production of an offensive smell which undoubtedly causes headaches". Nevertheless small local stations were set up in the West End and by 1881 the House of Commons itself was lit by electricity.

In 1883 Sir Coutts Lindsay of Grosvenor Gallery, New Bond St decided to change from gas to "the new smokeless electricity". He installed a small power-generator with overhead conductors mounted on neighbouring rooftops. Its great success led to extension of the supply to his neighbours. The system proved difficult to operate and Sir Coutts invited the young Ferranti to take charge.

Ferranti was born in Liverpool to artistic parents. He was sent to University College, London, at the age of 16 but had to give it up when his father became ill. He got a job at Siemens in Woolwich as a research assistant, inventing a number of revolutionary electrical devices which not only increased efficiency but could be manufactured at a fraction of the previous cost. He soon had his own company making alternators, arc lamps, meters and other of his inventions. In 1885 he patented his high voltage AC transformer system, which is basically still in use today.

At the Grosvenor Gallery Ferranti began to make changes, replacing most of the equipment with apparatus of his own design. Within three years he was supplying premises in 100 miles of streets. At that time the gas companies were rationalising their industry, moving over from local works to big plants. Ferranti took up their example in developing his own grand scheme for electric power-generation. The scale of his vision was undreamed of, an ambitious leap into the technical unknown. He planned a big power station capable of supplying all London, built on cheap land beyond the city and with the unlimited cooling potential of the Thames. Whereas the largest of the Gallery engines was 750 hp, the Deptford plant would have four of 10,000 hp each. The boilers would have 70 times more steaming capacity and there would be four 500-ton alternators, generating at 10,000 volts. This was more than 12 times the power of their Gallery equivalents and the new power station would be capable of supplying two million lamps.

Sir Coutts and his brother Lord Wantage established the London Electric Supply Corporation Ltd (LESCo) and, on Ferranti's advice, they bought up the three-acre site at the Stowage. Work progressed night and day to get the main building up by the summer of 1889. Ferranti was involved at every stage in the building works and the *Electrical Engineer* dubbed him "the Michelangelo of that installation...from first to last, from foundation to highest turret...all were specified or designed by one man". According to Ferranti's wife, Gertrude Ince: "The first thing I remember during those first months of married life was Deptford, and again Deptford. We talked Deptford and dreamed Deptford." Ferranti had staked his reputation, his personal fortune and many long months of labour to make the Deptford dream come true.

Eminent men of the time prophesied disaster. Ferranti wanted to use 10,000 volts. They said anything over 2,000 volts was dangerous. Thomas Edison himself visited the station during construction and spoke to the press about the risks but he added "Oh, it will go!" And it did, eventually, but first Ferranti had to design and manufacture his own cables capable of carrying the high pressure current. These were one of the most valuable of his inventions, carrying both 'out' and 'return' current in the same casing and self-insulated so they could be laid down in the earth without any further protection. LESCo were aware that digging up the streets would be disruptive and would require permission from dozens of separate parishes. To avoid this they came to arrangements with the railway companies to lay the cables along the tracks all the way from Deptford to Charing Cross, Cannon Street and Blackfriars stations. An agreement with the Underground meant tube tunnels could be used to get the cables to the main distribution points.

Ferranti's Deptford Power Station soon after completion in October 1889. The original building was retained in the growing complex until it was decommissioned in 1957 and demolished at the end of the 1960s.

The Board of Trade were so sceptical about the safety of these cables carrying 10,000 volt currents that Ferranti invited them to a most unusual demonstration. While one assistant held onto a chisel, another hammered it straight into a live main. According to a report "the cable was pierced, the fuses functioned and everything went perfectly", though Mr Kolle, who held the chisel, looks somewhat nervous in the accompanying sketch. Some of the cables remained in use until 1933 when they were replaced to provide greater compatibility.

Despite these initial successes, disappointments began to come thick and fast. The Board of Trade set up an inquiry under Major Marindin which recommended that Deptford's proposed area of supply be halved, that two of its four units should be located elsewhere and that small stations should be given the right to compete within every area. The results were catastrophic and were quickly followed by a major accident when an inexperienced operator at the Grosvenor Gallery site pulled a plug switch and panicked. Fire broke out and the Gallery was destroyed. Just when Deptford was taking over responsibility for generation, the whole system had to be shut down. Repairs were made and new transformers were purchased but a week later one of the repaired transformers failed, and the excess electrical load proved too much for the others which all burned out. This time the shut-down lasted three months. Customers deserted the company and the LESCo directors began to lose faith in Ferranti's plans. Why do we need the 10,000 hp machines they asked and the Chairman declared: "Ye're a very clever man, Mr Ferranti, but I'm thinking ye're sadly lacking in prevision." The order for the machines was cancelled. Seeing his dream in tatters while still knowing its worth, Ferranti left the London Electric Supply Corporation in 1891 and devoted himself to his own very successful business.

The power station continued to develop without its genius founder but frequent alternator failures and boiler fouling took their toll on customer confidence. In 1900 the station had to be shut down for major renovation. Those who could get work at 'the Light' were the lucky ones in these hard times. Now they faced six months without pay. In the early years of the 20th century Deptford Power Station expanded from lighting to transport with contracts for the LCC tramways and the suburban electric service of the London, Brighton & South Coast Railway. Other railways joined the network and the complexity of Deptford's electrical systems increased so much that it was said the station could "link up to anything - even the Gas Works".

In 1925 ten electric supply companies, including LESCo, merged to become the London Power Company which immediately planned a new station at Deptford on the dry docks to the west of the Ferranti building. Dr Leonard Pearce, the LPC's Chief Engineer, designed both Deptford West and the new super-station at Battersea. Building began in 1926, with every ton of building material dragged to the site by horse and cart. There was a terrible accident when a shaft ring fractured and five men were killed, caught between tons of falling earth on one side and the river gushing into the tunnel on the other.

During the General Strike the power station was run with help from the armed forces. Along with staff who continued at work, they stayed on site all the time. One of the few women workers at the station remembered how she helped to provide meals for everyone, setting off on her bicycle to Deptford High St when shopping was needed.

There was a friendly rivalry between Deptford East and West but whichever side you were on, 'the Light' was seen as a good place to work, combining reasonable wages with security and companionable conditions. For some there was also the possibility of a flat in St Nicholas' House, built for workers by the LPC. Like many trades, the work often ran in families. John Bauer from Canning Town, who has worked in every power station in the country, says he never knew how many cousins he had till he started work. Workers were reminded of their fortune by children outside the station gates asking "Anything to eat, mister?" and the men often brought double rations of sandwiches to give away.

In 1938 precautions were being taken against the coming war with air raid covers being installed over the switch house. There were still workers who remembered the 1916 Zeppelin bombing which killed a man on site but nothing prepared them for the tragedies of the blitz. Altogether 27 staff were killed on site by enemy action, the highest number of any power station in the country and testimony to Deptford's crucial position and purpose.

When Dunstan Thompson visited Deptford in 1947, he described the power station as "a giant complex of stone supporting two chimneys, twenty storeys high, made to look like colossal Doric columns...monstrous and magnificent. I thought of what a ruin it would some day make." The following year nationalisation of the industry created the British Electricity Authority which completed Ferranti's original work in creating a high pressure extension to Deptford East. This was the last extension to be built at Deptford, making it the country's second biggest station after Barking. After 1957 the Ferranti building was taken out of commission and stood

Deptford Power Station in the 1980s seen from Hughes Fields west of Deptford Green. The dramatic demolition of this great landmark in 1992 was captured on film by Deptford-born photographer Rice. One hundred years of the power station's records filled two large skips. Although a fraction of these were rescued by a local video group, neither the Lewisham Local History Society nor the Borough of Lewisham's archives were able to save the rest.

empty for a long time until demolition at the end of the 1960s. During the 1970s there were major problems with asbestos and the station was becoming less efficient. The last part of this monumental power station finally closed in 1983 and was demolished in 1992.

Although the Power Station site is now completely flattened, St Nicholas' House remains. With the old view of familiar chimneys obliterated many of the tenants feel Deptford has little left for them. Henry Campden was

111

born in the House, son of a power station worker, but moved to Downham with his parents as a teenager. His father introduced him to the work and both men travelled back to Deptford daily. Henry moved back to St Nicholas' House when he married and managed to get his parents' old flat. Now he is hoping to move again, this time out into Kent. It is not only the view that has changed. After their long years of work in the industry, tenants at St Nicholas' House feel cheated now that Power Gen, the privatised successor to the Central Electricity Generating Board, has sold the building to a private landlord. As 'the Light' is forgotten the rents get higher though the site beside the Creek remains empty.

At the turn of the 20th century Deptford was changing again. New industries had helped to get the town back on its feet after the closure of the dockyard but now the cattle market was threatened. Long-established shops were being taken over and whole areas cleared for new housing. Old Deptford Bridge was replaced, Blackhorse Bridge was widened by the Greenwich Board of Works and the ancient streets at the north end of the High St were changed beyond recognition when the new section of road was cut through to join Evelyn St to Creek Rd. The railway tangle was complete and no new lines would open in the coming century, though its effects would be more intense as new roads completed the isolation of areas stranded into islands.

Railwaymen had the ascendancy and navvying was a sad memory. The only sailors to be seen in Deptford now were the cattle-steamer men, though there were still proud families of lightermen, who passed the trade from father to son, and the docks continued to grow for many years. Farming was a thing of the past, and the allotment craze had not yet begun to take the place of the market gardens. There was work for women in the wood-yards and the rag factories, in the laundries and as domestic servants in the new rich houses of the hilly south. Italians had joined the Irish as long-term settlers and were slowly earning their way out of the stable lofts and into business via the organ and the ice-cream cart. Deptford faced the new century with the seeds of both decay and renewal already planted. A mess had been made, some of it was being tidied; new problems were arising from new ventures and the old terror of unemployment still loomed large.

9

Home and the Heart

"We often find it necessary to feed the children
before we attempt to teach them."
– Deptford Ragged School Report, 1868

The social researchers, moral improvers, charitable and church workers of the turn of the century based their judgements about what was necessary for Deptford and how it was to be achieved on a fundamental division of the working class into 'rough' and 'respectable'. This distinction could refer to individuals, families, streets or whole neighbourhoods. One outsider described his idea of Deptford: "This name to me meant unimaginable squalor. I was never taken there. Somehow I was brought up to think of it as a dark, dirty, common, low place." In the Booth notebooks the residents of Mill Lane were so rough as to be 'vicious'.

Respectability is a luxury commodity and very hard to maintain in the midst of poverty. Yet there was a notion, based in the doctrines of Protestantism, that success in life marked a person out as one of God's elect so poverty itself must be a mark of the individual's sin and failure. In a town like Deptford with high unemployment and large patches of slum housing the term 'rough' described a complex mixture of bad conditions and perceived immorality. Neither 'rough' nor 'respectable' should be taken as sociological categories describing real people or neighbourhoods. Rather they were emotive labels attached by observers to certain ways of life.

These observers were not always outsiders. Most knowledgeable about the gradations of respectability were those who lived in the heart of the struggle between hope and despair. Although there were similarities between middle class and working class ideas on this subject, it was not a simple question of the 'filtering down' of morality. Both versions stressed the central position of women as the guardians of respectability and the domestic realm as the stage on which it was acted out. "Women indeed embodied respectability or the lack of it, in their dress, public conduct, language, housekeeping, childrearing methods, spending habits, and, of course, sexual behaviour." (Ross, 1983). The most discerning audience for the small symbols of status was not the 'lady rent-collector' or the local parson but the neighbours. The ideal of privacy, another feature working class respectability shared with the middle class version, has for many of us gone too far and ended in isolation. It is easier now than ever before to ignore our neighbours. In early-20th century Deptford this was very difficult and, taken to its extreme, it would have been suicidal. Despite the cutting up of the overall district by the tangle of railway lines and roads, home was firmly planted in the immediate neighbourhood.

Ellen Ross has described the categories 'rough' and 'respectable' as two types of survival strategy chosen by women for their families in working class neighbourhoods. The 'rough' type was associated with a true street life where wives spent less money and time on cleaning and appearances and more on food, drink and recreation. Through 'gossip' they shared information about local households, allowing them to perform the roles later taken over rather inadequately by the state: helping the sick, providing meals for the hungry, taking in a child to help out a family in trouble. They operated the most local of insurance systems, lending pennies, food, clothes and household goods to neighbours and relatives, knowing that the favours would be returned in hard times. In this way links were maintained between separate households and a shared identity was created.

The 'respectable' kept themselves to themselves as far as possible, concentrating resources on improving their own family situation. Respectability demanded privacy and secrecy. Borrowing, lending and gossip were considered shameful and "the staunchly respectable were isolated from the sharing networks that provided both pleasure and a measure of security". Yet few families could take this to extremes because of the insecurity of most local employment and the unforeseen emergencies of illness, injury and death. The 'respectable' pattern depended on more formal institutions like friendly societies or insurance companies such as Prudential who would insure a young man's life for seven guineas on a premium of a penny a week collected door to door. Posters advertising Prudential schemes were pasted up on the trees all around old Deptford.

When George Glazebrook's mother had no ha'penny to give him for sweets in 1929 "she said she was short but I mustn't tell anyone". His friend, Joey, from a 'rough' family and with an accent to match, could not understand why he didn't nick one of the pennies for the gas stacked on the mantlepiece. George and Joey's friendship existed across the rough/respectable division. George's mother summed up many of the features of the distinction: "I'm not keen on him playing with that Joey Skinner. Rough lot they are. All those kids, cheap condensed milk scraped on door-step slices of bread. God knows how they manage with him out of work – and she's got one on the way, too." When George's grandmother made bread and dripping for him he did not tell her that his mother used margarine and that she said only poor boys like Joey ate dripping. The Glazebrooks were careful what they said in front of George and he got his "first primitive biology lesson" from Joey. The usual status markers appear – a piano, a wireless and a move in 1931 to a new estate out in Kent.

Huge numbers of working class Deptford children in generation after generation died before they could speak. Those who survived faced living conditions guaranteed to cause problems with rickets, dysentery and lung disease. Terrible diets arose not only from ignorance and simple poverty but because the "working class could be exploited as consumers as they were as wage earners" (Rule, 1986). Academic arguments about living standards have too often used wholesale prices as data, missing the true experience of the poor market shopper who tended to pay higher prices for shorter measures of inferior food.

Saturday was both market and pay day. In the morning the market was well equipped and crowded with well dressed and respectable people. At noon out came the 'coarse, diseased animal food' and the 'deteriorated vegetables'. Small dealers bought up the cheaper stuff for resale and by Saturday night, after workers got their pay, the following description from 1848 could apply: "From the butchers' and green-grocers' shops the gaslights flared and flickered, wild and ghastly over haggard groups of slipshod dirty women, bargaining for scraps of stale meat and frost-bitten vegetables, wrangling about shortweight and bad quality. Fish stalls and fruit stalls lined the edge of the greasy pavement, sending up odours as foul as the language of sellers and buyers. Blood and sewer water crawled from under doors and out of spouts, and reeked down the gutters among offal, animal and vegetable, in every stage of putrefaction." (Kingsley, 1848).

Deptford market was described in 1893 as "one of the best in the Metropolis, where provisions and clothing of every description may be purchased on exceptionally advantageous terms" and there were small grocery stores on most corners in the residential areas. However, buying in small measures or on credit was expensive and previous debts could make it impossible for shoppers to go elsewhere. The 'truck' system, where employers paid in vouchers only redeemable at their own shops, could milk workers of up to 10% of their wages. Food was often adulterated: alum was used to whiten bread, milk was watered down, sand added to sugar, earth to pepper, and sugar bakers were discovered using ground glass to 'frost' their cakes. Old tea leaves were re-roasted for resale and port was made by mixing alcohol and dye. The Food and Drugs Act of 1860 helped put an end to such practices but there is no doubt that working class shoppers remained at a serious disadvantage.

There were other ways in which the cost of living for poor families was disproportionately high. Heavy manual work meant the frequent purchase of shoddy clothing which wore out quickly. The greater risk of rent arrears meant that working class rents were usually set at a rate far beyond what the properties were worth. While it was just possible to make ends meet, familes of unskilled labourers lived constantly from hand to mouth. So long as the labourer was in work they would get by but a week's illness or slack employment meant short rations or debt, or both.

For most Deptford families the pawnshop had long provided a safety net. Some used it like a kind of bank, pledging and retrieving the same items on a weekly or even daily basis. Father's suit could go in on Monday to pay the rent and be taken out the following week when the wages arrived. If necessary the beds could be stripped in the morning to provide some money to buy stock for a coster's cart. At homecoming, if the day had been good, the blankets could be retrieved for the night. On a bad day it might be necessary to offer a coat in exchange. On a more long-term level, some women would pawn their wedding rings "at holiday times when we'd no wages coming...it threw you back all the year round". Other women found this a heavy emotional loss and pawnbrokers tended to view it with distaste.

Interest charged by the pawnbroker could be around 3 pence on a 10 shilling loan each week. Within three months the pledger would owe 13 shillings and may have to bring another little parcel to make it up. One pawnbroker admitted "I couldn't honestly say that I was any benefit to anyone that pawned, except it relieved them." Yet this 'relief' was a crucial part of maintaining everyday family life. Odd though it seemed to middle class observers with savings, some people even pledged to keep out of debt, raising ready cash at the pawnshop to avoid the heavy interest charged by the small shopkeeper for 'tick'. Here was a quite different view of material resources, seen as tangible assets to be drawn on when times got hard again. Looking through goods in shops, people would ask the assistant what they would fetch in pawn. A good watch or brooch, if it could be acquired, may prove a life-saver over and over again in the future. So, in a smaller way, could the family's Sunday best clothes. The household furniture itself was a form of insurance. Although one might lose it all for good in an exceptional depression, at least it provided a comfortable home in the meantime. During the First World War the unprecedented earnings of munitions workers were often spent on jewellery with a similar eye to the future. Besides all this, cramped living conditions could make custom of convenience: pledging provided not only cash but storage, especially for baby clothes which would await their next owner neatly wrapped in the pawnshop.

While the customer saw her pledge in terms of original value and cost of replacement, to the pawnbroker it was only worth what he could get for it in 12 months time. Nonetheless there were many odd items which pawnbrokers would accept: glass eyes, false teeth and artifical limbs were not exactly saleable but were very likely to be redeemed. Marriage cetificates could be safely accepted since a customer who did not return for them would see her 'marriage lines' prominently displayed in the pledge shop window. The neighbourhood pawnshop could be a flexible institution and mornings sometimes saw workers buying cigarettes with a loan on a basin of hot-pot wrapped in a handkerchief, to be retrieved at midday with a sub from work.

The pawnshops were known as the 'housewife's saviour' and it was true that men tended to pawn for a treat, women from necessity and often without their husbands' knowledge or consent. Women's possessions were first to pawn and last to redeem. While father needed his Sunday best, even if he only lounged about on the corner of the street until the pubs opened, mother seldom got new clothes and often did without boots since she had little need to appear in the light of day. Edward Buckmaster, who worked at Humphrey & Tennants at the riverside end of Hughes Fields, "was, as a boy, the lackey, running from moneylenders, credit drapers, and pawn shops". His mother had got into some small debt which snowballed and she finally fled from home in 1928 too scared to tell her husband. While many women would pledge items that technically belonged to their husbands, this was nothing compared to the washerwomen who rushed somebody's washing through and took it to the pawnshop for a few days before it was due back when it would be exchanged for the next load.

It was usually impossible for neighbours to help out with financial assistance, but they might lend a coat to someone who had nothing left the pawnbroker would accept. Any woman with slightly greater resources than her neighbours or whose husband was paid earlier in the week was likely to start lending money informally and a business relationship frequently developed. Charles Booth said of London's poorer districts that "every street has its lender, often a woman". It was also common for a woman to make some extra pennies as a 'pawn shop runner' charging others to save them the embarrassment of the pledge shop queue. During World War I many women became financially secure for the first time as they used their separation allowance to run small-scale moneylending businesses. The usual interest was a penny a week on every shilling, a massive rate of 433% but one which was generally accepted.

Neighbours also banded together to form paying-out clubs, known as 'didly' or 'diddlum' clubs. Stocking clubs, crockery clubs and Christmas dinner clubs made short appearances in many poor women's budgets. Sometimes it was possible to take out a club loan during the summer and pay it back with interest before Christmas when it was all shared out. In other clubs a lump sum was distributed monthly to each member in turn. Those who received early shares had only moral pressure and group loyalty to keep up the contributions for the benefit of the others. Most poorer people bought clothing and furniture on the 'never never', whether through a club or with the tally man who would call weekly to collect the next instalment.

Another kind of saving which was typical among the poor was burial insurance. The desire to 'lay something by' for the one inevitable landmark of a chaotic and unplanned life and to avoid a pauper's funeral was a very old aspiration. At the funeral of young Eliza Kendall at St Paul's in September 1844 the girl's sisters were "suitably attired in mourning...which had been purchased with sums raised in very small subscriptions amongst the working classes" in their area. Working people were likely to face the problem of burial early in married life at the death of one or more children. The poorer they were, the more likely this would happen. If they had not insured each child as it was born, death meant a choice between borrowing and the disgrace of a pauper funeral which carried with it the pauperisation of the father, a humiliation hard to bear alongside the grief. Middle class ignorance mocked the poor for squandering money on funerals but around 1913 the cheapest burial for a very young baby cost 30 shillings. Older children cost far more. For the majority of unskilled labourers this was nearly two weeks' full wages and undertakers gave no 'tick'. So housewives' budgets included one penny a week for each child, 2 pence for the mother and 3 pence for the father. With each individual separately insured, the money paid for a child who did not die provided no help in meeting costs. Worst of all, if the man lost his job or became ill, even years of regular payments would not save the benefit. His children were more likely to die in such circumstances and the family may face the dreaded pauper funeral after all.

Trying to answer the question: "How does a working man's wife bring up a family on 20 shillings a week?" Maud Pember Reeves and the Fabian Women's Group recorded the daily budgets of 30 working class Lambeth families 1909-1913. With a sympathy born of twice-weekly visits, these educated women did not presume to teach poor women how to run their homes. In their publication *Round About A Pound A Week*, however, they suggested to a wider world that had the Post Office initiated a weekly collection of pennies rather than the insurance companies the sum of £11 million a year paid by the poor could be used for life rather than for death.

Poverty affected domestic life in every way and at every stage of the family life cycle. If working class children were badly fed, their mothers also suffered terribly. Pressure from the Women's Co-operative Guild in the early 20th century secured 30 shillings maternity benefit in Lloyd George's National Insurance Act. In 1913 a lightning campaign was successful in having the benefit legally recognised as the property of the mother. In 1915 the Guild published under the title *Maternity* a series of letters from working women which revealed to a reluctant public the unpalatable truth of the agonies of motherhood among the working class. The impression these letters give is of perpetual overwork, illness and suffering, rooted in the conditions of life arising from the ordinary family wage of between 18 and 30 shillings a week. A middle class wife around 1910 would have had medical advice available during pregnancy and childbirth. She would be well fed and rested and able to remain in bed after the birth until ready to get up. "For a woman of the middle class to be deprived of any one of these things would be considered an outrage. Now, a working class woman is habitually deprived of them all."

From a husband's wage of 25 shillings, the woman would be lucky to receive 20 shillings a week with which to provide housing, food and clothing for the whole family. The additional outlay on maternity which ought to take around £5 was impossible from these utterly inadequate wages. A few shillings would be scraped together by the woman stinting herself when she ought to be well fed, "for in a working class home if there is saving to be done, it is not the husband and children, but the mother who makes her meal off the scraps which remain over". Most women had their babies at home. In 1910 the doctor would cost around one guinea (21 shillings). Poorer women would make do with only a midwife at 8 to 12 shillings.

In St Paul's churchyard there is a gravestone to Margaret Hawtree who died in 1734:
"She was an indulgent mother, and the best of wives
She brought into this world more than three thousand lives!"
Mrs Hawtree was an eminent Deptford midwife who had presented silver christening basins to St Paul's and St Nicholas' churches.
Around 1915 the local midwife was Mrs Harper, the chimney-sweep's wife, who lived in Mary Ann's Buildings. She was called to Hamilton St to help at the birth of Sophie Faulkner, but the baby arrrived first. Luckily Sophie's Aunt Emily was there to help out as she always was for births or illnesses, despite having four children of her own to look after.
A later Deptford midwife was Miss Elsie Walkerdine who had a room over a shop in the High St. Elsie is remembered affectionately by many Deptford people for her warm, calm manner and her flexibility about payment. Sometimes she would even go down to the pawn shop on a Sunday morning to retrieve some of baby's clothes if the birth was coming along quicker than expected. Mary Thorley, who worked for Elsie before and during the Second World War, remembers how husbands would come down to the shelter and say "Nurse, my wife's started labour. Would you come along? Or will you have to wait until this is over?" Elsie never refused, answering "If you've come round for me during this, I can come back with you." Elsie and others like her made a lot of friends in Deptford and are remembered by generations of mothers.

Overwork and underfeeding right up to the birth, left a woman weak and the child, if born alive at all, would be feeble and vulnerable in its early months. That first month was the time most infant deaths took place. Many a woman would be up and working at hard domestic labour within a week of the birth. Soon she may well be pregnant once more. One of the Guild's *Maternity* letters describes how "for 20 years

I was nursing or expecting babies".

These conditions, both pre- and post-natal, gave women varicose veins, neuralgia and 'fallen wombs', but they took these illnesses for granted, having been told by mother, midwife or neighbour that this was all 'natural'. The Guild's introduction to the *Maternity* letters attacked the idea that women must submit to a life dictated by "the satisfaction of man's desires and the bearing of children". Sketching the isolation of working class women "hidden behind the curtain which falls after marriage", the Guild was optimistic that women were at last raising this curtain themselves, aware of their ignorance and the horrific effects of poverty on their own and their children's lives.

These women who grew up in the new century trace their ignorance back to their mothers who "never spoke to us about anything like that". Even for the few women who had their babies in hospital very little information was forthcoming from the doctors. "When I had it I didn't even know where the baby was going to come from. Nor did my husband. And when he came to see me...he said 'Is that where they cut you open?'. 'No', I said 'it's come from the same place as you put it in'. And that was that."

Children's everyday lives depended as always on the relative poverty and stability of family life and the skills of their parents in 'making do'. Sophie Faulkner's family who lived in Hamilton St were very poor but her mother was a good manager. "Our clothes were patched and darned. My mother used to make nearly all of them." Children were often stitched into their underclothes for the winter and layer upon layer added over the top. "First of all there was a flannel vest, then a white cotton chemise and a pair of grey flannel 'trap-door drawers', which buttoned on the liberty bodice, on top of which we wore a cotton petticoat, and a dress, topped up with a white cotton pinafore edged with lace." Sophie's father used to mend the boots on Sunday mornings on an old stool in the scullery, heelballing round the edge to make them watertight. In summer the children would have new black plimsolls at 5 shillings a pair.

There were no 'mod cons' in those days and most older people have strong memories of washing day. First the old stone copper had to be filled and the fire lit underneath. A 'copper stick' was used to pull out the boiling clothes to run them through the big old mangle. Then they were put into the shallow cone sink for rinsing. The tablecloth, pillowcases, and pinafores were starched along with a dash of blue bag and then back to the mangle. On fine days they went out on the two lines in the backyard. Dinner that day had to be ready by just after 12 noon and would be cold meat with hot vegetables and mustard pickles (2 pence in a cup from Hawtons, the little shop on the corner of Hamilton St) or stew with dumplings. Breakfast was most often bread and beef dripping with a cup of cocoa.

Saturday night was usually bath night and the galvanised bath would be set out in front of the kitchen range, with children taking turns for the same water. In the cold weather mothers might heat an old flat iron, and wrap it in one of Dad's old flannel shirts to warm the bed. Most children shared a bed, sometimes three or four together. Bedrooms were usually bare boards and got horribly cold but if any of the children were ill they might be allowed the luxury of a coal fire in the bedroom. Sophie's mother was a good nurse. "She would bring a tray up with a bowl of water, soap, flannel and towel for washing and make our bed comfortable, and meals such as we could eat were brought upstairs."

Children had few toys but sometimes Christmas would bring a small doll. Sophie remembers having a black doll dressed in a red woolly suit. The four children in her family shared three comics a week which cost a penny each. They also got a penny per week pocket money as long as they did their chores. Hers was to clean her father's working boots. After chores the children went out to play in the street: cricket, football, rounders, hopscotch, skipping, marbles, charades, and a game known as "please we've come to learn a trade".

Old Attwood's Toy Shop i the 1890s. The shop, near th corner of Evelyn St an Grinling Place, was kept b old lady Attwood and he daughters but closed dow after her death in 1899.

As they got older most girls would take on more of the domestic work, 'cleaning through' the house, which usually meant scrubbing the bare board or stone floors, blackleading and polishing the kitchen range and whitestoning the hearth. Sophie remembers her home as always clean if a bit shabby. The light was by gas, paid for by a penny slot meter, and it was quite an event to watch the gas man make his shilling piles of coppers on the kitchen table. "Sometimes Mum was given back a shilling or two, and I can imagine how she must have saved this to buy something to improve the home."

Most children went to Sunday School and Sophie's parents sent them to the Baptist one in Octavius St because there were no main roads to cross. Annual outings to Crayford Sand Pits could never quite compensate for the lack of seaside holidays. "I left when I was 14 and went to St Paul's Church catechism classes in the hope of going to the seaside, but the year I was there they went to Crystal Palace for the Outing, so it was not to be."

ildren playing in Hughes 'ields Recreation Ground around 1910. Beyond the wall which went all the ly round the ground was Trevithick St leading to Butchers Row (now Borthwick St).

Deptford and Greenwich were renowned for their educational establishments long before private academies became popular in the 19th century. In 1617 pupils at the Ladies' Hall boarding school (near the Globe Inn at the junction of Watergate St and the Lower Rd) had staged an entertainment called 'Cupid's Banishment' for the wife of James I. Close to the court at Greenwich, the school was chosen for the education of the Queen's god-daughters. There were other, less superior, private academies, including half a dozen which grew up in 19th century Union St (Albury St). None of these establishments, of course, provided education for the poorer children of Deptford. These depended rather on charity, church and chapel.

Two important figures of 17th century Deptford were John Addey, shipbuilder (died 1606) and George Stanhope, vicar of St Nicholas' Church for 26 years (died 1727). Addey left £200 towards the relief of the poor people of Deptford which was invested in a piece of ground on the east side of Church St producing enough income to maintain schools for poor children. The Addey School was built in Church St in 1821 and enlarged in 1862. Stanhope founded a school charity in 1715 to clothe and educate 50 boys and 30 girls and the charity school in the High St was known as Dean Stanhope's or Bluecoats' School. Later the two charities amalgamated to form Addey & Stanhope School on New Cross Rd which opened in 1899. The old school in Church St became a laundry and later a factory before demolition in the early 1970s.

Dean Stanhope's school, 1871. Dean George Stanho[pe] founded a charity school which was built in 1723 where Revivals Café and Harvey & Thompson pawnbrokers (70-72 Depf[ord] High St) now stand. The school was demolished in 1882 to make way for sho[ps] but the statue of the chari[ty] girl is preserved at Addey & Stanhope school on New Cross Rd.

Another early educational institution for poor children was the National School which took over an old brick building in Flagon Row in 1816 to "disseminate the elements of useful knowledge among the poor...to check the progress of wickedness and vice, and to maintain the cause of true religion and virtue". By 1836 the school was crowded with 200 children in summer and 150 in winter. A school report explained to subscribers that less children attended in winter because their parents could not afford to clothe and shoe them. Subscribers were allowed to recommend children and then vote on a list. The harsh effects of the temporary dockyard closure in the early 1830s are shown by the boys recommended at this time: their fathers include seven shipwrights, two sailors, a tide-waiter, a sail-maker and a rigger. The National School, like others of its kind, taught the basics of reading, writing and arithmetic, with the Bible as textbook. It prided itself on instructing girls "in various useful modes of employment" and bringing them up "in a manner to become good Servants". Nineteenth century charity education did not mean to give poor children ideas beyond their station.

In 1844 William Agutter and his fellow workers at the Congregationalist Church in the High St (where the Job Centre now stands) founded the Deptford Ragged School "to battle physically and morally with the poor outcasts of Deptford". An overwhelming response to the small Sunday School held in a Giffin St stable loft led to a series of expansions, first to a larger stable loft in Flood St (later Addey St, now demolished), then to a loft over a skittle alley behind the

Lord Duncan pub which linked New Cross Rd with the top of Deptford High St. At first the school was held in the evenings for working youngsters but it soon became obvious that demand was high enough for a day school as well. With so little to keep them at home, children flocked to the comfort and warmth of the school.

In 1855 the local baptists moved to the new Zion Chapel on New Cross Rd, leaving their old chapel on the corner of Giffin St and Cross St vacant. Agutter and his helpers scraped together the rent for the building and the Ragged School project continued to grow in its new home. By 1862 the day, night and Sunday schools averaged over 120 pupils each. There was plenty more to do but the report explained "we have found our rooms full, our work continuous morning and evening, weekday and Sunday, leaving us neither time, accommodation, nor strength for additional schemes". By the late 1860s distress in the neighbourhood was increasing and the school was full all the time. Children had to be fed before they could be taught and "every winter reveals to the teachers many painful scenes of absolute starvation". In 1867 a New Year dinner for 600 children and 46 women was held in the Victualling Yard. The following year 420 children were taken on an annual treat to a field at Brockley where they were able to "enjoy a day's freedom and play in the pure air of the country".

Around this time education was changing throughout the country. The 1870 Education Act set up locally elected school boards and the Ragged School Committee handed over the day schools to the London School Board which also opened four other schools in the district. The Ragged School continued in the evenings and on Sundays and had time to develop other schemes, such as the blanket loan, the penny bank, the boot club and the Band of Hope. The teachers made great efforts to find respectable jobs in domestic service for the older girls. Ladies requiring young servants were invited to apply at the school on Monday evenings.

Teachers had always had problems with some of the children and were often pelted with mud in the streets. In 1867 a fence was placed around the door with a gate locked during school hours to stop children beating on the doors. In the 1870s there was rioting around the building and the police were frequently called to interfere until an ex-policeman was hired as doorkeeper. The children of Hales St were particularly 'wild and ignorant'.

In 1885 the old chapel was demolished and replaced with a huge, fortress-like building which older Deptfordians may remember. Conditions were not improving: in 1889 a census of Giffin St showed 1300 people in only 50 houses and one report describes a man, his wife and 10 children living all in one room. Other pitiful examples include the family where one pair of boots was shared between mother, daughter and son, or the sickly-looking boy whose coat was pinned so tightly round his neck that the teacher investigated, only to find that he had no other clothes on at all. Children who were at school one Sunday might be buried by the next. By 1885, however, there had been so many gifts of clothing that it was rare to see a Ragged School child actually dressed in rags. Other help came through grocery, meat and coal tickets distributed to the very needy.

The Ragged School was maintained by subscriptions, ranging from 2 pence to more than £1 collected by paid canvassers. Over the years the church of St Peter's in Wickham Rd, Brockley gave great help to the school. The vicar, Rev. Grundy (who said of himself "I am the most amusing parson in the Church of England") sent his congregation down to help at the school and encouraged Deptford's poorer parishes to regard Brockley as a hunting-ground for charity subscriptions.

Mr Williams' Academy, Grove St, circa 1880. Know as 'Bunny' by his pupils a always wearing a top hat lessons, Mr Williams ran last of the private schools Deptford, charging fees of between 2 and 6 pence per week for day school for be and girls, before the 1870 Education Act establishe Board Schools all around the area.

Girls were often taken out of school to help at home. Sophie left at 15 because her mother became pregnant again. She settled down to helping Mum with the housework and shopping, especially after the baby was born when her mother was ill for two months. Late babies were more than usually expensive because there were few hand-me-downs left in the family and, with Sophie's father on short-time, Mrs Faulkner had to borrow from a money lender to buy a second-hand pram and cot.

When her mother was well again Sophie found a job as a cashier at Haycrafts, the ironmongers in Deptford Broadway. She worked long hours for 10 shillings a week but enjoyed herself larking about and getting to know the other girls. Meanwhile she was taking evening classes three nights a week learning Shorthand, Bookkeeping, English and Typewriting. Most women worked, like Sophie, at least from school until marriage, and night classes were common for young people of both sexes.

Some young Deptford children earned pennies by following the horses round the streets and collecting the manure in a barrow to sell to Brockley people with big gardens. Those by the riverside sold driftwood for pcket money. As they got older, some went step-cleaning

Dressmaking class at Goldsmiths' Institute, circa 1900. Goldsmiths' also had classes in laundry, carpentry and bricklaying on their curriculum at this time.

or doing odd jobs for the maids in the grand Brockley houses. Most girls hated the idea of domestic service because it took all their free time away. One woman born in Deptford in 1901 worked in domestic service at the Rectory. Most of her money went on uniform. "You never had no free time. You'd get to the top of the stairs, take your cuffs off to get on with your work and at the ring of the bell you'd have all those stairs to come down, and put on your cuffs before you got to the door."

Mixing childcare with work is not a new problem. Many women had to work from home, taking in washing or doing 'slopwork' such as making up underwear from bales of cut pieces brought to the door. Those who did get outside work had to be ingenious. Mrs Cranfield worked in the Edward St soup kitchen at St Mark's Church during the First World War. She used to pay a woman from Milton Court Rd to mind her six-month old baby, Mary. This cost 10 shillings out of a weekly wage of £1 (20 shillings). To feed the baby Mrs Cranfield would go to the toilet and the minder would pass little Mary through the window to be breast-fed.

Additional questions about church or chapel attendance in the 1851 census had provided shocking statistics which showed that religion was fast becoming an irrelevance to huge numbers of working class people. Rev. Pring of St Luke's in Evelyn St saw the Church's decline as largely due to the fact that the clergy were "such fools". Rev. Kennedy of St James', Hatcham, agreed that the clergy were "so bigoted and amazingly unwise". Both believed prospective vicars should have to spend time in ordinary life before taking orders. They may well have been speaking about Rev. Pratt of Christ Church whose failure was so complete that his main funding had been withdrawn on the grounds that no one came to church. Pratt's work was in the poorest parish in Deptford and though he was "always about among the people" he admitted he "couldn't get at 'em...they are not infidels but they are ungodly". The total number taking communion was no more than 15. The Sunday School attracted around 200 children but Pratt commented that "the Ragged School gets the cream of them". Rev Townend of All Saints also admitted that his poorer parishioners never came to church but they were not unfriendly in their apathy. All the churches ran 'Men Only' services on a regular basis because it was recognised that men were the less religious sex and required special treatment to lure them to church.

The ancient parish of St Nicholas had been in the hands of the curate, Mr Wallis, for many years while its vicar lived quietly avoiding his many creditors. The previous year a Yorkshire paper had reported that the Vicar of St Nicholas' had disappeared from Scarborough owing £200 to a hotel. The debts would be finally paid off by 1901 and Wallis was worried the vicar would be let loose on the parish once more. Wallis had worked hard to turn the parish round. When he arrived the church was empty and the Sunday School was controlled by the powerful Skinner family who had refused to admit the parson for 10 years. Wallis managed to get on the right side of the Skinners and they gave him a lot of help in a chronically understaffed parish. He worked very hard, lived in the parish himself and paid visits every afternoon. The effect on church attendance was noticeable.

Dr Hodson, the Rector of St Paul's, was much more judgemental about his parishioners than Wallis but he also worked hard, visiting every house in the large parish over each three-year period. He had fought tooth and nail to prevent the granting of a drinks licence to the new Empire Music Hall, despite offers of personal bribes to keep quiet. Technically he was successful but the Empire management was more enterprising, securing a pub that stood just behind the hall and rebuilding it on a grand scale. The back entrance from the hall led to the doors of the pub and allowed theatre-goers to retreat there during the interval with no great hardship.

The Deptford Central Hall Methodist Mission opened in 1903 and became part of the South London Mission in 1912. Four years later the *Annual Report* prided itself on its social work, especially its three mothers' meetings a week. "The strain of incessant duties and the intense difficulties of slum home life render this work immensely valuable – the one bright spot in many a grey life." Other help, from cheap breakfasts to outings for young people, came from the Salvation Army with their base in the old Methodist chapel in Mary Ann's Buildings. Churches and chapels did provide useful services but they had to accept that the 'bright spot' of an annual outing was worth much more to parishioners than a year of sermons.

Neighbourhood and home, the High Street and the corner shop, the small markers of status which separated 'respectable' from 'rough' and the mutual aid which brought people together, these were part of the stuff of everyday life. Having babies, cleaning through, scrimping to pay the tally, keeping the family clothed, all took enormous energy and skill and tended to make women old before their time. From the teenager's first job to the family man gathering in 'the Pool' for jobs at the docks, work was an important aspect of most Deptford lives, but for the majority home was where the heart was.

10

Political Life

"trespassers on the public purse" – John Wade

Deptford changed enormously over the 19th century – from a naval powerhouse to a cattle slaughterhouse, from a maze of market gardens to a tangle of railway lines. There were, however, continuities in the experience of 'everyday Deptford'. Poverty was an old enemy even before the first dockyard closure in the early 1830s. After that disaster, and again after the permanent closure in 1869, Deptford reeled from the shock. The streets were deserted, the workhouses were full. By the end of the 19th century new industries, and especially the jumble of railway lines, provided new opportunities for many but unemployment remained high and living conditions shockingly low.

This chapter shows Deptford as a political arena, a stage on which all the political, social and religious struggles of the time were played out in their specific local form. It is not easy to pin down all the intersecting movements or explain the impact of tense political moments. Almost every paragraph here could be expanded into a book in its own right. Some describe local aspects of national developments in class politics and the growth of class consciousness. Others are labelled 'parish politics' but relate to big issues of taxation and religious freedom. There are also instances of social antagonism between gentry and common folk or between the people and the New Police. The actions of the poor could have important political effects at a high level. For example industrial unrest and concern about a working and middle class alliance persuaded Parliament into the 1867 Reform Act. Then there is the level of 'political life' most difficult of all to grasp yet surely relevant to all Deptford's inhabitants: the growth of local administration in the form of gas lighting, paving, dust collection, sewerage, public libraries and wash-houses.

It is not possible to cover each aspect in full or trace the long struggles of each section of the community. Instead we dip here and there into this busy political unit, cut across by networks of personal loyalty as well as lines of class and political allegiance.

Artisan Politics and the Shipwrights

Towards the end of the 18th century the older form of working class protest, the food riot, was dying out and being replaced by disputes which focused on wages. Workers' organisations like the friendly societies developed and popular literacy helped to spread new ideas of economic analysis, conflicting interests and working class solidarity. This was no simple result of a move from workshop to factory. Despite Britain's early and rapid industrialisation most people still worked in unmechanised trades and "the working class was born in the workshop, not the factory" (Prothero, 1981). It was these skilled artisans or 'mechanics' with their self-image of respectability and independence who formed the élite of the 19th century labour force and created its political identity. They considered their ability to maintain themselves by their own labour as their legal right and property. When it came under threat they were prepared to act and the strong solidarity established by trade practices was readily built up into formal trade societies and eventually unions.

Home to the Naval Yard and some of the largest private yards on the Thames, Deptford's special feature was its concentration of shipwrights. These had much in common with other skilled artisans. They had served a seven-year apprenticeship, often owned their tools, used traditional techniques and had a degree of independence at work. They worked in small teams with an elected 'leading hand' who would negotiate a contract for a certain job with the foreman of a shipyard. They tended to set their own pace, were free to take time off and were very mobile between the yards.

Shipbuilding was particularly hard work, demanding "not merely the customary skill and quickness of the handicraftsman, but great manual strength; they must carry heavy beams or woodwork from the workshops to the ship, or else they must convey ponderous timbers complete to the workshop for affixing in the ship, and with these they must ascend and descend the ladder" (Mayhew, 1850). Shipwrights were proud of their skill and stamina and their trade was one of the oldest and most honourable in the land. They set up trade societies to protect and further their interests. Most of the Deptford shipwrights belonged to the St Helena Society. According to John Gast, leader of the shipwrights from around 1800, there were "not ten men in the river who were not members".

Another distinct feature of shipbuilding was its special relation to government. Shipwrights were convinced of their unique value to a maritime nation whose great power was based on navy and merchant fleets. Only British-built ships were admitted to the Registry and British shipowners were given a trading monopoly through the Navigation Acts.

When John Gast came to Dudman's Yard at Deptford in 1797 a new era was dawning which would change the shipbuilding industry forever. The long wars with revolutionary France, beginning in 1793, would enormously increase the need for new ships and provide constant repair work. While the trauma of war and massive price rises shook the country, the shipwrights were on the up and they used the demand for their labour to gain wage rises. The wars brought prosperity to the mass of industries on the riverside.

In the wartime period between 1793 and 1802 the Thames yards built 73 ships for the navy, 69 East Indiamen and 316 other merchant ships. This was an age of prosperity and high earnings but when the Peace of Amiens was signed in March 1802 there were wholesale dismissals and wages were slashed. Strikes broke out among sawyers, caulkers and shipwrights but the Admiralty allowed men from the King's Yard to work as strike-breaking labour in the private yards. This provoked severe violence and troops were called in. Two thousand well-organised shipwrights stood strong and achieved their goals in wages, overtime and no victimisation. When the war began again the following year the new demand brought many back to work but after the Battle of Trafalgar in 1805 the pace slowed again, never fully to recover.

The fortunes of war were always a mixed blessing to Deptford. Such fluctuations meant work was unsteady. Government demands had kept the Deptford yards busy, forcing the East India Company to look elsewhere for ships. Instead of the old British heart-of-oak, they began to order teak ships built with cheap labour in India. The shipwrights' 'special relationship' with government did not save them and in 1795 these non-British ships were admitted to the Registry. Teak proved a durable material, needing less repair work. With the timber crisis of 1804 the navy itself began to move its custom to the Indian teak-yards.

When peace looked possible in 1814 the Thames yards faced ruin. The navy building programme ground to a halt and merchants bided their time, knowing that seven out of eight of the government transport ships would soon be on the market at knock-down prices. In April that year there was only one ship being built in all of the 23 main Thames yards. In 1811 Gast and others had tried and failed to organise a shipwrights' trade union. Another campaign ended in total defeat in 1814 when the government permanently extended all the privileges of British ships to those built in India. Gast also took a leading part in the apprenticeship campaign to maintain standards within the trades against those large employers who wanted to employ cheap labour and break the backs of the trade societies. In 1813, despite extensive opposition, the apprenticeship laws were repealed and the artisans faced another disappointment.

The situation seemed desperate. The 'special relationship' had been abused; the crucial role of the shipwrights in the war effort was ignored and, as Gast noted of Deptford, with "not a Ship to build or repair, workhouses became crowded, and the only consolation from Government was, times would mend – this was only a 'transition from War to Peace'". The wars had brought large numbers of workers to London. In the long post-war depression they joined the mass of men discharged from the army and navy, swelling the ranks of the unemployed. The last years of the war had seen rocketing prices and real wages were badly eroded by the time the boom collapsed in 1814. Masters discharged workers and slashed wages. The St Helena Society fell apart.

John Gast had his own disappointments. After his early apprenticeship to a Bristol shipbuilder he had gone to Portsmouth and immediately become involved in industrial struggle. He was discharged in 1797 in a wave of labour cuts and told "young man, you know too much for a shipwright". At Deptford he ran one of the biggest private yards in the country and he had confidently expected to become foreman. He settled into life as a Dissenting preacher in Deptford, taking over the King of Prussia pub in Union St (Albury St) in 1810. Three years later everything collapsed. Dudman sold the yard, Gast had to give up the pub and in December 1814 he hit rock-bottom when he was imprisoned for fortune-telling. His brother was already in the debtors' prison.

The Thames shipwrights were an extremely proud and skilled group of men. As part of the 'mechanic' class they had more in common with small employers and shopkeepers than with the dock labourers who worked with them. They were very conscious of the distinction, which was often voiced in terms of 'respectability'. This was not the same as the moralistic Victorian version of the term. It meant self-respect, pride and relative independence: an ability to maintain oneself without recourse to charity. A decent appearance and cleanliness were important but not paramount. Unlike the later versions it was not a question of superficial behaviour but of fundamental independence and the feeling of belonging to an honourable trade of recognised value to the community. In the post-war years, and again at the closure of the dockyard in the 1830s, many hundreds of these proud Deptford men were forced to apply for parish relief or starve. Some of them chose to starve or, like Gast, tell fortunes for farthings.

The massive Spa Fields political meetings of November and December 1816 marked the sensational opening of a new era of popular radicalism among such embittered artisans. Gast saw artisans suffering from wage reductions, unemployment and infringements of their rights. They shouldered the full burden of taxation on consumables which raised the cost of living, made British products difficult to export and reduced the spending power of the home market. Along with other radical artisans, Gast joined the Reform movement hoping to destroy the 'boroughmongers' who monopolised political power. The Reformers wanted 'universal' (manhood) suffrage so that artisans' voices in Parliament could keep a check on tyranny. Familiar with popular democracy from their experience of benefit societies, they justified it in terms of natural rights – anyone who paid taxes or could fight for the country should have representation.

These radicals were the forefathers of the Chartists, as the trade societies were the forerunners of the trade unions. Their aims – tax and trade reform, maintaining wage levels and apprenticeship, reducing unemployment – required a mixture of political and industrial action. Late in 1822 there was no shipbuilding at all on the Thames and very little repairing. Intense competition for orders put the men at the mercy of the employers. In such a period industrial action was unlikely to be effective and instead the shipwrights sought political solutions. At last in 1824 a general economic recovery put them back in a position to bargain. Resistance from the employers led to the founding of the Thames Shipwrights' Provident Union under Gast's leadership. This was possible because of the repeal of the Combination Laws which had been used to persecute the old trade societies. The ideals of the union were traditional: "It is the intention of the members of this society by a moral union to support their respectability in society." There was no question of class hostility. The union leaders expected the shipbuilders to welcome the possibility of ending the abuses of competition between the shipyards which they hoped to effect.

Once formed the new union spread very rapidly and gained a total of 1,400 members. Based on existing solidarity and common attitudes, it was able to accumulate funds and conduct the Great Strike of 1825 which "lasted so long that the grass is said to have grown up in the building slips". Co-operation from the shipbuilders was never forthcoming: fear of the power of the union overwhelmed any consideration of its policies. Instead they fought hard, clamouring against 'combinations' and pressuring government ministers to crush the union through legislation. The Select Committee inquiring into the matter was petitioned furiously by both sides. Its report was hostile to combinations and, though there were few legal changes, it directly attacked the shipwrights' strike. The struggle continued throughout the year but when the government opened the royal yards to any ship needing repair the strike was doomed. Despite everything the union survived and the struggle left Gast more than ever convinced of the need for unity among the trades. He remained at the heart of the struggle and continued to work for his beliefs into old age.

Education and the Mechanics' Institute

By the 1820s a clear trend could be seen throughout Britain in favour of education at all levels, stemming from a belief in education as the great means of human progress, the triumph of the rational over the 'animal'. Education would counteract wicked thoughts, improve morals and manners, reduce crime and drunkenness, and make people more orderly both in life and work. The London Mechanics' Institution was founded in 1823 after an appeal in the *Mechanics' Magazine* received an encouraging response from leading liberal figures including George Birkbeck. The group recognised that an industrial nation needed literate skilled workers. They were also reformers who hoped for social change through education. Mechanics' institutions offered to meet widely-felt needs including the hope of rising socially. Educational self-help activities were already widespread among artisans and many heroic sacrifices had been made in the cause of self-education.

The Deptford Mechanics' Institute opened in November 1827. Dr Birkbeck gave a speech to a well-attended meeting on the advantages of knowledge. A librarian was available in the evenings to issue books to members and newspapers and periodicals were laid out in the Reading Room. In 1838 the Institute reopened, in a High St building near the Broadway, with a series of lectures on science and literature. One of the problems of mechanics' institutes was that they appeared with all their ambitions in a world which required elementary education before it could master the abstractions of chemistry and algebra. At Deptford, Mr Pease of Woolwich gave a talk on Practical Geometry for civil engineers, architects, surveyors and mechanics. Ladies were assured that they would find the lecture useful for their drawing studies. The Deptford Mechanics' Institute was successful among the lower middle class but, with charges at 4 shillings a quarter, it made little impact on the artisans who preferred their own less formal arrangements for mutual education. In 1848 John Wade (see below) bought up a piece of land by Deptford Station for a new Mechanics' Institute building. Facilities included a reading room for newspapers and magazines, open from 9am to 10.30pm daily, and a library open until 9pm daily, except Wednesdays when it closed early for the weekly lecture.

Parish Politics and the Church Rate

High taxation during the war period continued for many years but in the 1830s, just when Deptford was less able to pay, the land tax was raised. A dispute arose over whether the King's Dock and Victualling Yards should be exempt from payment. The yards had previously contributed as much as a third of the total bill, now Deptford townspeople would have to pay it all. This was blatantly unfair. The 'public work' of the yards was nationally important work which protected and supplied the entire country, not just the people of Deptford. The yards occupied three-quarters of the waterfront, the most valuable land in the area. The government had paid no local poor-rates since 1805 yet the bill for the families of men formerly employed in the yards was more than £2,000 a year. It was a notorious fact that many of the poor of the parish had been able to obtain settlement there through their parents coming to work in the yards. The government had made few efforts to protect the British ship-building industry and Deptford was now suffering the consequences. The petition sent to Parliament on this issue came from a "Deptford, depressed, dilapidated, and almost deserted by trade and employment for its people".

In January 1836 Powle and Wade, the local tax assessors, notified the government that the proportional value of the yard land had increased due to new buildings and the general depreciation of other property in the area. The bill remained unpaid and the assessors decided to distrain goods. They went with a posse of men and seized 19 different

Mechanics' Institute, Deptford High St. The Institute moved into this building in the early 1850s and it retained its use as a library and lecture hall un the end of the century whe it was known as St Mary's Hall. In 1908 it opened as Deptford's first cinema, th Electric Theatre. In 1915 it was purchased by Fr. Felix Segesser of Our Lady of th Assumption although LCC regulations meant that the profits had to be channelle into Roman Catholic schools other than St Joseph's. When the Broadway Cinema opened 1916 the competition prove too fierce and the Electric closed until 1921 when it became a billiard hall. The area was redeveloped into shops in the 1980s.

items totalling nearly £100. The solicitor to the Admiralty immediately paid the arrears but gave notice that legal action would be taken against the assessors for trespass. This led to a spate of local meetings but in the end the matter was dropped.

During the 1830s and 1840s another struggle was being waged in the Deptford parishes. This was the question of church rates and it brought out some of the best speeches in Deptford's political history. The star character was John Wade, a draper who lived in Evelyn St and had a shop in the High St. Wade was a Guardian of the Poor, a liberal and a religious Dissenter and central to nearly every political and charitable initiative in both St Nicholas' and St Paul's parishes throughout this time.

The church rate was a separate tax on all householders to pay for additional parish expenses such as candles, clothing for the Beadle, a robe for the Vestry Clerk, the organist's wages, wine and biscuits both for the communion and for the vestry officers and any other incidental costs decided by the vestry or the churchwardens. Sometimes the abuses associated with the church rate were truly scandalous as when money for church repairs was spent on lavish dinners for the vestry committee, when the charge for lighting the church at evening service was raised from 30 shillings to 30 pounds, or when officers' rounds for issuing 'distress warrants' turned into pub-crawls costing the parish £5. Beyond these particular cases, however, it was the basic principle of the church rate which upset Wade and the other Dissenters. What right had the established church to force men to pay to uphold a religious creed in which they did not believe? Why should they pay out twice, once for their own chapels and Sunday schools and then again for the corrupt practices of a church they never attended?

The growing hostility between the two parties – for and against the rate – can be clearly seen in newspaper cuttings and other evidence held at the British Library. Although the rate had already caused contention at St Paul's in November 1833 when Wade had declared "it was useless to talk about law when they had not justice", early the next year the *Greenwich Gazette* complimented the parish on its 'good feeling' despite differences of opinion. By June 1834 Wade was becoming increasingly irritated by the use of public money for vestry boozing. In November he was furious when St Nicholas' vestry passed a rate of 6 pence in the pound at a sneaky unpublicised meeting. When Wade demanded why the notice of the meeting had been taken down and the gates shut he was told that it was to prevent the notice getting wet and the goats coming in. "Yes", said Mr Wade, "I was one of the goats which they wanted to keep out".

In April of the following year he made his first major speech against the rates saying "it was the duty of every man to support his own religious creed" and that if every denomination was allowed the luxury of a rate the gentlemen opposite would be "declaring against the gross injustice of such an attempt to force money from their pockets". He talked about common justice and religious freedom, declaring that true Christianity required no temporal prop and "established religions...are established wrongs". He suggested voluntary rates but already he was aware of the possibility of the use of the Ecclesiastic Court against him if he refused to pay.

This ancient court had recently tried a parishioner of Bethnal Green for non-payment. It had actually decided that he was justified in resisting a demand for 6 pence for church rate but then saddled him with legal costs totalling £54 and 17 shillings. Wade knew of this case and he ended his speech: "I shall not resist to extremities the collection of this rate if carried, having the fear of the Ecclesiastic Court before my eyes."

The political antagonism was illustrated in January 1836. Wade quoted Milton that forced rates were "no better than forced vows, hateful to God, who loves a cheerful giver". David Showell, the conservative churchwarden involved in almost as many local issues as Wade himself, responded that Milton was "an author of indisputable talent, but one of the vilest republicans". In November, Wade "charged the gentlemen opposite as trespassers on the public purse".

In the early years Wade lost most of his arguments in the vestry itself but in 1836 he managed to get a majority vote for a year's delay in the rate-setting. A public poll was demanded by the churchmen and the adjournment was lost. This happened several times over the next few years and we are lucky to have some fascinating evidence of the different tactics of each side. The anti-rate party called large public meetings and developed an imaginative range of propaganda from plastering Deptford with posters about the church seizures to short stories about "naughty boys" who were "fond of Music and Wine and...riding in Coaches" and robbed the people to pay for it.

Propaganda from the other side could be just as powerful. The Useful Tract Society published a cheap booklet called *The Church Flag* in which a Mrs Wilkins explains to her son Teddy that "the Flag is hoisted to tell the country round, that our Church is triumphant, and also to let the naughty people know that the Church Broker will take their goods if they do not pay the rate just made". More usual tactics for the churchmen were letters like the one from St Paul's churchwarden William Pembroke to conservative David Showell who lived in Hatcham, asking him to use "your influence with your friends in the Hamlet and favour us with your Company" to swing the vote.

In 1839 Wade finally gave up his tactic of arguing the toss while staying on the right side of the law by paying the rates. This time he took a stance of non-payment and in May he was called before the Ecclesiastic Court. The court authorised the churchwardens to seize his goods including a side of bacon, tobacco, a table and chair and five waistcoats. The anti-rate party saw this as an attack on civil rights and a subscription fund was set up to help Wade. His friend, church-warden George Shove, praised Wade's "unflinching, manly, and truly English resolution, which, in a good cause fears not to brave the terrors of the Ecclesiastical Inquisition". Two years later Wade was presented with a silver cup "by the friends of civil and religious liberty in Deptford, for his manly conduct in resisting in the Ecclesiastic Court the payment of a church rate in St Paul's Deptford." This was far from the end of his involvement in parish life. He continues to crop up at almost every meeting and we will hear from this 'Gulliver of Deptford' again. In October 1844 St Paul's parish finally did away with the church rate in votes at the vestry and at the poll. That year the voting was far more widespread than previously and the anti-rate majority was huge (at least 616:350).

Local elections for vestry officers were serious occasions with each side producing their publicity and the three or more competing colours plastered all over Deptford. The parties had names like 'Parish Economy' and 'Parish Improvement' but reflected the general division into conservatives and liberals. Even the post of Grave Digger was hotly contested with the sympathy vote going to William Cockle from Tanners Hill whose election sheet begged "most respectfully to offer myself as Candidate". Cockle had been brought up to the trade of Sugar-mould Potter which had been superceded by the invention of the wrought iron mould. He was now "TOTALLY WITHOUT EMPLOYMENT, not understanding any other business". With eight children all depending on his wife for support he promised that "should I be the fortunate candidate, I will do my utmost for the satisfaction of the parish generally". He lost on this occasion but was soon elected as Parish Beadle.

Local Administration: the Vestry and the Council

In April 1821 St Nicholas' parish put out the following advertisement:

St Nicholas, Deptford, To Scavengers and Others.
The Commissioners of Pavements…will receive tenders from such Persons as may be willing to CONTRACT for the cleaning of the said Parish, and removing the DUST, ASHES, &c therefrom, FOR ONE YEAR.
N.B. The Commissioners have given directions to Prosecute all Persons found taking away Dust, Dirt, Ashes, or Filth, from any part of the Parish, without being legally authorized by contract to do so.

Local authorities as we understand them, with their social and leisure services, their planning and development role and their responsibility for housing were a product of the 20th century. However, the idea of local government is an ancient one stretching from Saxon moots, through 16th century ward-motes, to the council meetings of today. The early-19th century solution to specific local needs was often to call a meeting of local householders to establish, for example, a Gas Light Company or "to consider obtaining an Act of Parliament for lighting and paving the streets of the Manor of Hatcham". The Acts of Parliament relating to a particular area could be numerous and created a number of overlapping authorities.

Not until the Metropolitan Management Act 1855 was the system reorganised to create a patchwork of administrative (rather than church) vestries and district boards like the Greenwich Board of Works which covered Deptford. They were responsible for sewers and drains, roads, lighting, open spaces, cemeteries, baths and wash-houses. With the Local Government Act 1888 London was finally favoured with a popularly elected County Council which was granted additional powers relating to housing, asylums, reformatories, licensing, technical education and public health.

On the local level, the *Kentish Mercury* (forerunner of the *South East London Mercury* whose head office is in Deptford) was opposed to this Act and worried about the political aspects of the coming election. "Let us imagine what would be the condition of things in London for example if a strong majority of Aggressive Radicals...dominated the new Council. The new body would be used as a powerful engine for promoting the designs of Anarchists and Revolutionaries." They warned fellow conservatives who were standing as 'non-political' that their strategy was naïve and would not fulfil the *Mercury's* goal of "the

Unionist party obtaining the control of the new Council" but would leave it open to "the most dangerous Socialistic and Anarchic attacks on the peace and prosperity of London".

After the election the *Mercury* ran an editorial 'I told you so'. More than 80 of the 137 elected Councillors and Aldermen were radicals (Progressive Party) giving them a majority over the conservatives (Moderate Party) of around three to two. Ten years later the London Government Act 1899 split the County of London into 28 boroughs and established borough councils to replace the old vestries and district boards. In Deptford the Progressives were outnumbered by one member on the new Borough Council. Mr B J Hall, the Secretary of the Working Men's Club and Institute Union and a labour activist who had lived in Deptford for 14 years, failed to win a Brockley ward for the Progressives and one seat was lost in an otherwise Progressive ward when a popular publican was elected instead.

There was a strong line of continuity between the old vestry and the new Council. The Mayor, Benjamin Jacob, had been a long-standing vestry member and Mr Marchant the Vestry Clerk was appointed as Town Clerk. One of the 46 original aldermen and councillors was Ernest George Simmonds who remained a member of the Council until the elections of November 1945.

The first meeting of the new Council was held in November 1900 in the old two-up two-down vestry offices at 20 Tanners Hill. The 'atmospherical conditions' of the small unventilated hall used as a Council Chamber "did not tend to moderate the heat of debate". Soon the Council agreed to rent two rooms at 493 New Cross Rd and Mr Marchant allowed them to use a room at his London & County Bank

Old vestry offices, 20 Tanners Hill. These offices were used by the Deptford Borough Council from 19?? until the opening of the Town Hall on New Cross in 1905. With only the two second-floor rooms for the whole of the Council's clerical staff together with the Sanitary Inspectors during the daytime and meetings in the evenings, the offices were horribly cramped.

in the Broadway as the Cemeteries Office. Office space was one of the main preoccupations of the early years and led in 1902 to an architectural competition to design a town hall. The architects appointed, Lanchester, Steward & Rickards, must have worked at an incredible speed by modern standards. A contractor was found in May 1903, the foundation was laid in October and the building was officially opened within two years. For three days in July 1905 the hall was open for inspection by the public. A total of 17,130 people visited – an incredible average of 800 every hour.

Some fascinating details emerge from the early Council minutes and reports. One frequent subject was horses. In February 1901 it was noted that horse No. 56 had died from lockjaw. Large quantities of rye grass and clover mixture, straw, oats, bran, hoof oil, harnesses, brass polish, cart grease and dust-cart wheels were purchased by the Council. The Finance Committee were asked to provide in the next budget for purchase of six horses, six slop-vans and four dust-carts. The Council even entered its horses for competition at the Lewisham Horse Show on Whit Monday 1902. Some months earlier a tender was accepted for the repair of 37 'loincloths'. The mind boggles!

The first woman mayor of Deptford was Beatrice Drapper. Born and bred in Deptford, she was a swimming and gymnastics instructor and actively involved in the local public world. For many years she was a member of the Greenwich Board of Guardians, whose relief fund for women and children during the dock strike of 1912 served up 1,000 meals a day at the Central Hall Methodist Mission. Beatrice was elected to Deptford Borough Council in 1919 and chaired a number of its social committees including the Maternity and Child Welfare Committee. In 1927 she was elected Mayor of Deptford, opposed only by one councillor who said he did not want to serve under a woman.

Doris Burley was elected onto Deptford Council in 1946 at the tender age of 22. Six years later she was appointed Mayor of Deptford and, with her sister as Mayoress, she presided over the area's celebrations in Coronation Year, 1952. Doris stayed on Deptford Council until 1965 but although she was still relatively young she did not wish to make the transfer over to Lewisham Council.

Deptford in Parliament
The Reform Act of 1832 made Deptford part of the Parliamentary constituency of Greenwich which returned two MPs though its electorate was less than 3,000. In the 1830s and 1840s these included Captain Dundas who was appointed Lord of the Admiralty in 1846 and the shipbuilder Edward George Barnard from Deptford Green (Ch.7). In 1851 David Wire, who lived at the Stone House on Lewisham Way and had twice been Lord Mayor of London, was elected with another Liberal called Salomons but the following year Conservative Peter Rolt took his place. Salomons remained an MP for the area as its electorate grew. In 1868 he was joined by Mr W E Gladstone who became Prime Minister that year. Gladstone did not stand in Greenwich in the 1873 election but was returned again the following year.

Deptford first elected its own MP at the General Election of 1885 and has had 10 MPs since then. The turnout in the early years was substantial but the electorate remained little more than 15,000 until after the First World War. Deptford's first MP was the Conservative squire W J Evelyn, based at the old family seat of Wotton in Surrey. He resigned in 1888 and was replaced by another Conservative, Charles Darling. Darling became a judge in 1897 and was replaced by Deptford's third Tory, Arthur Morton. who had been the Vice Chairman of the LCC Housing of the Working Classes Committee and "would support measures calculated to ameliorate the conditions of life among the industrial classes".

Morton lost the seat in 1906 to Deptford's longest-serving MP, Charles Bowerman. Bowerman was a printer by trade and became General Secretary of the London Society of Compositors, President of the National Printing and Kindred Trades Employees' Federation and President of the TUC. He also served as an alderman of the LCC and as a Privy Councillor. Bowerman was defeated by Conservative Denis Hanley in 1931. This may have astonished the 28 year old Hanley more than anyone else although there were some very surprising results in that Depression year as solid Labour seats tumbled. Deptford was regained for Labour in 1935 by Walter Green, a long-standing councillor for the borough (1909-56) and its mayor in 1920-21. He may have preferred local to national politics because he did not fight the 1945 election. J C Wilmot won the seat in that year against Squadron Leader Eric Cuddon, the composer of the *Deptford Dip* dance hit (Ch. 12). Wilmot was Minister of Supply and Aircraft Production in the post-war years and became Lord Wilmot of Selmeston just before the 1950 election when Sir Leslie Plummer took over Deptford. The 1950 election list included the Communist Les Stannard, an electrician who had lived in Deptford all his life and is presently a leading light of the Pensioners' Forum. Plummer was succeeded in 1963 by John Silkin, Labour Chief Whip and a cabinet minister. Silkin resigned before the 1987 election and the list of hopeful successors to this safe Labour seat extended to 36 names. Joan Ruddock, Vice Chair of CND, became Deptford's first woman MP that year and extended her majority in 1992 to a healthy 12,238.

'The Mass of the Poor'

Social historians are acutely aware of the difficulties in uncovering the lives and attitudes of the poor. As with the crime reports in the 17th and 18th centuries there are ways of reconstructing the lives and opinions of 19th century lower working class people but to do so in a particular area like Deptford takes years of systematic research and to report on that research would take a whole book. Here again we must confine ourselves to one or two examples.

The great majority of Deptford's working class population was not active in formal political agitation. Their situation was usually too insecure for involvement in benefit or trade societies or the luxury of self-education at the Mechanics' Institute. They were more likely to become involved in spontaneous outbreaks of unrest like the Sailors' Uprising of 1774 (Ch. 5).

Certainly there was hostility to the New Police established by the Metropolitan Police Act of 1829. In April 1830 Henry Sheldrake, the toll-keeper on Deptford Creek Bridge, charged two policemen with violent assault after they tried to cross the bridge without paying. In their defence they said they had heard of a robbery at Lewisham and had been told there that the thief had gone to Limehouse. They were pursuing him and had no halfpenny to pay at the toll-gate. The magistrates trying the case were sceptical. How did the police expect to catch the thief on foot with no money to pay the ferry? They replied they would have gone round via London Bridge. Thomas Shipman, the magistrate, exclaimed: "What! a distance of five miles out of your road; upon my word this is a very bad beginning." Despite the assault being proved, Shipman did not deal harshly with them "lest any prejudice should be created against them in the minds of the lower orders of Deptford". Six years later James Gibbons was fined 10 shillings and costs for assaulting the police in the High St on a rowdy Saturday night. In another case "five athletic and ferocious looking Irishmen" were charged with assault on PC 127R on Blackhorse Bridge after closing time one Monday night.

The first Deptford police station, Princes St. The ⸱ion was built in 1854 and ᵓsed in 1912 when the new ₜion opened in Amersham ℓ. This photograph shows ℓ station after it had been taken over by Fleetwood Chemical Works.

Occasionally police interference was fatal. One Sunday evening in September 1839 George Stevens, PC 165R, was on duty in New King St when Mary Hoble, who kept the Navy Arms, called him to sort out a nasty scene in her pub. It was against police orders to go into pubs unless the disturbance was very serious so it was only when John Pine and another man began to wrestle outside the pub that Stevens interfered. His orders to go quietly home met with threats from Pine. Stevens followed them as they 'booted off' along the New Rd and when he went up again Pine struck him. A large mob began to gather but Stevens collared Pine and another PC, William Aldridge, came up to assist. They drew their staffs and dragged Pine to the toll-house at the top of the New Rd where they were surrounded by a 500-strong crowd. Stones began to fly and both constables "lost our hats in the row". Two more police came to assist and they got Pine to the Telegraph pub in Broomfield Place before a stone struck PC Aldridge in the head. He fell to the ground and died some hours later.

At the Coroner's Court most of the local people summoned as

witnesses spoke of the violence of the crowd but refused to identify the prisoners as present, preferring to confuse the coroner with incidental detail. A timber dealer from outside Deptford who had happened to see the action identified William Calvert as throwing the fatal stone. The prisoners, who had "showed great levity and appeared to be a reckless set", were shocked when a verdict of murder was brought against Calvert, Pine and two others. They were committed to Newgate Prison to await trial. At the Criminal Court the judge railed against mobs and stated that this was a murder case but made clear that "on account of the suddenness of the transaction" the jury may want to lessen the blow. After an hour of debate the jury returned a manslaughter verdict. Pine was "transported beyond the seas for the term of your life", William Calvert was transported for 15 years and the others received two years imprisonment with hard labour.

Agitation and Reform

Local politics cannot fail to relate to national developments but they do not simply reflect the national scene. Working class politics in Deptford and the rest of Kentish London were influenced by the specific community experience. Most important was the lack of any sustained sense of class hostility. This led to working class willingness to ally with middle class liberal leadership emerging from the social élite of the area. John Wade commanded great respect among the tradesmen of Deptford and the Dissenter David Wire, who moved into the Stone House on Lewisham High Rd (Lewisham Way) in the early 1840s, soon found strong support not only from the Dissenting community but also from the poor 'Mill-laners'.

The radicalism of Kentish London remained rooted in the early 19th century tradition of independent artisans with their social ideology of respectability. Class-conscious politics appear elsewhere in the country during the 1840s and 1870s but the response in Kentish London was a radicalism of the small man rather than the worker. It sought to dismantle the traditional political structure and the power of the landed élite. "The issue was not the poor against the rich or employees against employer, but the people versus the parasitic elite." (Crossick, 1978). Traditional radicalism developed into a brand of liberalism concerned with justice, dignity, political equality and an end to privilege and corruption.

Chartism, the hope of millions to introduce full political democracy, did not fare so well in Kentish London. Not until May 1841 did the Deptford branch appear, and only after the massive open-air demonstration in Deptford Broadway (July 1842) would it be realistic to describe a serious Chartist presence in this area. The next two years were quiet ones and simply maintaining the organisation seemed a full-time task. There was a brief revival in 1846 until the march from Kennington Common to petition Parliament. The arrest of national leaders at this time marked the efective end for the movement in Kentish London. Greenwich police noted that "the Chartists appear, since the apprehension of the Chartist leaders, to be becoming gradually more lukewarm in the cause".

Despite this weakness, which is partly explained by the social diversity of the Deptford community, Chartism did create a positive political force in the area and could mobilise large crowds for the great occasions. Around 2,000 were in the Broadway in July 1842 and twice that number converged on Blackheath the next day. As well as numbers Chartism provided a continuity which ensured that any revived agitation would appear under the Chartist banner. Three men dominated the movement in the area: Joseph Morgan, a young tallow chandler; George Floyd, a Deptford baker; and Thomas Paris, an elderly Scottish smith who had moved to Greenwich in 1819 bringing wide-ranging political experience.

Relations between the Deptford middle class and the Chartists were far from hostile. John Wade was active in the Metropolitan Parliamentary Reform Association which hoped to moderate Chartist demands and begin joint agitation. Chartists congratulated the anti church rate party on their victory in 1844 and when David Wire stood as a Liberal candidate in the 1847 election he was supported by local Chartists even though he rejected many of their goals.

As political activity declined in the 1850s some of the Deptford Chartists turned to other forms of organisation including the Mechanics' Institute, the Deptford Working Men's Co-operative Provision Assocation and the Deptford and Greenwich Co-operative Shipbuilders. Others moved into the Reform League and the Deptford Radical Assocation or even into local temperance societies. For many working men in Deptford the initial experience of Chartism was a vital part of their later involvement, providing the skills of political organisation, self-expression and self-confidence.

Concentration on political freedom and equality rather than social or economic change increased as the 19th century wore on and was represented by the co-operation between artisan and middle class radicals in the Reform League. However, Deptford provides examples of every kind of political and industrial action. The industrial activities of the poorer working class helped to produce the divisive 1867 Reform Act by convincing the rulers that something must be done to prevent an alliance between respectable artisans and the labouring poor.

The 1865 strike at George England's Hatcham Ironworks in Pomeroy St showed a high degree of militancy against the "objectionable rules under which the establishment was worked". England played some nasty tricks on the strikers. He posted up a notice withdrawing the offensive rules and ordering the men back to work where they found the gates locked aganst them and were interviewed one by one by Mr England. After a whole day of this no-one was allowed to start work but some were told to call again on Tuesday, others in a few days, the rest not till the following week. The men, angry and confused, met at the Crown & Anchor pub on New Cross Rd where a resolution was carried unanimously that no-one would return to work until England had given a proper statement of his intentions.

A deputation from this meeting had no success with England who would see them only one at a time and "had proved by his strange, and in fact very reprehensible conduct, that he only intended to play fast and loose with the men". His deceit about the rules and his letters to the press about 'roughs' involved in the strike, were intended to blinker the eyes of the public and prevent the men receiving sympathy. He told the chairman of the Strike Committee that he was saving £400 a week wages during the strike and could put the screw on the door and save more. Another member of the deputation said his interview was cut short "by his sincere desire not to come into collision with Mr

England's stick". England had got worked up and threatened the man before turning him out of the office.

In January 1867 unemployment was high and the St Paul's parish relieving officer was kept very busy. One afternoon, after a great number of tickets for bread had been distributed, hundreds of people were still waiting around Mary Ann's Buildings near the bread depot. When it was announced that there was no more bread the crowd moved off angrily down the High St. One baker's shop was completely sacked, at another the baker gave out all his unsold bread to protect his windows. Towards the Broadway another bakery was attacked. With the arrival of the Superintendent and a body of mounted police, order was restored but the next morning large numbers of men assembled again and the tradesmen closed up their shops. The men marched off to the Greenwich Union House where the Poor Law Guardians were holding their weekly meeting. This group however, were not the "disorderly characters with which the lower part of our town is infested" and they were treated leniently.

The local correspondent of the *Daily Telegraph* had his own ideas about the origins of the Bread Riots. They came, he thought, from the bad management of St Paul's parish and the terrible quality and short measures of the parish bread. The poor would not eat such bread and instead they offered the nasty, black, musty loaves to the local butchers who made it into 'beef' sausages!

The following day business as usual was proclaimed in Deptford after a strong police presence in the main roads the previous night. At the junction of the High St and Creek Rd where the unemployed tended to congregate there were "not more than 50 persons in groups of eight or ten each...and the usual number of straggling 'roughs' idling in the principal streets of Deptford...nothing of an unusual appearance". That day five tons of bread were given away and the behaviour of the poor was "most orderly". Something like the Sailors' Uprising of the previous century, the Bread Riots had been a temporary and spontaneous lapse into disorder in an area which, despite hunger and unemployment, could usually afford to ignore the suffering on the doorstep or meet it with charity not political change.

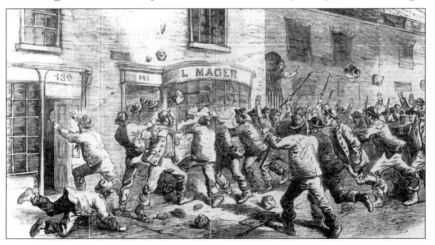

'Bread Riots in Deptford', January 1867. This drawing is from the 'Illustrated Police News' so we should be a little wary about taking it at face value. The "disorderly characters" involved in the sacking of bakeries in Deptford High were responding to unabated hunger and years of "nasty black, musty loaves" from the parish relief.

11

Dealing out Bread and Morals

*"The raising and improving of the poorer part of the
population of Deptford, religiously, intellectually,
morally and socially" – Objectives of the Deptford Fund, 1898.*

Although we hear of them through the court records and the
occasional riot report, most of the information we have about the
Deptford poor is through the concerns of charity. This chapter
investigates the charitable response to Deptford's poverty and follows
from the last in showing the shifting relationship between politics and
charity. In the 1830s eminent local men were involved in every aspect
of public life from the Coal Institution to the Conservative Association.
They signed political petitions and they gave charitable subscriptions.
By 1894 when a public meeting was held to establish the Deptford
Fund which would become the most important charitable effort for the
coming century, it was West End Society types who took the lead.
Philanthropy in Deptford had become an outsider's game and duty.
The social mix was all but gone and Deptford Town itself was now the
pitiable pauper.

The State of Deptford Debate

In 1833-4 a spate of letters appeared in the *Greenwich Gazette* which
soon became labelled the 'State of Deptford' debate. The leading
correspondent called himself Veritas and lived in New King St in the
heart of old Deptford. He complained that if Deptford had been
properly represented in Parliament the dockyard would still be open,
that Deptford people had done their best with public meetings,
petitions and letters to the King but "all have met with the usual fate
of such applications...left to lie on the table". The closure did not
reduce the national expenditure but simply shifted it elsewhere and
large sums were being spent building new docks like "Sheerness, that
grave of millions of the national treasure". The paper's editorial
accepted Veritas' view of the "train of incalculable evils, that has filled
our poor-houses with paupers, that has depopulated our streets and
houses and which I defy anyone to prove has benefited the government
a single shilling". One problem was that men who had passed their
lives within the walls of a dockyard knew too little about other
employment. They had taken jobs at low wages, dislodging others who
then became burdens on the poor-rate.

Another letter writer, calling himself Subscriber, asserted that
Deptford people had tempted the blow by their political activity and
the "high and independent spirit for which they and their predecessors
have been distinguished". Subscriber accused Veritas of self-fulfilling
prophecy. Asserting that "the town is full of poverty, abounding in
wretchedness, deserted by every respectable class and loaded with
poor-houses" was likely to increase the flight of the 'respectable' from
Deptford. Subscriber drew readers' attention to the handsome new
houses around Hatcham and Lewisham Rd and argued that, though
the Lower Town was much deserted, it had improved since 50 ships
had been removed. Instead of its "close and narrow streets pouring out
their improvidents in nightly and disgraceful riots" all was now quiet

and peaceful. Presumably this 'peace' was the silenced voice of the hungry unemployed.

Veritas responded caustically. His concern was with the centre of Deptford not the stately mansions on the periphery whose residents spent their money in London not Deptford. He accepted that perhaps Deptford would be better off without the vulnerable and unstable employment of the dockyard but wished that the government would give up their useless occupation of the valuable river frontage to allow a proper use for it.

Other groups were interested in the waterfront. For a while in 1833 there was a rumour that the land would be taken up for the Post Office packet establishment but the plan fell through because the dock gates were not wide enough for the larger paddle-steamers. The following year the Deptford Pier and Improvement Company released a prospectus bemoaning the "distressed state to which the town of Deptford has been reduced by the abandonment of the Government Establishments". The Company, which employed George Landmann as its engineer, raised plenty of capital but failed to obtain the necessary Acts of Parliament and the dockyard remained virtually closed for a decade with only occasional breaking-up work.

The 'State of Deptford' debate provides some idea of the level and causes of poverty in the area. Now we should take a look at the types of charitable work which tried to deal with it.

Bread and Morals

By the 1830s there was a proliferation of charitable agencies in Deptford. Most of them were seasonal such as the Deptford Coal Institution (est. 1837) and the Deptford Soup Institution (est. 1809). The DCI spent around £100 in its first winter. Over 90% of the funds went on coal itself. The DSI distributed 20,000 quarts of 'wholesome good soup' and three and a half tons of bread from the Soup House in Crossfield Lane every winter.

Charities at this time raised funds through subscriptions. Some would pay collectors to knock on doors, usually around Brockley, asking for money. Unlike today, when charities are usually run by professionals and making a donation does not entitle the donor to decide on the use of the money, subscribers would often be given tickets to distribute as they saw fit. Those subscribing 6 shillings a month to the DSI received 48 tickets worth one quart of soup each. A similar situation was found in the educational charities which gave subscribers the opportunity to put forward one child a year for the school and vote on a list of possible children. This provided the wealthy with an efficient patronage system and maintained the dependency of potential receivers. It also contributed to an attitude to charity work which provided the foundation for the whole of 19th century philanthropy: dealing out bread and morals from on high.

For example, the Board of Health were very clear that clothing and blankets would be delivered only to those poor known to be "cleanly in their persons and habitations, to the extent of their means". The committee of the Deptford Benevolent Institution for Educating Youth, founded in 1802, "scrutinised the character and conduct of parents of potential candidates" and children would only be accepted for schooling if their parents conformed to the moral standards of school patrons. Many of the eminent local men involved in the Coal Institution were also to be found in the Deptford Christian Instruction Association and the Deptford Auxillary Tract Society. They were among those who felt that the 1839 proposal for educating poor children did not treat the inculcation of religious principles seriously enough and they petitioned Parliament to reject it.

There was a strong feeling that providing charity gave one the right to interfere. Many of the girls of the DBI school found work as domestic servants for lady subscribers but the money they earned was kept by the charity to use for the benefit of the girls as the committee saw fit. It is no wonder that 'charity' became such a dirty word among the working class. Artisans often preferred to pay school fees of one penny a week rather than send their children to the free schools. As John Gast declared in the 1830s: "Attempt not to destroy the ideal of the skilled workman by sundry offers for the care of his children. The man wants work...The approach of the philanthropist is a mockery to this."

One of the most successful and useful of the area's charitable initiatives was the Kent Dispensary established in December 1783 at the Roman Eagle pub at the junction of Church St and Bronze St to give free medical advice and help to the poor. It soon moved to Deptford Broadway and by 1813 it had 'cured and relieved' 57,516 people and delivered babies for over 8,000 poor married women. By 1836 the total number of patients seen was 140,664. In that year the Duke of Wellington chaired the anniversary dinner and the charity was certainly gaining some high-powered support. By 1843 it had obtained the official patronage of Queen Victoria. The Duchess of Kent was Vice Patron and Lord Bexley was President. There were 12 Vice Presidents including the Duke of Wellington, two Earls, a Viscount and a sprinkling of Right Honourables.

When a controversy blew up in 1841 between the Medical Officers and the management committee, John Wade managed to get six tradesmen appointed to the special committee dealing with the matter. He also complained about holding the meeting on a Saturday since few tradesmen could attend. He was supported by the *Woolwich Gazette* who thought it would be a good idea "to infuse a little of the leven of the working classes into the committee".

In 1836 the Dispensary was anxious that "the larger part of the poor fall a sacrifice to ignorant vendors of medicines" but ignorance is relative; they still spent £32 a year of their own funds on leeches!

West End Society Charity

A later version of the High Society involvement in local charity was the Deptford Fund which was to establish the Albany Institute. In 1894 a public meeting was called to draw attention to the dire poverty of Deptford people. In attendance were the Viscount and Viscountess Templeton, Lady Maryon Wilson, Lord Tarleton and the Conservative MP Charles Darling. The Fund set up at this meeting received royal patronage from the Queen's daughter-in-law, the Duchess of Albany from March 1895 until her death in 1922. She was succeeded as President by her daughter Princess Alice, Countess of Athlone.

There was no contact between the Albany and other clubs in London and there is little sign of the desire to learn from the poor and share their lives found in the Settlement Movement and the City Missions of the time. Rather the records reveal a sense of superiority and patronage mixed with concern about working class deficiency. Poverty was seen as a 'moral cancer' and the Fund's objectives were to raise and improve "the poorer part of the population of Deptford, religiously, intellectually, morally and socially". Appeals for the Deptford Fund appeared on the *Times* business page and within two years a Sick Kitchen, a School of Domestic Economy and a Girls' Club were up and running.

The Girls' Club was originally set up for the Gut Girls (Ch.8). The organisers believed they could improve these 'rough and unkempt' women through contact with 'refined ladies' and by providing them with useful and wholesome activities. The club proved popular with an average attendance of 28 during the first year. By 1898 the Gut Girls were joined by women from bottle washing, tin works, laundry and rag sorting. Evenings opened with a lecture and a magic lantern show, followed by needlework or singing, and ended with coffee and cake. The magic lantern shows were very popular and the girls begged for a repeat of 'Life of Our Lord', but there was much nudging and giggling during the lectures. At a talk about Easter it emerged that all except two Catholic girls knew nothing about the religious aspects, though they did promise not to riot on Good Friday afternoon when they went up to Blackheath!

There were frequent comments about the working girls' conspicuous clothes which were thought to suggest independent and unwomanly behaviour. These women earned a fair wage for their work in the gut sheds but they liked to spend it on large hats and had to be encouraged to sew underwear. According to the *Daily Telegraph* "not a single member of the original club possessed an undergarment beyond a single petticoat". Within a couple of years the girls had learned to consider it "desirable to possess a change" and were spending more money on "necessary undergarments". By 1907 the Albany's *Annual Report* commented proudly on the "rows of respectable girls, most tidily dressed, with neat sailors hats" and less of the "cart-wheel hats and dishevelled plumes of but a few years ago". A local vicar had claimed some Deptford girls were prepared to spend a week's wages on an ostrich feather.

In 1898 the Corporation of London stopped importing Argentinian meat and there was high unemployment at the cattle market. The Duchess of Albany set up a relief fund for the 40 girls thrown out of work. The fund paid for gifts of food and money and retraining schemes which helped girls find work in laundries and domestic service.

The club was seen as "redeeming the girlhood of Deptford" and preventing their young lives "running to waste". The image of the 'fallen woman' was very powerful as a constant backdrop to the club's civilising efforts. The reports pay much attention to clothing but are also proud of changes in the girls' standard of thought, voice and gesture. By 1911 they were buying more flannelette to make into undergarments, there were less coarse jokes and rough horseplay and "their whole outlook on life is higher, purer, a step (if only a little step) nearer to the Christian ideal of womanhood".

Although the girls' conduct was improving, they were far from easy to manage. Mrs Annie Lamert, the paid secretary of the Deptford Fund and organiser of the Girls' Club until 1919, worked hard to win their loyalty and obedience. Sometimes she lost her battles. When she had them to tea they stuffed all the food into their pockets even before she managed to say grace. At times the girls were "naughty and restless". They gossiped, giggled and interrupted: "Their one idea of enjoyment is to talk when they are not eating." On an outing to Gravesend in 1901 some girls 'broke ranks' and were found in a pub. In 1910 they listened to Mrs Lamert's long speech about the life and death of the King but spoilt their good behaviour by booing through the hymns.

During the First World War women whose husbands joined the services needed work more than ever and a toy factory was started at the Albany in 1915. Attendance at the Girls' Club fell because of the abundance of overtime available at the local factories and "the unrest and excitement occasioned by the large number of young soldiers in the streets". The girls were reported as dispirited and anxious about the air raids but they seemed better nourished and clothed than before. Dancing was introduced during wartime, though the girls were never very graceful at the 'Society Tango' or the 'Hesitation Waltz'.

In 1919 attendance started to pick up. The club was split into under- and over-18s and a gym was set up under an LCC teacher. New activities were added in the 1920s, including French, roller skating, swimming, literature, cooking and Morris dancing. Before this time the Deptford club had been unusually isolated with a narrow curriculum. There was little or no interest in the girls' rights as workers. During the January 1910 General Election in which Labour won Deptford with a majority of 522, Mrs Lamert was worried by the girls' interest in socialism. In the early years the girls chose lecture subjects such as 'Nelson' (1903) or 'Flowers' (1908). By 1919 they were hoping for 'Labour' or 'Courting'. Unlike other clubs which stressed a 'home-like atmosphere', the girls sat on row after row of form benches and there is no mention of a canteen or a girls' committee.

The Albany Institute provided a comprehensive system of welfare for the poor of Deptford. The School of Domestic Economy had begun in October 1899 with 30 scholars and two teachers to train girls in cookery, laundry, needlework, dressmaking and simple hygiene. Finding domestic work for the girls was uphill work. Some refused to take jobs away from Deptford and for those who had worked in the cattle market and had their evenings to themselves the prospect of 'domestic slavery' did not appeal.

A Clothing Guild distributed free or cheap clothes to poor people and 'Happy Evenings' were held for children. At the 1908 Annual Treat 339 boys ate 1,000 rounds of bread and butter and 96 pounds of cakes as well as dozens of buns and oranges. The Sick Kitchen provided meals to convalescents at one penny each. In 1907 the charity's work was very heavy because many large firms in the area were closing down or cutting jobs. Humphreys & Tennants gave notice to 800 men in one month.

One important aspect of the Fund's work was the Refuge which took in girls and women labelled as 'fallen' (often unmarried mothers). They also took in 'preventive' cases of young girls in danger of running wild because they came from broken or bad homes. One example was a 14 year old girl whose Refuge report stated: "Mother died at birth – father lived with another woman. Father died suddenly. Widow got £10 and has been drunk ever since."

Another offshoot was the Babies' Hospital which opened in 1913 in Albury St to care for badly nourished babies. By 1922 it could accommodate 16 to 18 babies. It moved to Breakspears Rd in 1933 and the new hospital – with beds for 20 children, an out-patient's department and a large garden – was opened by the Duchess of York (now the Queen Mother). In 1940 the hospital was evacuated to Leicester and just one week later the building was almost completely destroyed by a bomb.

During the 1920s the Institute modernised. In 1921 a Boys' Club opened and in 1926 there were joint singing classes. Clubs for mothers, grannies and granddads were started and by 1927 there was an orchestra, a babies' band and a penny bank. In 1928 a 'poor man's lawyer' service was on offer to those earning less than £2 a week.

Grannies' Club sing-song at the Albany Institute, Creek Rd. During the 1920s the Albany broadened its appeal with clubs for mothers, grannies and granddads, an orchestra and a babies' band. The Albany's provision for Deptford's old folk petered out after this until the 1950s when it opened the first all-day club for the elderly.

The Albany's progress through the decades was an indicator of social change. Unlike many other charities it survived the upheavals which brought in the welfare state and it thrived on the community activism of the 1970s. The paradox of the 1980s – social commitment, financial nightmare – was played out in its local form, leaving the 1990s Albany close to empty and tangled in internal battles unknown to most Deptford people. The watershed moment of the early 1990s may be a turning-point for the Albany and we can only hope it will prove its worth in time for the Deptford Fund centenary in 1994.

In 1925 a row broke out over bad relations between voluntary and paid workers. Lady Florence Pelham-Clinton, who had been a strong supporter of the Albany for many years, left to form her own Institute in Deptford Broadway, probably taking some of the Girls' Club members with her. The original Lady Florence Institute is now inhabited by Futures nightclub.

Another rival was the old Ragged School which became the Princess Louise Institute in 1919. The list of meetings from the 1922 *Report* includes morning, afternoon and evening Sunday Schools; bible classes for women, older lads and older girls; a children's lantern show and a young people's service; scouts, girl guides, brownies and wolf cubs; a young men's club, a junior boys' club and a girls' club; a penny bank with 680 on the books and a slate club with 94 members. The Institute also ran an infant welfare centre with 60 to 70 mothers present each week. Women would queue for the weighing room and see the health visitor or visit the doctor. In another room was the 'shop' where infants' foods and simple medicines were sold at a reduced rate. "Sometimes there is a useful word from the Doctor or Health Visitor to the assembled mothers; sometimes instrumental music, and always a hymn or choruses for them to sing and the ever welcome cup of tea." This was quite a different place to the modern clinic.

Most mysterious was the 'Cripple Parlour' held on a Friday evening with an average weekly attendance of 28. This continued until the mid-1930s but no further details are available. Attendance at the schools averaged 650, at the services 220 and at the clubs 230. Those who conducted the clubs and services lived almost exclusively in Brockley and included five of the Wigner family. The Wigner connection began when Arthur Wigner first came to work the Magic Lantern at the beginning of the century. The Wigners were a large family and Arthur encouraged all his grown children to involve themselves in the Institute. He owned the Medina Refinery, the big oil works on Creekside, and gave money as well as time to the Ragged School. Of course he did not give it all away – George Maslin remembers him as the president who drove up to the gates of the Princess Louise in a huge, pink Bentley!

The Albany and the Princess Louise Institute did great work for the children of Deptford but there was another tradition, based in the working class itself, about how to improve the lives of the next generation. It seems appropriate to place the Co-operative Guild in with 'charity' rather than 'politics' because it aimed to provide an alternative means of feeding, clothing, entertaining and educating working class children and adults which inspired pride rather than humiliation. Mrs Cranfield, born in Deptford at the turn of the century, was part of the Co-operative Women's Guild which fought for family allowances in 1913. She volunteered to start a junior circle, taking children on outings and trying "to drum into them about the Labour Party and push all that...we've realised that conditions make people Communist, if the boot pinches you're going to shout". When a friend's son went to prison for six months for "shouting on the streets about communism" his mother and Mrs Cranfield "consented to take the children and try to train them our way...we used to make them sing and shout...*Jerusalem* and the *Red Flag*". Mrs Cranfield was a fighter but even she could be humiliated by the harsh attitudes of the Relief Office. Her husband was a porter at New Cross Station and during the Railway Strike in the 1920s she was told "there is a job for him...you are his responsibility. You can't expect the ratepayer to keep [your children]." In the end they gave her 4 shillings in food tickets but insisted her husband was to have none of it and she was not to return.

The Children's Champion

Middle class socialism could also prove its worth in Deptford as shown by the remarkable Margaret McMillan and her sister Rachel, remembered in the name of the nursery school they founded at Deptford. It was Margaret McMillan who swept away old ideas in her tireless crusade to break the vicious circle of bad nourishment, poor conditions and disease. She was a crusader in other ways too and tackled every issue from shopworkers' hours to votes for women. A socialist from an early age, she claimed it was her school life at the Academy in Inverness, where the girls were in training to be 'ridiculous snobs', which made her a rebel and a reformer. She left home in 1877 and started work as a governess. Ten years later she was living in London with Rachel, working as companion to Lady Meux of Park Lane and observing at first hand the excessive materialism of the aristocratic world. The sisters became interested in William Morris and went to socialist meetings together. They became involved in the campaign for the dockers' tanner (a minimum wage of 6 pence an hour) and Margaret held classes for the jam-girls and mill-girls of Whitechapel. In 1892, when Margaret made a speech in support of the dockers, Lady Meux accused her of "going about with dreadful people".

Margaret was invited to Bradford by the Fabian Society and became a founder member of the Independent Labour Party whose leader Keir Hardie gave a speech in Deptford in 1895. On the Bradford School Board she used her position to begin the first recorded medical inspection of school children. Under her influence Bradford became "an educational Mecca". J B Priestley remembered her from his own Bradford childhood: "She could not see a child looking neglected, hungry, dirty or weary, without instantly going out to battle for it."

Margaret moved back to London in 1902 and lived with Rachel in Bromley. This was the time of the Booth surveys and the revelation that over a third of recruits to the army for the Boer War were physically unfit for service. The old idea that poverty was the result of weak character or idleness was undermined and it became obvious that charity alone could not solve this problem. The report from the Inter-Departmental Committee on Physical Deterioration recommended systematic school medical inspection and feeding of needy schoolchildren by the local authorities. By 1908 local councils could provide school meals and Margaret collaborated on a pamphlet of detailed advice about feeding children weakened by malnourishment. Despite her efforts school meals for all were not available until the Second World War.

The two sisters explored South East London. After a visit to the Greenwich Observatory they found themselves wandering in Deptford's "dark, noisy courts...sodden alleys all hidden behind roaring streets". Margaret was horrified by the "women who care no more, girls whose youth is a kind of defiance, children creeping on the filthy pavement, half-naked, unwashed and covered with sores".

In 1910 Margaret established the School Treatment Centre in the Old Vestry Hall at Deptford Green to work with local schools in the oldest and poorest part of Deptford. This was an area of casual waterside workers living in old houses. Overcrowding was severe and infant mortality rates were shockingly high. As many as 80 out of 500 babies died before their first birthday. If they survived they were more than likely to suffer from skin diseases, tuberculosis, rickets and scabies. In one school a third of the children were in bad health.

The building was rent-free courtesy of Greenwich Borough Council and LCC grants helped pay for doctors and nurses. The upper room served as a nursery, consulting room and dental surgery. This dentistry was the earliest known treatment of its kind available to working class children. It soon became obvious that home conditions were thwarting the clinic's work. In three months the nurse treated 927 cases of skin disease and minor ailments; 723 of the children returned re-infected. When W J Evelyn, Deptford's first MP, offered free tenancy of Evelyn House (353 Evelyn St) the clinic began to take on remedial work by training the children in exercises to improve breathing and straighten out spine defects.

Still children from the clinic were being sent back to homes where they slept three or four to a bed. With poor diet, bad ventilation and dirty surroundings, infections spread all too easily. Hoping to find a solution using fresh air, exercise and wholesome food, Margaret decided to let some of the girls from the Treatment Centre stay overnight at Evelyn House as an experiment. The back garden was cleared and levelled and a corrugated iron shed erected as a shelter. An ingenious hot water system was constructed by linking pipes across the garden fence to a neighbour's boiler. A young woman was engaged as Camp Guardian to watch over the camp girls who ranged from 6 to 14 years old. Sometimes there were as many as 17 of them sleeping overnight in the garden.

When the girls arrived after school they were given duties around the camp. 6.30 pm was wash-time and each older girl supervised a younger one to ensure proper cleaning of hair, teeth and nails. Wooden beds were put out, facing south east to catch the early morning sun. By 8 o'clock everyone was tucked up in bed with the lantern glowing reassuringly. In the morning the girls made porridge for breakfast and then left for school. Good food, regular exercise and the great outdoors behind Evelyn St soon wiped away all the marks of poverty. The whole neighbourhood was amazed to see these fit and healthy children.

Margaret negotiated the use of St Nicholas' churchyard to set up a boys' camp. The council forced her to remove the shelter she built near the grave of Admiral Benbow but the camp went ahead and the boys learned to cook even if they could not read or write. There were problems though: "The boys broke the crockery at a great pace. They lost the towels. They did all kinds of strange things with the new toothbrushes." After a while local pressure forced a move to a piece of wasteground in Hughes Fields. In 1914 Margaret managed to acquire a vacant plot in the Stowage from the LCC for a peppercorn rent of one shilling a year. She had use of the buildings on the corner of the site and this is where the first open-air nursery school was founded. Rachel McMillan Nursery School still survives on the same site, opposite the junction of Church St and Creek Rd.

Margaret wanted to extend her work to pre-school children, hoping to influence their development and counteract the disastrous early effects of poor conditions at home. When women were called upon to work for the war effort the Ministry of Munitions authorised a childcare allowance for very young children. The grant of 7 pence a day per child for minding the children of workers at Woolwich Arsenal helped Margaret to establish the baby camp.

In the Board Schools young children had a gallery of little benches of their own and "the turbulence of the streets is subdued into industrious calm. Ragged little urchins run quietly in harness, obedient to a look, a gesture, of the teacher in command." The McMillan method was radically different. She wanted children to think for themselves and discover the world through play. It took time, however, to erase the memory of the cane which made these toddlers hide their hands behind their backs whenever they saw a teacher. Parents were also suspicious and the old habit of sewing children into their clothes for the winter died hard but eventually both parents and youngsters were convinced of the benefit of a daily bath at the nursery school. Encouraged with smiles and gentle words, the children came to enjoy wash-time. Clean clothes meant an end to the terrible fidgeting caused by infested clothing which was noted by every slum teacher of the period.

Queueing for school milk Lucas St Primary School Tanners Hill, circa 1923. Boots were also supplied the schools in cases of hardship and it looks as though some of these children are wearing them

The nursery grew during the war with both sisters devoting themselves full time to running it. The Mayor of Deptford had arranged for a regular grant to be paid to give Margaret an occasional rest from work but when he wrote stressing it was to be used for her own personal benefit she had already spent it on the nursery school. Rachel died in 1917 after a short illness and Margaret became increasingly indifferent to her own needs. Sure that her sister was guiding her work and giving her strength to continue, she dedicated the nursery school to Rachel's memory.

Margaret was well known for her persistence at the Board of Education where she would wait on the Ministry steps all day if necessary. In 1919 Queen Mary visited the nursery and soon a cheque for £300 arrived from the Palace. Margaret's reputation brought students from all over the world to work with her in Deptford. Against the general opinion that any decent woman could care for young children, Margaret insisted that nursery teachers needed proper practical training. Many were shocked out of their sheltered opinions by the conditions around the training centre, especially because they boarded in local houses and were expected to make home visits. Some of the students took children home at the weekends to give them a taste of life away from Deptford. Other entertainment included the toys donated by rich patrons, music on the piano or gramophone and the menagerie of animals Margaret kept in the early years. Visits by prominent people increased as the outside world became fascinated by the McMillan success in Deptford. George Bernard Shaw came to give lectures to the students and was easily converted to the cause of nursery education by Margaret's "lovely brats", even allowing one toddler to pull his beard and call him 'Beaver'. When the camp children were invited to Easton Lodge, home of Lady Warwick, an Edwardian beauty and close friend of Edward VII who had converted to socialism, they were so well-behaved that the butler declared he preferred them to trade unionists any day.

With the help of her friend the Conservative MP Nancy Astor, Margaret managed to acquire a site opposite the Albany Institute in Creek Rd to build a training college which Queen Mary opened in 1930. Already awarded a CBE, and given the freedom of the Borough of Deptford, in 1930 she was made Companion of Honour, arriving at Buckingham Palace for the ceremony with a safety pin in her hem. She died in March 1931, remembered fondly by Bernard Shaw as "not only one of the best women of her time...but also one of the most cantankerous, and she owed a great deal of her effectiveness to the latter useful quality".

In the last two chapters we have seen some instances of charity and some moments of political tension. In all the charity there was compassion but it was ever fed by fear. Charity from on high is always a political statement, though the language changes. The 'many-headed monster' of Tudor times readily became the 18th century 'mob'. The Victorian 'criminal classes' were the 'rough types' of the 1920s. We have made them 'problem families'.

TESTING THE SPIRIT

12

Depression and the Good Old Days

"I wouldn't like to see those times come back.
They say 'The Good Old Days', but they weren't.
They were very hard. You had to look at every ha'penny
before you spent it." – Age Exchange, Fifty Years Ago

Oral history research is not for the faint-hearted. Apart from the hard work, the hours of transcribing and the impossible decisions over selection, there is a more fundamental problem for the tidy-minded. People are different, both personally and sociologically. Each life experience is a unique reflection of dozens of factors. On top of that, memory itself is a slippery thing, much misunderstood, constantly transforming and making new patterns as times change.

So oral history is full of contradictions, paradoxes and confusion... a bit like real life! The Deptford people who talk about the interwar period as the Good Old Days will tell you, in the next sentence, about unemployment, short-time and the hated Means Test; bad housing, outside toilets and epidemic sickness; making do, going short, moneylenders and pawnbrokers and the continuing horrors of childbirth in a time of rising maternal mortality. On their minds as well was the betrayal of Ramsay MacDonald, the growing fear of another war and above all, the insecurity of life in a world slump. "In the district in which we are concerned, there is much casual labour and unemployment and consequent distress, while the conditions of living are, in many cases, such as to render morality and decency very difficult." (Princess Louise Institute, *Report*, 1934).

Whatever was good in this period must have existed above and beyond these fears and hardships. Often it lay in everyday things, taken for granted at the time but lost since and much mourned. This is the time of the 'community spirit' based on streets in which everybody knew each other and would gossip, help out or fight with almost equal readiness. This is the time when the rent collector and the insurance man came once a week to collect the pennies left on the kitchen table or the chimney-piece. This is when the house key could be left on a piece of string inside the door without fear.

The perceived safety of children is one issue which clearly marks the boundary between that time and our own. Neighbourhood children were seen as just that – belonging in some way to everyone, watched over by all the adults of an area, free to roam but easy to punish for any mischief. Parks like Hilly Fields were crowded with chidren during the school holidays but fenced in with iron railings and watched over by LCC park-keepers in their brown uniforms. "They would be watching out for any misbehaviour, but also keeping an eye on the children. Any tumbles or minor accidents and we would go to them for help." (Age Exchange, *Leisure*).

Children continued to go to Sunday School long after their parents had given up on church. Partly this was to get the kids out of the house and give them the opportunities for learning and leisure which the churches and chapels provided. We saw in the previous chapter how the Princess Louise Institute provided highly moral 'entertainment' for every age group. The other institutes and the churches offered similar clubs and outings, including Christian Endeavour and the Band of Hope. Girl Guides, Boy Scouts, Boys' Brigade and the new Co-operative Guild Woodcraft Folk provided camping holidays for those who could afford them. The Salvation Army, with its hall in Mary Ann's Buildings, was a source of mocking amusement for many Deptford folk. Sophie Lake remembers chanting "Salvation Army, all gone barmy" as a child in the 1920s but she joined up as a teenager and has remained with them ever since.

Salvation Army 'Deptford Chums' with their leader Mrs Burridge, circa 1923. There were youth groups of all kinds run by the churches and chapels to offer entertainment and discipline to Deptford's youngsters.

Some families would go up to Greenwich Park on a Sunday afternoon, taking a couple of jam sandwiches and some tea in a screw-top lemonade bottle. On Sunday evenings the youngsters would stroll along the 'Monkey Parade' on Blackheath, Hilly Fields or down in Greenwich. "This was where small groups of boys and girls (separated) would walk up and down, call out the odd remark, and sometimes get into conversation...it was all quite harmless fun. Later still, courting couples would take over, so the Parks were well used." (Age Exchange, *Leisure*).

'Courting' was an important part of life then as now but it was hedged round with difficulties. Apart from the parks, always remembered as cold comfort for young lovers, there were very few places courting couples could be together. There are endless stories of strict and interfering parents. One woman describes how even when she was engaged "we couldn't sit down on the sofa and hold hands. My mum would say: 'What are you sitting there for? There's another chair over there'." Sometimes the porch provided a haven for the good-night kiss. One mother used to say "Go and see that boy don't pinch the door-mat, but don't be more than five minutes". Fathers were more likely to rattle on the window or come out and see the lad off. Neighbours were always on the look-out for gossip. If the boy was well known to the family he might share in their social occasions. At a Glazebrook family dance in the grandmother's house in Oareboro Rd, cousin Cissie and her young man Mick were 'spooning' in Granny's big kitchen armchair. They got caught but the parents were calm enough, "anyway they're getting married soon".

If most parents over-protected their children, they were usually reluctant to let them know exactly why. "Our parents...were the offshoot of the Victorian Age, and we were greatly influenced by them", says one of the Age Exchange reminiscence group. Although contraception was known to many people, especially after Marie Stopes' publicity campaigns, it was still a taboo subject and ignorance about sex was very widespread. When Joan Tyrrell had her first kiss she called out "Mum, what shall I do? He's kissing me. I don't want a baby". Her mother was very embarrassed, "that was how Mum was. She was old fashioned." Another woman remembers her mother as "very prim and proper and we were brought up in total ignorance. When sanitary towels were first advertised, my mother asked my sister what they were...They were things that were never discussed." With a mixture of strictness and threats ("Your dad used to say, 'If you get in trouble, I'll shoot you and the fellow as well'") parents did their best to avoid 'trouble' without ever discussing it. "Although we were ignorant, we knew it was wrong, so you just didn't do it. You'd be disgraced if you were found out or got pregnant." Many women, of course, did get pregnant. Some would have a rapid wedding, others would be left to fend for themselves, inevitably stigmatised as 'fallen women'.

"We went to Blackpool for our honeymoon. It was a rude awakening actually. Well, you got to know things second-hand sort of thing and then you suddenly realised what was happening you thought, 'Oh my God, what's this?'."

"Marriage came as quite a shock to most people. You had to do what came naturally – we managed! They need instruction nowadays because they have so many different ways."

"Then, of course, after you've had one baby you know. And I said 'never again, I'm having no more'." The woman who said this was pregnant again 16 months later but after the second child she was taken to the Walworth Road Clinic by her sister to get fitted with a cap. As long as you were married (and could prove it with your 'marriage lines') it was not difficult to get a cap and women of this generation considered themselves lucky when they looked at their mothers' lives. "They didn't have nothing at all. They couldn't stop it then. The husband used to go out drinking..." Women give away snippets about this aspect of their lives in oral history interviews: a 'good husband' was one who did not drink too much or lose his temper. Economic dependency and sometimes religious conviction kept women with mean and violent men but they developed their own ways of coping. One of these was to keep their secrets among themselves. The woman described above never told her husband about the cap but she certainly spread the word to other women.

Entertainment features strongly in memories of the Good Old Days. It was readily available, cheap and escapist. The Broadway Theatre and the New Cross Empire were great centres of live variety entertainment. The Deptford Electric Palace and the Broadway Picture Playhouse were the nearest 'flicks'. Some of the older picture palaces closed in the interwar period but a number of huge new cinemas took their place.

Tragedy hit the Deptford Electric Palace at 197 High St in 1917. It was a packed Saturday afternoon show with many parents waiting outside because of concern about Zeppelin bombers. One small child, bored with the silent movie, pulled two small pebbles from his pocket and flicked them one at a time into a nearby ventilator fan. As the blades of the fan hit the pebbles and the noise reverberated around this 'bug-hatch' cinema, the children panicked and trampled each other in the rush for the door, shouting 'bombs'. Parents were banging on the door, screaming out their children's names. There were no Zeppelins but four children had died, none more than 10 years old.

New Cross Empire Music Hall, opposite Addey & Stanhope school on New Cross Rd, opened in 1899. closure of the Empire in 1954 and demolition four years later reflected the ise of live entertainment. site became a car lot but was up for sale in 1993.

Shows at the popular New Cross Empire ranged from 12-girl dance troupes on the revolving stage to Phyllis Dixie the Fan Dancer, a tall blonde with a beautiful figure who danced naked but was so skillful with her fans that she avoided official censorship. Halls like the Empire were solidly grounded in the local community. One night a week they held the 1930s version of karaoke, getting the audience up on stage to dance, climb ropes or fool about. Ethel Penfold's memories of the Woolwich Empire sound like the *Generation Game* – competitions drinking all the milk out of a 'titty bottle', eating cream buns from a plate with no hands, or washing a doll with "electric all going up your arm". Ethel used to win the 'wash the baby' competition regularly. Once she reached the final and came home with a prize box of kippers. The New Cross Empire advertised in 1932 for local talent to appear in the show *Paris in New Cross*, pointing out that Gracie Fields had been a Mill Girl and Harry Lauder a Pit Boy but they had seized their opportunity: here was Deptford's grand chance. Costumes, make-up, music and tuition were provided free. The call-up – "Your Stage Chance has arrived" – must have been irresistible for many young people. A bigger undertaking was the *Greenwich Night Pageant* held outdoors at the Naval College in 1933 with a cast of 2,500 local people.

A typical 'night out with the lads' was a fourpenny seat at one of these live music halls with a two-hour show followed by a supper of fish and chips or pie and mash. Cigarettes were purchased loose by the half ounce between half a dozen lads. "Fabulous Turkish, Balkan, Egyptian, Virginia and Empire tobaccos with tips of gold, silk and cork, they smelled abominably, and tasted the same, but were witness to our man-hood." The whole evening cost less than a shilling. Many young women used to skip work once a week to go to matinees at the local cinema. Often girls paired up to go cycling or walking in the country or for trips to the new open-air swimming pools built by local authorities in Bellingham, Eltham and Charlton.

These were the dancing years with 'sixpenny hops' held at almost every school and church hall, not to mention the indoor swimming baths where weekly dances helped to keep the pools financially viable. Boys would meet their partners "inside after they had paid their own entrance, and in the interval we retired to the toilets until they had bought their refreshments!" Dances included slow and quick foxtrots, waltzes and tangos as well as the 'Paul Jones' which helped sort out almost-random partners (although, of course, if you didn't like the look of whoever was coming your way when the music stopped "you scurried past him or hung back, anything to avoid your fate"). One favourite was the Spot Waltz with a revolving central spotlight throwing out specks of coloured lights and focusing when the music stopped on one couple who won a prize. The modern dances – the Black Bottom, the Charleston and the Blues – "horrified our elders", but when the *Lambeth Walk* became an international hit in 1938 its appeal crossed generations as well as class and nationality.

The *Lambeth Walk* was followed in 1939 by the 'dance hit' the *Deptford Dip*, written and composed by Eric Cuddon who served as Squadron Leader in the war and stood as Conservative candidate for Deptford in the 1945 General Election. The Labour majority that year was 14,254.

This was also the golden age of cinema and many young people went at least once a week. The cinema was a great favourite: for courting in the double seats, for escaping the cold, wet, mundane reality outside, for thrills, romance or a good weep. In the early silent cartoons a little old lady rattled away on the piano at the front. At the Broadway Cinema, the well-loved 'Auntie Grace' played at matinees until closure in 1960. A session at the pictures was a total experience. There were always two films as well as the Movietone News and a travelogue and often a live variety show in the interval. In a world without television the newsfilms and travelogues gave the audience something special and intriguing which we take for granted: an immediate view of the world beyond home. There was endless crunching on a 'pint of peanuts' or a bag of monkey-nuts, an orange or apple and maybe some popcorn. Usherettes would walk up and down the aisles with their trays selling ice-cream, chocolates and cigarettes and flashing their torches during the showing. It could be distracting but it was part of the fun. "When the performance was over, you couldn't see the floor for orange peel and monkey nuts and shells. We always took an orange to the pictures. What with all the sucking and all the kissing, you can imagine what it was like." Likewise, for the kids who went to Saturday morning cowboy films, cheering for the goodies and hissing at the baddies was integral to the entertainment. These matinee performances always finished with a cliffhanger. "See next week's thrilling installment..."

In 1932, the worst year of the Depression, four new giant cinemas opened in South London. "Pictures are my first choice," said one unemployed Deptford man, "because they make you think for a little while that life is all right."

During the 1930s the miracle of wireless spread throughout the country. The schoolchildren's craze for making a wireless out of an empty match-box and a cotton reel lasted only as long as they were entertained by the very limited noises it could make but magazines like *Practical Wireless*, available for 3 pence, published plans and instructions enabling many families to build their own sets. Tuning with the cat's whisker on the quartz crystal was horribly frustrating. The wireless had to be kept completely still and the accumulator (a jam-jar full of acid) needed charging at a cycle shop every week. The single pair of earphones made wireless a rather solitary entertainment until loud speakers were developed and it was a while before the content of broadcasts became worth the effort. In the mid-1930s the valve replaced the crystal, sets were manufactured in large quantities and the wireless became a way of life. Another important piece of new technology was the gramophone. These were a great status symbol and owning one meant taking it round whenever you went visiting. "When we put the gramophone on, neighbours all around used to open their windows to hear."

Many working class families would save up for a week's bed and breakfast holiday at the seaside: Southend, Clacton, Margate or Ramsgate. It was usually only possible with some extra help from family or by using a 'mutuality cheque' from the Co-op which would have to be paid back week by week. The beaches were crowded with happy kids clutching tin buckets and spades. There were donkey rides and fairgrounds, entertainment on the piers and beauty competitions in the local parks. Men wandered the beaches hawking pineapple or ice-cream and the roads were lined with stalls selling cockles and mussels with salt and vinegar for tuppence a plate. In the heatwave of 1933 sand was deposited on 'Greenwich Beach' so that poorer families could "have a holiday feeling".

For some families a day trip to Southend was a holiday in itself. Paddle-steamers left Greenwich four times a day and the bars on board sold beer for tuppence a pint. "You'd stagger straight off and fall asleep on the sand. Then on the way back you'd be drinking again."

Firms often paid for an annual staff outing, a beano, once a year. The workers would fill up the back of the coach with beer and sing all the way there and back.

Charabanc outing from Milton Court Rd, circa 19 Day trips and staff outing (beanos) provided a welc break for many Deptford families. The pensioners' trips to Margate and Southend organised by Fr David Diamond in the 19 and 1980s must have bro back memories of outings like this one.

Taking a holiday meant losing your money and could be a risk to the job itself. For many Deptford people a hop-picking September in Kent provided a working holiday for the women and children while the men would come down for weekends. Now that hops are collected with machinery, memories of the Good Old Days are all that's left of going 'down hopping', a tradition which stretched back with few changes to the mid-19th century. Hopping is often associated exclusively with East End families but the streets and schools of Deptford were also much quieter at hopping time. Ellen Chase described how some of the Green St (Mary Ann's Buildings) tenants at the end of the 19th century "spoke familiarly of Squire Evelyn and went to his country seat regularly for the hop-picking".

Whether the women saw hopping as a holiday or as paid work depended partly on their financial circumstances but also on their skill and speed as pickers. For women with very large families it could be the only way to work at all. For others it raised the extra money to clear the year's debts or save up for a winter coat or a special Christmas. For those with less pressures the money was spent at the time in the form of regular 'subs' for the weekend drinking and the final pay-off may be only a few shillings. Most agreed that the healthy living for women and children was at least as important as the money. Everyone could go hopping and be watched over: the elderly, the less able, very young children and even household pets. For some women leaving the husband behind was as much of a relief as taking the children with them.

Families would write to the farmer from January onwards asking if they could come, and could they have their usual hut please. At the farms the pace was building up through the summer with the mad rush to get the harvest in and the sheep shorn before the hops were ready. Once the date was fixed, postcards were sent out to the

Londoners telling them when to come. A wave of excitement went up and down the roads as the postcards arrived and preparations began immediately. Many regular hopping families were able to keep the same hut and leave tables and chairs, dressers and babies' cots down there. Even so there was a lot to transport and during the year all sorts of things were put in the 'hopping box'.

The different ways of getting to the Kent farms depended on available finance and skillful borrowing. In the 19th century overloaded wagons made their way slowly towards Kent and in 1853 thirty pickers were killed in Hadlow when a bridge snapped beneath their heavy cart. An old tradition for Deptford folk, and some East Enders, was to walk all the way. Sometimes it was possible to borrow a lorry from a local tradesman though the temptation to take more stuff was dangerous: "Used to take the piano on the back of the lorry. Down hopping! Bloody great Alsatian dogs, canaries, all sorts! A right turn out!" Most people in the interwar years went by train, making their way up to London Bridge railway station early in the morning to catch the 'Hop Picker's Special', a cheap train of old coaches fitted into the slacker hours of the timetable. Children were hidden under the seats, in the luggage racks or even in the hopping box itself. The hop-farmers sent horses and wagons to meet the pickers from the station while the locals looked on.

Relations with locals differed from place to place and year to year. One hop-farmer's daughter remembers: "Those London girls used to come down in velvet frocks and button boots and we thought they were all rich. We country girls used to love to see those Londoners come down." More often the Londoners were looked down on as poor and rough, 'dirty foreigners'. Pubs often charged a shilling deposit on a glass and some even had 'No Pickers' signs. The village shop counter would be fitted up with wire netting, while 'home dwellers' were served at the back door. Local pubs and shops faced a dilemma – the promise of all that custom weighed against the risk of offending regular customers. Cottage wives often cooked Sunday joints and cakes to sell to 'hut dwellers' and their husbands grew an extra allotment and reared cockerels to sell to the Londoners on their pay-off at the end of September. The wagons taking the pickers back to the station were laden not only with luggage and children, but with sacks of potatoes and fat cockerels strung up by the feet.

Accommodation at the farms was, by our standards, primitive and overcrowded but for many of the women it was little different from home life in terms of bedding, plumbing or numbers per room, though the toilets are usually remembered with horror. What was different was the quality of the air, the feel of open space and the communal working and living which all remember with great affection. "Sit on the bin. Talk. Pick. Talk. Have a cigarette, have a laugh...while you carried on picking." Companionship and sharing were central to the pleasure of picking. Childcare became so much easier when everyone looked out for each other's kids and all the neighbours were known as 'aunts'. The hand-me-down network grew to mammoth proportions. If someone was sick the others would muck in to keep their picking going or help out with the nursing. Less obvious but well remembered was the feeling of friendliness and the time for women to talk together, knowing they were "all in the same boat".

Breakfast – a bit of bacon fried on the embers of last night's fire – would be around six o'clock and work began at seven. Pole-pullers, who were always men except during the war years, used sharp blades on long poles to cut the bines free and pull them down to the pickers. Family groups would strip the hop cones off the bines and into the hop bins. Each 'bin' was a large open sack supported by poles resting on trestles at each end. The bines were covered in harsh prickles and at the beginning of the season hands would be scratched until they bled. Gloves only slowed down the picking speed. At regular intervals the tally man would come round to see how many bushels had been picked and pack them up to be taken to the oasthouses for drying.

Around five or six in the evening the cry 'pull no more bines' echoed around the hop-fields and the day's hopping was over. The women would walk back to the huts carrying their youngest children and their

Deptford women hop-picking in the 1930s. 'Going down hopping' provided a working holid. for women and children ir tradition which stretched back with little change to the 19th century. Septemb. found the streets and sch. of Deptford strangely qui. while the Kent hop-fields were busy with Londoner. The photo shows Mary Granger, who was a Deptford market-trader during the 1940s and 1950s (Ch.14).

empty baskets and kettles but there was plenty more work to do. Fires and lamps had to be lit before it got too dark, food and laundry had to be organised. Chores never stopped, not even down hopping, but eventually, when a hot dinner had been magicked out of the iron cauldron ('the hopping pot') and the washing had been hung out, the women could relax for a while around the fires, talking, singing and laughing. Some women would go to the pub but weekday drinking was not generally approved except for the 'grannies'.

By midday Saturday picking was finished for the week and preparations began for the arrival of the menfolk. Local missions often provided hot baths on Friday nights and old working clothes were replaced with 'best'. For the children the men's arrival was an opportunity for fun: "There was a great 'Hooray!' when all the men appeared, half-sozzled most of them, but they were there. Saturday night was the night." Although most of the women also looked forward to it they had more work to do. "You had to feed them and then go to the pub. Do your shopping. Then start cooking again. Up the pub, home and bed! On Sunday...some of the men went for a walk, ended up in the pub, of course. You ended up in the pub about half hour before shutting up time. Come back, wash up, and it was time for them to go!" The pubs were crowded at weekends and the dark country lanes rang out with singing on the way back to the farm. Some of the best stories came out of the weekend larks and surprises were never far away on the farm. One lad who was down for the weekend called out in the night. When his mum got up to have a look "it was only a bleeding cow. Stuck its head in the hop-house door licking his feet. What a treat, licking his dirty feet!"

The Salvation Army and other missionaries often tried to provide alternatives to what they saw as the hoppers' drunken immorality. They would come round with tea and cake for a penny or get the children singing hymns on a Saturday night. Encouraging the adults to join in often ended in chaos and rude words would quickly replace the pious hymns. Despite the mockery, there was nothing but praise for the medical missions and the hot baths.

At the end of the season the atmosphere was jubilant. Whoever got to strip the last bine would have luck for the coming year. The young girls were thrown in the bins, photos were taken and there was the pay-off to look forward to. The huts were tidied and the women queued for their money which could amount to around £60 for a hard-working family. Then it was time for the party. "It was the best night, a goodbye night." Dressed in their weekend best for the return to Deptford, the hoppers made their way back to a different life, happier, healthier and a little bit wealthier.

Nevertheless, although much about the 1920s and 1930s was good with hindsight, it was a hard time for most Deptford people. After the First World War, British economy and society never regained the stability and confidence of the pre-war years. The Peace Parties of 1919, held in streets throughout Deptford, expressed a genuine joy at the end of war but their context was one of sickness and uncertainty. Influenza spread throughout Europe killing off vulnerable populations in one of the most deadly epidemics since the cholera waves of the 1830s.

During the 1920s it was widely believed that depression in the basic industries and the acute industrial unrest leading up to the General Strike of 1926 when 160,316,000 working days were lost, were merely the aftermath of post-war economic dislocation. In the later 1920s normal peacetime economic rhythms seemed to be returning. The prosperity of the United States was held up as the shining example of enterprise capitalism wedded to modern mass production technology. This highly productive, high wage economy, which seemed to serve the interests of business and labour alike, was shattered by the devastating economic crisis which began with the New York stock market crash of 1929 and spread rapidly throughout the world.

Armistice Day, 1918, at the Royal Victoria Victualling Yard. There were Peace Parties and bunting strung up throughout Deptford to mark the end of the First World War. These building the old rum stores, were renovated by the GLC in t mid-1960s as part of the Pepys Estate.

Great sections of the British population were faced with a breakdown of the whole economic system under which they lived. One of the richest countries in the world was shown to be unable to provide huge numbers of its people with any way of making a living. The sense of insecurity was acute.

At the junction of Deptford Broadway and the High St "where the public lavatories form an island in the middle of the road, men in grubby coats and cloth-caps lounge against the railings. Some are cupping their hands to their mouths to capture the warmth of their breath; others are slapping their arms across their bodies and stamping their feet. Their faces are the colour of dirty, yellow soap." George Glazebrook's mother explains that they are out of work and waiting for the coffee stall to open. This is 1928.

By 1932 one Deptford man in six was unemployed. The national figure had reached a record level of 2.7 million in August 1931. Nearly a fifth of them had been out of work for more than six months. Most of these were drawing unemployment insurance benefit from a fund into which workers, employers and the state paid weekly contributions. To get the benefit you had to sign on twice a day. There were fights between counter staff and the unemployed at Deptford Labour Exchange and one man remembers mounted police on duty controlling the unemployment queues. A couple with two children would receive 30 shillings a week, each extra child only merited another 2 shillings a week. This was a poor labourer's rate and was enough to keep the family from outright starvation but not much else. Diets became unbalanced, dominated by bread and margarine and tea with condensed milk. Clothes and shoes wore through and could not be replaced. Breaking a cup or plate became a minor disaster and after a while the blankets were all in pawn, the rent fell into arrears and families became desperate. Suicide and crime rates soared while entry figures at the Maudsley mental hospital rose by 13% in 1932.

August 1931 marked a political watershed with an impact in countless working class homes. The Labour government resigned and its Prime Minister, Ramsay MacDonald, formed a new coalition with the Conservative and Liberal leaders. This was the culmination of months of working class disillusionment with wage cuts in every industry and the Employers' Associations blaming unemployment benefit for the 'artificial' maintenance of wages. Faced with much higher levels of unemployment than expected, the Unemployment Insurance Fund was now deep in debt to the Treasury and the new government was desperate to make reductions. Legislation was rushed through the House of Commons to cut all benefits and introduce a new system which included the hated Means Test.

When the Conservative leaders forced a general election in October 1931 a million voters refused to go to the polls at all. With the apathy and disillusion of Labour supporters and the poor organisation of the Liberal Party, the result (known as the National Government until 1939) was a government of unusually old men, predominantly Consevatives, who looked back longingly to the values of pre-war Britain.

Not all the unemployed had been entitled to employment benefit. Many had to apply for help to the Poor Law Authority, the local Public Assistance Committee (PAC). These committees now became a central part of government policy. Benefit was restricted to 26 weeks and hundreds of thousands of people were disallowed by the various new criteria, including those who had been longest out of work. These people would in future have to apply for 'transitional payments', first undergoing a means test by the PAC. Payments were not to exceed the new benefit level of 27 shillings for a family of four. They were often far less than this if the local PAC's own relief scales were lower or if the Means Test showed any household income which could be set against the payment.

Many of the people who now faced this test were skilled workers who had paid insurance contributions for many years and had never been near the Poor Law before. The PACs had previously been mainly concerned with the relief of the old, the sick, widows and orphans. These paternalist agencies, with their ingrained attitudes to the poor, now became involved in scrutinising 'respectable' households, prying into Co-op and Post Office savings accounts, penalising parents for the few shillings their children might bring home and forcing the sale of furniture and 'spare' clothes before giving out measly relief, usually in the form of food vouchers, one for the butcher, one for the baker and one for the milk. The PAC even considered docking the 1s.8d a week earned by an unemployed Deptford man for digging a clergyman's garden. "You only got what would do you: in fact not enough to do you really. Everything was doled out by the little bit. You were only allowed milk if you had a baby and couldn't feed it, and then you were only given so much. My God, let's hope that never comes back. Never. Those times should never come back." (Age Exchange, *50 Years Ago*).

A Deptford vicar organised weekly community singing in church for the local unemployed: "I think it can relieve a man's feelings if he can sing as loudly as he likes" he told the *South London Press*. At the Albany there were boot-repairing classes and a Physical Training Centre was opened to try to keep unemployed men from becoming unfit and demoralised while out of work. The 1932 *Annual Report* described the Boys' Club: "It is no light matter to carry on with these lads fighting all the time against poverty, lack of clothing, boots and food." The tricks to disguise shabby clothing – scarves to hide the lack of a shirt, wearing three jumpers so that the holes of one were covered by the material of another – read as pitifully as any from the early Victorian Ragged School reports.

If church and charity were appalled by the resurgent poverty, the local authority was also disturbed about the effects of benefit cuts and increasing unemployment. When the Deptford Medical Officer surveyed the food supplies of a number of poorer local families he concluded that there were at least 80 families who, after rent and allowing one shilling a week for all other expenses, had only 4 shillings per head to feed the family for a week. Borough councillors were horrified and sent reports to the Ministry of Health, County Hall (HQ of the PAC) and the Save the Children committee to show "the shocking conditions under which some of our people live in Deptford". The unemployed themselves were making their own protests. Many joined the National Unemployed Workers' Movement (NUWM) and the Deptford branch grew to 1,000 members. The Movement depended on well-organised activists who held meetings outside the Relief Stations, at factory gates and on street corners. By collecting weekly subscriptions of one penny from the queues at the Relief Stations they kept in touch with every one of the members and could influence many non-members. Individual cases of injustice or particular hardship were taken straight to the officials responsible with the activist accompanying the member to give moral support. Many trade unionists, like the well-known Deptford NUWM organiser Alf Lucas, had not had work since the 1926 General Strike and became increasingly militant as benefits were cut. The 1930s was a time of marching, including the national Hunger Marches as well as countless local deputations, public meetings and protests. Many of the descriptions sound like battles, with hundreds of people arrested, thousands knocked about in police baton charges and tens of thousands chased by mounted police.

In 1931 a mass deputation of 5,000 unemployed marched to the town hall followed by children singing 'Daddy's on the Dole'. Alf Lucas spoke for the NUWM, urging the Council to undertake housing schemes to clear the slums and provide work at trade union rates. He also demanded free office accommodation for the Movement, free baths and free maternity treatment for the wives of unemployed men. Later that year, as people gathered on Deptford Broadway for the

NUWM march to the PAC at County Hall, they were told by the police they must leave their banners behind. They were led by Kath Duncan, a great speaker, a resourceful activist and a friend in need to thousands of Deptford families.

Kath Duncan was descended from the famous Scottish cattle-thief, Rob Roy, who was said never to steal from the poor. She was influenced by the Suffragettes and by the first Independent Labour Party meeting in her village. In 1923 she moved to Hackney with her husband, Sandy. Both LCC teachers, they had been staunch supporters of Ramsay MacDonald, Prime Minister of Labour's first government, but the General Strike of 1926 took them to the Communist Party.

The Deptford NUWM published a newspaper during the General Strike called the *Unemployed Gazette*. Along with a short history of the struggle, adverts for jumble sales run by the Women's Section or Esperanto classes at the NUWM offices in New Cross Rd, there were general articles about war, Christianity, fascism, local personalities and national developments on the strike front. Each issue also ran a column called 'Things We Would Like To Know' which ranged from wanted ads for bicycles to sarcastic jokes about local Conservatives, from gentle reminders about coming events to odd items such as the following: "How much longer the Deptford Borough Council will allow the ratepayers of the borough to be harassed in the High Street on Saturdays by cumbersome, profit-making vehicles (buses etc)?"

In 1930 the Duncans moved to South London and Kath stood as the Communist candidate for Greenwich in the 1931 election. Soon after the election they moved to Deptford and Kath threw herself into the unemployed movement there, becoming a powerful and prolific street speaker. Margaret Kippin tells how, against orders from her parents, "we would hang about on the edge of the crowd when Kath Duncan was holding one of her meetings. We did not understand what it was all about, but there was a sense of excitement, especially when there was barracking from the crowd." Kath, like all outdoor speakers, got plenty of such heckling, especially in the early years. Bill Jones remembers her outside the Lord Clyde pub: a small woman making powerful speeches. All the young lads heckled if they had managed tuppence for a glass of beer.

The government established a system of training centres and 'Slave Camps', where unemployed men worked for a meagre allowance of 1s.6d per week while their families starved at home. Kath denounced the centres on every street corner and feeling against them grew so strong that Labour PAC members refused to send Deptford men to the Belmont residential training centre and the PAC began to have difficulty dealing with the large numbers of cases.

One afternoon in 1932 Alf Lucas arrived at the Relief Station to find more than 100 men waiting for their money. They were told the PAC could not meet that day so there would be no money, only food tickets. "What are food tickets to us? Our landlords won't take food tickets. And how will we cook our food?" the men grumbled. Alf told the official to telephone County Hall and get these men paid before the weekend. Police rushed in with batons drawn and the men were thrown out onto the pavement where Alf opened an impromptu meeting on the kerb. Before he was moved on by the police he called "Comrades, we'll all meet in Edward St tonight to fight

Kath Duncan giving one o[f] her powerful speeches in t[he] 1930s. This is the only photograph of Kath and n[o] details are known about i[t]. She campaigned against rises in gas prices and for [the] rights of the local market-traders as well as her mor[e] famous denunciations of t[he] Means Test and the Slave Camps.

this sort of thing. Kath will speak there. Go and rally all the people you can." That night's meeting led to a decision for a strike at the Woolwich training centre. About 250 men came out on the Monday but their inexperience of industrial action had led them to 'excuse themselves' from attendance! Alf suggested they go back to work that day but prepare for a true strike on Wednesday. He himself went to the Area Office to persuade the official to contact the PAC and get the money paid. Next morning at the centre all the men were pleased: they had been sent three times the usual relief.

Local work like this needed resourcefulness, courage and a scorn of bureaucratic red tape. It could be dangerous but it was often successful on an immediate and local level. There was a constant stream of callers at the NUWM office. Women often preferred to come direct to Kath but her special role was as public speaker, arousing indignation against the "whole system of unemployment benefit that keeps the innocent victims of capitalist slump at starvation level".

At first Kath had not been taken seriously by her opponents, who described her as 'Kath Bunkum' and her supporters as 'chasing a red herring in skirts', but by the winter of 1932 she was known as the 'leader of the Deptford and Greenwich unemployed' and as someone to be reckoned with. Her open-air meetings became a feature of the political life of South East London. She preached socialism like a pioneer and always linked the manoevres of the capitalist class to the various weapons of Hunger, War and Fascism, bringing the latest news through stories of the scandalous extravagance of Lord This and Lady That!

Every Sunday in May and June 1932 hundreds of workers from the riverside boroughs marched through the docklands calling on dockers not to load the 'murder ships' sending British war materials to Japan. Kath led "her merry men and women" through the Blackwall Tunnel every week. Late one Sunday, after Kath and Sandy had spoken to a 3,000-strong crowd at a Woolwich anti-war meeting, the small band of tired comrades arrived at Deptford Broadway. A police inspector who ordered them to stop singing the *Red Flag* was ignored and suddenly a crowd of policemen appeared, batons drawn. Injuries were sustained on both sides and Sandy had to be taken to the Miller Hospital. Six of the marchers were arrested, including Alf Lucas. When the news came out on Monday there was great indignation in the streets. Men in the training centres went on strike and 5,000 people gathered in the Broadway to cheer Kath when she demanded the dismissal of the inspector. At the end of the meeting mounted police tried to disperse the crowd but they fought back and scattered the police instead. On Tuesday there were crowds in the streets all day and the *Daily Worker* reporter found "groups of police patrolling about, and the place is like an armed camp". The week continued with meetings at all hours and all kinds of local organisations passing resolutions of protest. Kath made sure the case was at the forefront of discussion on the streets of Deptford, selling photos of the arrested men to raise money for the Defence Fund.

Six months later, on 19 December 1932, Kath herself was arrested and charged with being "a disturber of the Peace of our Lord the King, and an inciter of others to commit crimes and misdemeanours". The charge was based on a 14th century statute originally designed to prevent the Peasant's Revolt. A few weeks earlier the veteran Battersea activist, Tom Mann, had been imprisoned under the same law. Both 'disturbers' refused to sign an undertaking to cease political activity and Mann, aged 76, spent two months in Brixton Gaol while Kath was in Holloway for a month. George Lansbury, leader of the Labour opposition, said in Parliament: "Of all the tomfool laws to apply in modern times this one takes the biscuit." Criticising the detective presence at public meetings, he declared "it is no business of the police to know what any of the citizens are thinking about; let them mind their own business and look after burglars".

On Kath's release the people of Deptford flocked to greet her in the Broadway but a few days later the LCC Education Committee wrote saying they were removing her name from their list of teachers. A lightning campaign resulted in a petition signed by 5,700 people, two testimonials from headteachers, resolutions of protest by local union branches and an offer of legal advice from the NUT. Soon the *South London Press* ran the headline 'KATH DUNCAN WINS'. Kath plunged straight back into public meetings, ranging from support for the All-London Bus Strike to protests against heavy sentences for trade unionism in India. At a meeting in Greenwich Kath appeared with Wal Hannington who had served three months for a 'seditious' appeal to the police to join the working class movement to fight their own 10% wage cut. In February Kath was the NUWM speaker at the massive

TUC Hyde Park demonstration.

It was 1933 and the Reichstag building in Berlin was burning in an atmosphere of growing hysteria as the Nazis presented themselves as the saviours of Germany. Hitler's power was consolidated over the next two years. In Deptford Kath spoke out: the burning of the Parliament building was a symbol of Nazi determination to destroy democracy. Would the British capitalist class be any less callous to the unemployed, would they hesitate to use fascism in Britain? The NUWM banner carried to County Hall in May said 'Forward in the Fight against Hunger and Fascism!' Kath received a friendly warning that the fascists would be down in Stockwell St in central Greenwich that evening. She rushed around to spread the news and when the Blackshirts arrived in a military lorry they found a huge crowd who drove them out of the street. On another occasion fascists trying to reach Deptford were put to flight by an enormous crowd flooding up New Cross Rd. Attempts to hold fascist meetings in the Broadway were drowned by mass singing of the *Red Flag*.

Deptford's long tradition of welcoming visitors was put to the test in October 1932 when Kentish marchers stopped over on their way to the mass demo in Hyde Park. The Salvation Army lent blankets and the Council allowed the marchers to use the public baths. Sandwiches were supplied by the Royal Arsenal Co-op Society and Isaacs of Greenwich provided a fish supper while a Mr Murray of Deptford High St helped with accommodation. Two years later Deptford opened its doors to 30 Scottish men on the National Hunger March. The PAC supplied three blankets per man and the Council were once more persuaded to allow hot baths and clothes washing. The local Solidarity Committee planned a full programme of activities and the Scottish visitors were kept busy doing the rounds of union branches.

Deptford NUWM also did its own marching. In September 1933 a Hunger March was organised to the Trades Union Congress conference at Brighton to appeal to "the employed section of the working class to join with the NUWM in mobilising the whole Labour movement against the Means Test". The TUC was not supportive but the march went ahead. Vic Parker, the NUWM organiser for South East London, described the stopover at Redhill where the marchers spent the night in the sports stadium: "It turned very cold that night and I shall never forget trying to get a little sleep stretched out either on the long narrow wooden forms or on the concrete banks of the stadium. Was it hard! And was it cold! We were half dead in the morning!" Despite the cold, the marchers received great welcomes everywhere, including high tea at Croydon. Kath's job was to collect money to pay the marchers' train fares home. Vic remembered staggering into a Brighton bank with bags heavy with silver. At the TUC conference the block vote was cast against hearing the deputation and the marchers returned home bitter at the betrayal.

The LCC election of 1934 attracted far more interest in Deptford than the previous one and the total votes were up from 28% to 50%. People were aware by now that this Council controlled the all-important PAC. Kath and Vic stood as Communist candidates for Deptford. Their policies would repeal the 10% cut in benefits, abolish the Means Test and provide work for around a quarter of a million London men through slum clearance, building work and other public works such as strengthening the river banks against further flooding and supplying piped water to all houses. A bouquet of red carnations arrived for Kath "with best wishes and good luck from the boys of the Surrey Commercial Dock" from the dockers who had once thrown red ochre over her. The Labour candidates received nearly 15,000 votes each but 2,564 Deptford people voted for Kath and Vic.

Kath did not confine her attention to the big issues of unemployment, war and fascism but got involved at a local level. For example, she spoke for the Lewisham street-traders against the Council's objections to barrows in Lewisham High St. In September 1936 the South Metropolitan Gas Company, based in the Old Kent Rd and providing gas for 1.5 million South Londoners, brought in a new scale of charges which increased prices for the poorest consumers while cutting bills for big users like the local authorities, shopkeepers and the better-off. These were the very customers who were changing over to electricity and the new scales were a blatant bribe at the expense of small consumers. A protest movement developed all over South London but the initiative was taken by Deptford.

On the official level, the Borough Council passed a resolution of emphatic protest and speeches at public meetings had to be relayed to crowds outside in the streets. A joint committee was formed in Deptford Town Hall of all the MPs, LCC members and mayors for the whole of South London. On the popular level, protest meetings were organised by the Labour Party, Communist Party and by ratepayers and tenants' associations. Letters were sent to MPs and councillors and on 30th September a procession of 2,000 marched from Deptford to the Old Kent Rd offices. In a short while New Cross Rd was blocked by 10,000 people and police had to divert the traffic. A week later a group of 200 women marched from the Broadway carrying posters and pushing prams under the banner of the Women's Co-operative Guild. One woman played a mouth organ while the others sang the pop songs of the time. On 13th October a procession of the dignitaries of the Joint Committee, led by the Mayor of Deptford, marched from Camberwell to the gas offices. With this united expression of the will of the people, the company surrendered and the tariff was withdrawn.

There had been talk of going over to electricity but few Deptford people could afford to make the change. Instead many boycotted gas stoves and raked out old oil stoves or bought second-hand ones. There was talk for days about the miraculous meals achieved, though there were also some frightening accidents. Along with mass unemployment, the dispro-portionate cost of fuel for poorer people has arisen again more than half a century later. Perhaps some lessons can be learnt from the 1930s, though we sorely miss Kath Duncan.

The fight for gas came in the midst of political struggles which made London a bustling centre of activity. Kath and many others from Deptford were in the East End to face Mosley's fascists, and a mass of people turned out in 1937 when the Blackshirts tried to march through Long Lane, Bermondsey. Meanwhile the Deptford Spanish Aid Committee collected £100 to buy an ambulance for the Spanish Republican government fighting Franco's Nationalists. Kath was personally responsible for interviewing Deptford men for the

International Brigades and she threw her usual energy into the Aid for Spain campaign, selling the *Daily Worker* on Saturday afternoons, holding evening meetings in the Broadway and collecting aid money door to door every Sunday.

Sandy Duncan died in Scotland during the war and Kath returned to Deptford to work in the Labour rooms for the 1945 election. A long illness had crippled her hands but still she addressed envelopes and used her unrivalled knowledge of the borough to help towards the Labour election victory. At last her sister fetched her away to return to Scotland. While she waited in an ambulance at Euston Station the driver looked in and recognised her, saying "Poor Kath. But you weren't always like this, Kath; and I'll remember you as last I saw you." Kath Duncan died in 1954. Like the ambulance man, we should remember her as she was in the 1930s. "Whenever there was a job to do, Kath was always with us...She would march off at the head, leading the way, full of vitality and purpose. She was always a striking and imposing figure with her neat black costume, spotless white collar, and a black wide-brimmed straw hat, worn at an angle showing her auburn short-cropped hair." (Communist Party, *Tribute to Kath Duncan*, no date).

The chaos of unemployment, wage cuts and struggling small shops in 1930s Deptford did not hit all residents in the same ways. Of the 12 million families in Britain it was estimated that two-thirds "even if they sold up everything they had, realised all their insurance and put all their savings on the table, would have had less than £100 – in other words they had no capital". This figure would, of course, have been much higher in Deptford. In 1936 Rowntree had published standards of 53 shillings a week for a couple with three children and 31 shillings for a single woman. Very large numbers of workers, and all the unemployed, did not reach the standard "below which no worker should be forced to live".

However, there were families in Deptford in which the bread-winner's earnings were above these standards. Eva Warren, whose father was a skilled worker, described the sharp contrasts: "A labourer got perhaps £1 and 10 shillings, but my father got £2 and 10 shillings. John's dad [her father-in-law, a foreman] got £3 and 10 shillings." Both fathers had work throughout the 1930s and considered themselves fortunate. George Glazebrook's father worked in the printing trade and George's account brings out both the similarities (the pawnshops, penny-scrimping, the world 'where no flowers grow') and the differences (the comparison between himself and his friend Joey whose "old man's out of work...Got no soddin' money, see?"). So, although many Deptford families had a common experience, wage differences and job security were vital in the internal grading of living standards which fed the opposition between 'decent families' and 'rough types'.

Hard times indeed. When poverty falls like a cloud over an area its effects are determined by the 'cultural infrastructure' – from issues like quality of housing and the number of children in families to value systems and everyday beliefs. The extreme sexual divide of this period caused terrible tensions in families where the man was out of work for many months but the high value placed on neighbourliness and mutual aid certainly helped many through the worst times. In the recession of the 1980s and 1990s we have greater state provision but the isolation and boredom of long-term unemployment bite far deeper.

For some Deptford families the interwar years offered a completely new beginning – out 'in the country' in the new LCC estates at Downham and Bellingham. The suspension of the building programme during the First World War had led to worsening conditions in the slum areas of Deptford. Fulfilling the government's promise of 'homes fit for heroes' would mean providing thousands of new working class cottages, as well as clearing the slums. In 1917 the Local Government Board admitted that private enterprise could never provide what was needed and the 1919 Housing Act gave generous grants to the LCC and London boroughs "to provide for the whole need of the working class in their district as far as it was not likely to be met by other agencies".

The housing shortage was recognised by Deptford Council in 1918 but lack of available building land led Deptford to team up with other councils – Greenwich, Bermondsey and Lewisham – in a bid to build a 'garden city' between Grove Park Station and Bromley Rd. The suggestion was at first well received by all parties but progress was chaotic with Greenwich refusing to participate, Bermondsey withdrawing from the scheme and then the final blow in 1920 when Lewisham rejected the proposals. The Lewisham branch of the Middle Classes Union may have lobbied Council the against the idea of potential 'rough types' but there were also stronger forces at work. The LCC had already purchased large tracts of land to the west of Grove Park and in 1922 they extended the scheme to form the new estate of Downham. Meanwhile Lewisham Council pursued its own plans to the south of Grove Park, completing the work in 1929. It was the LCC schemes, with their quotas for inner city families, which had the greatest impact on Deptford.

People's reasons for moving were varied. Men who had fought in the war and heard the promises about the better life for its heroes were disappointed when they returned to overcrowding and poor conditions. They put their names down for LCC estates but it could be many years before they were offered a place. Often illness in the family and a doctor's recommendation to find a healthier life spurred Deptford people to apply for rehousing though there were strict criteria to be met. Priority went to civil servants, postmen, bus drivers and all those with regular jobs. Family income had to be at least £3 and 10 shillings but not more than £5 a week. Processing the application meant a visit from the Council to check on domestic standards and circumstances. Families who were offered accommodation were envied by others in their neighbourhoods and the move could mean losing some old friends though many kept in touch with their home towns through work or family.

Arriving at the new estates could be a shock. In the early years the new home would be surrounded by a sea of mud and building materials. "We knew nobody, not a soul, and the building of the estate went on all around us...noise, dust and activity...They roared away all the time, cutting down trees, digging up roots and gouging out holes all around us." (Age Exchange, *Just Like The Country*). Often the roads were not yet laid out and transport could be a nightmare for those who had to get to work at the docks or the tram depots early in the morning. People used to the bustle of Deptford life found the new areas desolate and lonely and one man complained to his wife: "Burying yourself in the country. Nobody's even been past the front door." Men quite often came to the estate for tea after work and then went straight back to their old haunts. Women's reactions were mixed. The new houses could feel like a castle after overcrowded conditions back home but that also meant much more cleaning. Breathing the fresh air and looking out on the cows and horses in nearby fields was described by some as paradise: "It was country you know, the spaciousness of Downham, it was absolutely beautiful." Others found the quiet isolation unbearable and some moved back to the old areas.

There are different opinions about the friendliness of the new neighbours. One woman felt "we didn't really have neighbours because Mum had her own gateway...not like being under a porch, which is more neighbourly". The mixture of people from all parts of the country could cause difficulties but most were young with small families and shared a working class background. Once the ice was broken between neighbours "they'd help you when you got married, they'd help you give birth and, if you wanted somebody laid out, they'd come". This sharing of human resources and expertise at the three major life processes (birth, marriage, death) is typical of working class neighbourliness and, though shaken, it was not lost in the move from traditional life-styles. What really did change it was the penetration of state services into these processes.

These working class estates in the south of Lewisham obviously had an impact on political life in that borough. In the 1931 General Election Labour retained only five seats in London and was expelled even from the solidly working class areas of Deptford and Bermondsey but despite this overwhelming victory a Tory peace did not settle over the capital. Labour won control of the LCC in 1934 and increased its majority in 1937. Both Labour and Communist Parties were growing in strength throughout the 1930s. London in this decade was alive with political activity, at least as strong in the suburbs as in the older centre. There was a resurgence of radicalism, a new interest in national and international affairs and dozens of organisations raising funds for Republican Spain.

In the eyes of local politicians the newcomers brought the threat or promise of political change. The estates were an important base for Labour organisation, although at Downham there was intense rivalry with the National Unemployed Workers' Movement. They certainly helped Labour in the LCC victories but in Parliamentary elections they carried the party to the edge of victory and no further. Towards the end of the 1930s there was a fundamental change in the approach of the Left to the middle classes. Many middle class Lewisham people joined Mass Observation or the Left Book Club, became involved in raising funds for Spain and followed international affairs through the Penguin Special series. This cross-class work, along with 90% support from the estates, helped to create the Labour victory of 1945 when they won all 19 South East London seats.

Lewisham had been substantially middle class, proud of itself as a haven of health and respectability. There had always been pockets of quite stark poverty but it was the new 40,000-strong population of Bellingham and Downham, with its strong links to the riverside working class, which impinged on the respectable heart of the borough. To their middle class neighbours they seemed to bring a disreputable air, crime, unruly children, unemployment and charges on the rates. A line grew up dividing old middle class Lewisham from the new working class enclaves. This was represented most blatantly in the Downham Wall, a high concrete structure embedded with broken glass, built by private residents to distance themselves from council tenants. Despite considerable controversy the wall was not demolished until 1946.

13

Deptford Under Fire

"a certain fatalistic cussedness,
a dogged determination to survive"
– Christabel Bielenberg

Although it is the Second World War which is best remembered for air raids, they were also a feature of the First and Deptford had suffered badly in these raids. In September 1915 a Zeppelin raid killed 16 local people when a trail of bombs destroyed a crowded house in Hughes Fields, started a fire at the Foreign Cattle Market and devastated a six-room house and a school on Clifton Hill. The Zeppelin drifted westwards, leaving a wake of explosions in Edward St, Childeric Rd and Hunsdon Rd and a crater in Monson School playground. At Ilderton Rd a large tenement house was destroyed causing five deaths. There were other raids throughout the war but this first attack, one September midnight, caused most damage and stayed longest in people's minds. As the war progressed, anti-aircraft defences were improved, the Miller Hospital at West Greenwich became swift at treating burns and shock, and people slowly grew more used to scenes of rubble: "within a little while such a spectacle became almost a commonplace, and did not stir us to the like extent." (*Kentish Mercury*, 24/1/1919).

At the beginning of World War I a postal censorship officer found a newspaper being sent to a suspect address in Amsterdam, believed to be a German intelligence 'letterbox'. Chemical tests revealed a brief message: "C has gone north. Am sending from 201." A Special Branch inspector was put on the case. His only clue was the postmark Deptford. He contacted the local police for a list of all streets with a house number 201 and was told that in all of Deptford there was only one, 201 High St. This turned out to be the shop of Peter Hahn, a German baker and confectioner. A bottle of chemical ink was found on the premises and neighbours described a frequent visitor: a tall, well-dressed man, thought to be a Russian. Inquiries were made at boarding-houses all over London and eventually a landlady in Bloomsbury reported that a Russian named Müller was one of her lodgers but had gone away to Newcastle-upon-Tyne. He was caught by Newcastle police and it emerged that he was an important German agent who had been sending naval intelligence by inserting adverts in English newspapers – articles for sale, rooms to let – according to a pre-arranged code and posting the papers to various 'letterboxes' in neutral countries like Holland. After Müller's execution British intelligence continued to send the coded messages, all with false information, and before the Germans discovered the deception they had sent £400 to the dead spy.

This chapter is not a history of the war but an impression of what happened in Deptford, of what it felt like to live through the terror and strange times which seemed to last forever, of how people adjusted and how they stayed the same. It is a story of survival, as all war histories must be, but it is also a commemoration of fear and chaos, rubble and death in every street.

Understanding the war means unpicking the 'myth of the Blitz' and recognising that the propaganda of national unity and the notion of the Great British sense of humour were essential crutches which helped people 'take it' but that they created a false picture of heroic jollity. Nevertheless, respect is due both for individual courage which saved many lives and for the stubborn determination of communities to keep up the spirit.

The Admiralty Yard, the docks, railways and dense population made Deptford a primary target. By the end of August 1944 not a single house, shop, school, factory, office or public building was left undamaged in the whole borough. 648 people were killed by enemy action.

The term Blitzkreig, the 'lightning war', was first used to describe Hitler's swift invasion and conquest of Poland. In the late summer of 1940 'Blitz' became slang for air raids and as the bombardment stretched into months the word came to represent the total experience. The central idea of aerial bombardment was to destroy civilian morale by side-stepping the military engagement of equals and targetting the weapons of terror on untrained, unprepared, ordinary people. The notion had been developing among both German and British strategists for some decades. The Italian General Douhet had foreseen wars fought by droves of bombers and had advised "hammer the nation itself to make it give in". Mussolini agreed and dreamed of an air force such that "the span of its wings should intercept the sunlight". British military intelligence also believed in the power of air raids to create a state of panic and to bring productive work to a standstill. These ideas were fed by a deep-seated contempt for the civilian masses. Both sides put enormous energy and resources into the destruction of civil structure and the human will to resist. Neither side was successful in this, despite huge and lasting damage. The 'morale' of both Londoners and Berliners was battered and bruised but, as a British observer said of Berlin, "those wanton, quite impersonal killings...did not so much breed fear and a desire to bow before the storm, but rather a certain fatalistic cussedness, a dogged determination to survive and, if possible, help others to survive, whatever their politics, whatever their creed".

Although this account concentrates on the Blitz as experienced in London, we should remember two facts: 1) while 29,890 people died in London from enemy action, fatalities among British aircrew engaged in the equivalent action in Germany were almost twice this figure; 2) the British bombing of Dresden in South East Germany in February 1945 killed as many people as in all Britain's blitzed cities put together.

Official expectations of the impending chaos of aerial bombardment had major effects on the preparations made before the war. Stanley Baldwin had predicted tens of thousands of mangled people before a single soldier suffered a scratch. Clement Attlee, the Labour leader, asserted "we believe that another world war will mean the end of civilisation". The Air Raid Precaution (ARP) sub-committee first met in 1924 and continued into the 1930s under Sir John Anderson (patron saint of the Anderson shelter). By 1937 it was predicting 30–35,000 casualties a day once the bombing started. The statistics are macabre – 2.8 million hospital beds, 20 million square feet of timber for coffins, £550 million worth of property destroyed in the first three weeks and so on. Others expected organised machine-gunning of refugees on the roads out of London and mass deafening by the sonic waves following bomb blasts. Such fears led to a very particular development of emergency services. The emphasis was on death and destruction and on 'crowd control', with little consideration for those side-effects which actually proved most common: confusion, anxiety, dislocation and distress.

In 1938 a group of eminent psychiatrists advised the Ministry of Health that a massive psychiatric system would be needed to deal with the 'broken spirits' of bombardment. They estimated that there would be four times as many psychological as physical casualties. This 'expert' pessimism was again allowed to dictate planning and thousands of physically sick patients were cleared from hospitals when war began "to make space for the trembling hordes" (Harrison, 1976).

In 1935 responsibility for air raid precautions was handed over to local authorities. Calls went out for volunteers and by the end of 1938 1.4 million adults had offered their services as wardens and firewatchers. Eventually 2 million people were incorporated into this 'fourth army'. Many of these volunteers were awarded medals for bravery, dozens lost their lives. Without them the damage and confusion of war would have been far greater.

18th October 1940. The windows of the Victorian terraced houses in Clyde St were blacked out, the old Board School had been evacuated, the Lord Clyde pub had closed for the night and the Old Town Library was locked up. The only sound was the bustle of seven volunteers in the warden's post next to the school. A sudden rushing sound was the only warning before a flash of light and a mighty explosion as earth and stonework spurted from the top of the school. All along the street doors and windows were blown in, glass, slate, bricks and timber showered from the sky and a suffocating dustcloud swirled around the roadway. As the rubble settled and light grew over Deptford, only the smoking remains of the warden's post marked the death of seven dutiful volunteers.

When war came on Sunday 3rd September 1939 Chamberlain's announcement on the radio was swiftly followed by the first of South East London's 1,225 alerts. This time, and again early the next morning, the screaming sirens which became an integral part of wartime experience sounded a false alarm. To most people's surprise the war began very slowly and this early period became known as the Phoney War or the Bore War. Although enemy reconnaissance flights were seen that November around Woolwich, it would be another eight months before the Battle of Britain began in earnest.

Schooling was immediately reduced to half-time. One South East Londoner who was five years old at the time has told how she was just learning to read and was upset that no-one would help her. "They were too busy rushing round deciding what to do with the black-out, or what to wear in the shelters. This apparently was very important, in case you had to go down in the middle of the night and the neighbours saw you." The general confusion at the start of the war is illustrated further by this woman when she spoke of "having all the dogs and cats put down. The vets had queues and queues during the first few weeks, and people brought the animals home in little brown sacks because there was nowhere to bury them."

The official response to the outbreak of war was the order for widespread evacuation to prevent panic fleeing. In the first few days of 1939 1.5 million people were officially evacuated from London. There was a mass exodus of South East London schoolchildren with their teachers and many mothers with pre-school children. They were sent to towns and villages in Kent, Surrey, Sussex and Devon in one of the greatest social upheavals of modern times. Children from Deptford's poorest areas, with no experience of country life, were squeezed into the 'reception' areas where their hosts often had even less idea of the ways of the urban slums. Had the Luftwaffe attacked Britain at once, fear and sympathy might have overcome the mutual resentment. As it was, although some evacuations were successful, complaints streamed into the billeting offices, mostly from 'hosts' angry at the dirty and infested condition of the evacuees and the effects they expected it to have on their own children. A letter to the *Windsor Express* openly suggested 'concentration camps' for evacuees and mass segregation was discussed by some local councils in reception areas.

By Christmas the majority of those evacuated had returned to familiar backstreets, despite government worries that the closed schools would leave young people to mischief. There was a second exodus in June 1940 when fears of invasion were high and as the bombing started in September a continuous stream left London under Blitz conditions in packed buses and trains. Two months later many returned and the outflow was reduced to a trickle. Reasons for going or staying or coming back were complex and varied, often relating to family details rather than any factual assessment of risk. "Whatever else they were, these people were not docile. They would not all go away when they were told to, and those who did returned before they were expected....By their behaviour they made planning difficult; they made a good plan look, in the end, like a bad plan." (Richard Titmuss).

One of the most outstanding and remembered aspects of the Home Front experience was the way work continued against all the odds. As we saw with the long 18th century wars against the French (Ch.5), Deptford's experience of war was never simple. At that time war brought increased work to the shipyards and all the subsidiary industries around them; it also brought press-ganging. In the 1940s, while large areas of Deptford were being reduced to rubble and hundreds of people were losing their lives, others found increased work opportunities after the long struggle of the interwar years. Molins Machine Company in Evelyn St had made cigarette machines in Deptford since 1919. This successful family business now diversified into weaponry and provided work for hundreds of Deptford people.

For those who remained life went on. Much of everyday life had changed but the consistency of heavy night raids actually allowed people to adjust to new routines more easily than if the bombing had been more erratic. Many found, to their own mildly pleased surprise, that they were much tougher than they had thought.

On Sunday 7th September 1940 hundreds of Luftwaffe bombers

came in waves across South East London in the first and largest mass air raid of the war. There were 93 incidents in the borough and the bombs left more than a million tons of burnt timber smouldering at Surrey Docks. Huge fires blazed along both banks of the river sending up a blanket of smoke thousands of feet high and nearly 10 miles long. Many smaller fires burned in the streets and the clang of firebells added to the general pandemonium. By morning 430 Londoners were dead, 1,600 seriously injured. People were stunned: all the predictions and precautions had not prepared them for this. "The shock of their experience and the loss of their homes seemed to have numbed their minds and reduced them to the depths of despair." (*Kentish Independent*).

While refugees from Silvertown were arriving by the hundreds on the Woolwich ferry, clutching bird cages, babies and rescued possessions, Deptford Borough Council faced similar housing and feeding problems with bombed-out Bermondsey families. Raids continued nightly and soon the new terror of the parachute mine appeared. These were huge cylinders containing hundreds of pounds of explosives. They drifted silently earthwards and impact could occur just as people relaxed once the bombers had passed. These mines often failed to explode on impact which could cause even greater disruption. Sophie Lake remembers with a shiver how one got caught on her chimney in Brockley. Unaware of it, she had a bath and settled down for a rest before an anxious policeman appeared, ordering her to vacate the house. Evacuation in these circumstances covered a 400-yard radius and two unexploded mines in the Milton Court area made 2,000 people homeless.

11th September 1940. The basement of the Methodist Mission in Creek Rd was being used as a public shelter. At four o'clock that Wednesday afternoon it was crowded with frightened people caught by the siren in the course of their everyday lives. The bomb brought down large parts of the building and started a fire. At least 23 of the shelterers died. The splendid mission hall was renovated after the war but still lacks one of its ornate corner domes.

Official attitudes to sheltering were based squarely on the 'chaos' theory of mass reactions to air raids. The government was concerned to avoid allowing a 'shelter mentality' to develop. It was believed that if big, safe, deep shelters were established people would simply live in them and do no work. Communist Party agitation for deep shelters reinforced government fears that such shelters would become breeding grounds for subversion.

Those who had gardens built government-issued Anderson shelters which held four to six people. Others, like Sophie Lake's landlady who had no shelter because she was a pacifist, slept in the coal cellar. Some had an indoors Morrison shelter as tested by Churchill at 10 Downing St in January 1941. Those with neither would have to run to one of the public shelters, either brick surface huts like those outside the flats of New King St or the basements of large buildings like the one stretching from the cellar of Pecry's clothes shop under Deptford High St. Ann Franklin and her father preferred the Pecry's shelter to their Anderson because "you could not hear the planes going over or bombs dropping. We all used to have a good laugh singing old songs." South London's tangle of railway arches provided emergency shelter, especially for homeless people or those who got claustrophobic cooped up in the Andersons.

Some of the bigger public shelters organised themselves a social life with amateur concerts, darts matches and even 'house magazines'.

Deptford Air Raid Precautions workmen building a surface shelter Deptford Park, August 19 These public shelters wen up all over Deptford to provide refuge to the man who had no garden in wh to build an Anderson she

The *Kentish Mercury* introduced a social column called 'Shelter Sidelights'. The Mayor and Mayoress of Deptford attended a New Year party at the Albany Institute shelter in 1940. A Christmas party in a Speedwell Estate shelter even managed a Christmas tree and balloons. Half a century on, eerie traces of these shelters remain on some of our walls in the shape of the big S with an arrow and a sign indicating how many yards one had to scurry to get there.

Although the government was eventually forced to modify policy and open the Underground, few South East Londoners used it, whereas the huge Chislehurst Caves did provide a sociable shelter for many Deptford people. A direct bus left Deptford in the early evening and returned each morning. Special trains also ran to Chislehurst and New Cross Station was crowded with mothers and children, laden with bundles of possessions, bound for the caves. Some managed to keep alcoves reserved for them with bedding and bunks, especially in the inner caves where whole families lived in cut-out rooms with curtains for privacy. There were proper toilets and electric lighting and soon the caves developed into a private enterprise zone with a cinema, a chapel, a barber, a dance floor and a gymnasium. Spread throughout the caves, families gathered in groups playing cards and chatting, or queued at the canteen holding jugs, teapots or cans to fill up with tea. Feelings were mixed about the caves. Some say "it was horrible there, all damp and chalky" but many were simply grateful for a rest from the sound of bombs. There were around 8,000 people in the caves on many nights from mid-September 1940 through to the late spring of 1941.

By 5th October there had been 694 incidents and over 300 serious casualties in the two and a half square miles of Deptford borough. Home Intelligence reports showed morale steady and most people "settling down to the new air raid life cheerfully". Conversation was almost exclusively about air raids but was gossipy rather than panicky. It centred on personal matters – the 'bomb at the corner of our street' – rather than the war as a whole. It is clear from the Mass Observation social survey that the more intensely involved people felt in the war at home, the less interest they had in news from the fronts except, of course, where they had family or friends to watch out for.

All through October there were heavy night raids often involving the hideous oil bombs, precursors of napalm bombing, which

Bomb damage in Etta St, 10th January 1943. Eleven people died that lunchtime in Etta St and nearby Treboro Rd. This was the same day a fighter bomber dropped its 1,000 pound bomb on Sandhurst School Catford. The old costers' barrows were put to use moving the few remaining possessions of bombed-out families to new houses.

contained around 16 gallons of crude oil and a TNT charge to splatter the blazing fluid over a radius of 30 yards. The 'Hope & Glory' image of bomb-sites as adventure playgrounds for children fits uneasily with the oil-blackened houses and scorched streets of Deptford in 1940. The dark evenings were drawing in and the nightly chore of 'doing the black-out' became ever more dreary. The gloomy atmosphere was increased by the dismal call of the 'Moaning Minnie' sirens and the prospect of a night cooped up in a cold, clammy shelter. That November saw the longest alert in Britain of the entire war when the All Clear did not sound for 14 hours. Those who remember both wars say of the First: "The policemen used to go round on bikes with placards on them saying 'Take Cover' and blowing their whistles. That was nothing like the Second World War." (Age Exchange, *War*).

It was a terrible Christmas. Many servicemen were home on leave and evacuated families had come back to be in their own homes for Christmas but everyone knew how quickly the holiday would be over. People were determined to enjoy themselves to the maximum after surviving so much and with so much danger, fear and uncertainty still to face. Two days before Christmas the Railway Tavern in New Cross Rd was an oasis of light and warmth in the blacked out street. Late in the evening the sirens sounded their miserable warning but many remained in the smoky bars, hoping to forget about the war for just one night. Six bombs hit New Cross that night. One of them slashed straight through the roof of the Tavern and exploded in one of the bars sparking a fire. When the rescue teams arrived, 15 bodies were dragged out. The pub stayed in business for many decades with its one remaining storey nuzzled up against its much taller neighbours, eloquent testimony to the attack on civilian life. It now sells catering equipment and has lost its appeal.

Christmas itself was quiet but on the day after Boxing Day 1940 South East London was hit by 90 bombers and within an hour there were fires burning all over Deptford and New Cross. Eighteen people died when the tram depot (now the bus station) in New Cross Rd was completely destroyed, though the 'perpetual light' was reported to be still shining in the devastated synagogue next door. Two days later there was an incendiary raid on the City of London which began the Second Great Fire of London. Viewed from Deptford it seemed as if the heart of London must really be finished as a huge mass of smoke and flame stormed skywards. Evelyn had described the first Great Fire (1666): "All the Skies were of a fiery aspect, like the top of a burning Oven, and the light seene above forty miles about." This time Deptford burned as well: houses in Evelyn St and Prince St were destroyed and there were fires at Goldsmiths' College, J Stone & Co and the London Spinning Mills in Trundleys Rd.

The New Year brought little hope after three months continual air attack. Morale was lower than anyone dared say and Mass Observation found large numbers of people, especially housewives and mothers, weary with the discomforts and uncertainties of the war. Nevertheless productivity continued to rise, strikes were rare and most people made it to work eventually, with transport difficulties a favourite topic of conversation. Essential services were maintained and raid incidents were tackled with increasing efficiency. The Albany Institute and many evacuated schools were turned into 'first line' rest centres for the bombed-out. Staff in these centres knew their clients as 'the population'. Some were carried in, black with soot and completely confused. Along with providing food, clothes and help with finding alternative accommodation or claiming compensation, much of the work was "pure comforting". Some people came back to the Albany to sit and talk with welfare advisors even after they had been rehoused: "They felt safer in the centres because of all the people." (Age Exchange, *War*).

At first such services were difficult to plan, especially given the official tendency to over-provide for death and destruction (for example, mass production of papier mâché coffins). They tended to be an extension of peacetime services laid down in the 1930 Poor Law Act and were often based on a Means Test mentality with little room for the compassion necessary in wartime. For those who stayed in South East London the war could be a constant round of moving to new flats only to be bombed out again. Anyone used to the delays of modern state bureaucracy must sympathise with a bombed-out mother doing the rounds of the authorities to find a new home, claim compensation, organise new documents, check up on family members and still find the strength to queue for food, often with the thought of husband, brother or son in danger in the back of her mind. "When the Blitz burst upon London it brought an entirely new element into people's lives, one for which they had to find not only the courage and the stamina, but also the time." (Harrison, 1976). One local woman whose father died in 1941 remembers her brother going to arrange the funeral and having "to queue half way round Lewisham to get into the undertakers".

One good thing about the queues was that people talked more. "Every time you went for your rations, or you made your daily or weekly trips to the shops to pick the rations up, you could be up to two or three hours in a queue, and people talked. They would relay their experiences of a raid, or talk about food, and different things you could do with making the rations stretch." (Age Exchange, *War*). The ration books themselves took some of the stress out of the long wait since at least everyone knew they would get something in the end.

There were other frustrations and fears. Staggering bleary-eyed out of the shelter you never knew whether your house would still be there and if you left a damaged property for too long it was likely to be looted for anything that was left. Notices appeared around the streets warning that the penalty for looting could be death but one South East Londoner remembers his parents' house stripped of everything, including the kitchen sink. Many remember the irritation of never undressing completely for weeks on end, washing each bit separately: "You wouldn't dare have all your clothes off in case the sirens went." Although people got used to the black-out, as they were forced to get used to so many things, it still held its dangers: "Don't forget, trains were blacked out, streets blacked out, stations blacked out, and one morning I had to get a very early train to work. A drunken Canadian soldier got into my carriage. I won't go into the horrible lurid details but it was very unpleasant...Mind you, our boys could be just as bad. You used to get the old tale: 'Well you know, I might be dead tomorrow'." On the rare times of home leave even the happiest reunion could be spoiled, "when he got into bed of a night time you'd find him waking up screaming, and you'd have to calm him down...I expect there's a lot of wives like me." (Age Exchange, *War*)

Early in 1941 the press reverted to the normal diet of accidents and petty crime but in March the heaviest raid on South East London caused a massive fire at the Victualling Yard which destroyed 70% of the yard's buildings. During one of these raids Henry Sweetland of the Deptford ARP earned the George Medal for outstanding courage, continuing in his rescue work despite heavy injuries. April started quietly and people began to feel the worst was over. The *Lewisham Borough News* warned that sheltering was at its lowest level. On 16th April 12 people died in Malpas Rd. Three days later as the sirens screamed out the 545th alert since war began, Mrs Emily Lloyd and her children headed for their basement in Reginald Rd. A direct hit brought their house tumbling down, filling the refuge with rubble and swirling dust. 14 year old Tommy Lloyd squirmed his way through a narrow opening into the devastated street, helping his sisters to safety and refusing to leave until he had helped recover his mother's body from the ruins.

The last significant bombardment of the London Blitz came in May

1941, damaging 11,000 homes and killing over 1,400 citizens across London. For a year and a half from June 1941 London experienced a much-needed break. Hitler's response to the RAF bombing of the ancient German town of Lübeck were the so-called Baedeker raids on historic British towns such as Bath, Norwich, York and Canterbury. With the provinces under fire, many evacuees returned to London. Some found only an empty space while others moved back into houses with deep cracks in the ceilings, broken windows and doors that no longer closed properly. Some terraces were virtually obliterated and vast quantities of Blitz rubble were used as ballast in ships returning to America: some of Deptford's old houses ended up as hardcore in New York's famous Franklin D Roosevelt Drive. Emergency water tanks were erected on bomb-sites for use in future fire raids. Iron gates and railings disappeared from all across Deptford to provide scrap for munitions. The parks were taken over for agriculture in the 'Dig for Victory' campaign. Things had changed back home and Londoners faced a "long, grim, uphill slog, stripped of virtually all glamour, romance and adventure. An air of grave realism replaced a lost innocence. Already there was an inclination to look back on the summer of 1940 with nostalgia." (Blake, 1982).

In May 1941 Deptford held a War Weapons Week, releasing an emotional appeal to raise money for munitions through Saving Stamps and War Bonds. The Mayor wrote that "a bitterness words cannot express clouds our memories of that sturdy, historic Deptford we have loved so well" and a photo montage of Deptford's bomb damage was overlain with a picture of Churchill promising "for all the tears, there will be retribution...punishment fitting the wanton crime". While allowing that 'grousing' (complaining) "is our British characteristic and our right", the brochure urged a recognition that without a steady output of munitions "we'd be silent as the graveyard, with Hitler to write the epitaph".

The following year Warship Week was marked with a souvenir brochure referring back to Deptford's glorious maritime history –

Dip Deep Deptford! War Weapons Week, May 1941 An emotional appeal to re money for munitions included a reminder from Mayor of the vulnerabilit of "that sturdy, historic Deptford we have loved so well."

"They that go down to the sea in ships carry England in their souls; her glory in their hearts. In the cavalcade of triumph Deptford bears a proud and honoured place." Behind all the blarney was a very real need and Deptford people responded with money, voluntary work and another heavy sigh.

London's peace was shattered once more in mid-January 1943 when Hitler sent out his reprisal for the heavy RAF raid on Berlin. It had been so long since the sirens last churned the stomach that the sound was received with surprise and uncertainty until the new improved anti-aircraft (AA) defences erupted on Blackheath, firing over a hundred rockets accelerating to 1,000 mph in 1.5 seconds and exploding all together with a roar "like an express train passing through the living room before crashing in the back garden" (Blake, 1982). Days later the horrific bombing of Sandhurst School in Catford filled South East Londoners with fury. A fighter bomber had roared up Sandhurst Rd with its machine guns firing straight at terrified pedestrians, before circling at 500 feet and dropping its 1,000 pound bomb directly into the school building. Thirty-eight children and six teachers were killed, many more were seriously hurt.

Within minutes there was death and destruction in Deptford itself. The Chichester pub in Evelyn St was destroyed by a direct hit leaving only the publican's pet monkey alive. In Oscar St 11 died and more still in Etta St and Oareboro Rd. A wave of criticism spread about the failure of the defence system to warn and protect the population. It was admitted in Parliament that the South East London balloons had been kept close-hauled due to 'essential work'. After that the AA uproar was more intense. "Sometimes it seemed almost as if the guns fired at an empty sky in an elaborate deception to give the gunners practice and to remind everyone else that there was a war on." (Blake, 1982). Residents became a little blasé. Few allowed the sirens to interfere with nights out. The shelters "were stuffy and there was no privacy, and we know what married people get up to!" (Age Exchange, *War*). Theatres, cinemas, dance halls, pubs and youth clubs were well attended. The cinemas normally flashed a message on the screen advising of an alert (known as 'red roses') but the films would continue and those who left were urged to be quiet about it.

The children's writer Noel Streatfield, whose book *The Bell Family* (1954) was set in Deptford, had been active in local social services in the area from the early 1930s. She was involved in Deptford's basic efforts towards childcare provision, including serving on the Deptford Child Care Committee. During the war she organised children's parties and salvage schemes. In the summer of 1940 she helped with evacuation and civil defence in the area and she worked for the Women's Voluntary Service running the mobile tea wagons which set out at sunset to take tea round to the shelters. The tea service also attended incidents and Streatfield later wrote of the amazing effects a cup of tea could have on shocked and wounded people. Where rescue work took days, as in the Chichester pub incident, the canteen set up as a single spot of normality in the midst of chaos. Jacko, the publican's monkey who was the sole survivor of the blast, was wrapped up in rugs as a shock case. A policeman brought him a cup of sweet tea in a bone china cup as a joke but according to the warden, when Jacko had finished "he gives 'isself a shake as if to say 'that's a bit better'. Then 'e acts perfectly natural and turns round and bites the policeman". In the Woolworth's incident (see below) the canteen service sent trays of tea up and down the grieving queues. Later it moved to the mortuary where the cups of tea helped to calm the bereaved while they waited for the horrific task of identifying the remains.

From January 1944 London suffered 'the little Blitz'. This three-month bombardment caused much less damage than previously but the night sky was full of 'ack-ack' gunfire, cursed for keeping people awake but welcomed because it undercut the sense of helplessness which is the main feature of aerial bombing. There were many fires and once again the Victualling Yard was aflame. At this time it was being used as the US War Supply Depot and 15 stacks of flammable material, each the size of a house, burned for several hours. This was the last manned raid on South East London, but for Deptford there were many more months of horror still to come.

In June the first 'vengeance' weapon, the V1, shot through the sky parallel with Trundleys Rd before landing in Bow. This new terror, known as the 'buzz bomb', soon found targets closer to home and the South East boroughs bore the brunt of London's baptism of fire in this new form of attack. Deptford's first V1 crashed in Reginald Square destroying the small terraces of 1870s houses and causing 23 deaths and widespread damage to the whole area, forcing the Odeon cinema to close. Then followed 11 weeks of V1 bombardment with 10 hits per square mile in the South East boroughs (three times the average for Greater London). These mass produced weapons were a very cost-effective way to destroy buildings and kill non-combatants. When one fell near Convoys' Wharf, killing 13 US Navy officers, the damage extended to Palmers' cold storage plant at the old Foreign Cattle Market where leaking ammonia caused severe burns to firemen and rescue workers.

Sometimes the engine of a V1 would cut out mid-flight leaving it to glide several miles with no warning of approach. Local people were in the front-line that summer, facing the same kind of danger as troops under artillery fire. At one point the authorities decided that, rather than disrupt working life, no warning at all should be given for single V1s. Such ruthlessness was unnecessary when most people went about their business as best they could and years of experience had brought the capital's Civil Defence to a high pitch of efficiency. There were warden's posts in every neighbourhood with rooftop spotters strategically placed to observe bomb falls as they occurred and good communication between wardens, fire control, first aid posts and rescue workers. While rescue teams turned over the wreckage, engineers shut off leaking gas or water and firemen doused the last of the flames. Services were restored as soon as possible and salvage, demolition and site clearance teams arrived. Goods would be removed to a council store while the homeless were taken to the nearest rest centre. Eventually building workers would arrive to patch up the property though they could never keep up with the rate of damage. The buzz bombs strained these resources but help came from all over the country. Wardens from Northamptonshire arrived in Deptford and many Deptford families took in building workers from all over Britain as lodgers.

Eventually Allied troops overran the French launching sites and

186

relief came to 'buzz bomb alley' at the end of August 1944. In September the Chairman of the Secret Weapons Counter-Measures Committee reassured the press that the battle against the buzz bomb was over but he did not mention that the launching sites had been moved to Holland. Within days the first V2 rocket produced two massive thunderclap explosions and killed six people in Chiswick. Nothing was said officially and the population was left mystified and uneasy. That September rockets caused multiple deaths in Dairsie Rd, Eltham and Adelaide Avenue, Lewisham. People began to report sightings of the rockets which appeared as vapour trails of brownish smoke. The sonic boom was heard for more than 10 miles around but no sirens warned of the rockets which travelled at speeds of up to 3,600 mph. These were Hitler's 'bolts from the blue'.

After a brief lapse when British forces descended on Arnhem in Holland, the rockets resumed their attack on South East London from Germany itself. The government imposed a newspaper black-out on the subject but media speculation had to be allowed to go on or the Nazis would quickly realise what the government wished to hide: that some 160 rockets had indeed struck the country. Moreover it was important to stem the flow of returning evacuees who had been told the worst was over. To ordinary people it seemed that the newspapers went mad, painting a terrible threat but giving no space to the actual incidents people saw around them. More rockets fell that October around Deptford. November started badly and grew steadily worse with incidents all over South East London.

Deptford has a unique place in the history of these second vengeance weapons. Although other boroughs were hit by more rockets, they killed more people in Deptford than anywhere else. The borough suffered nine V2s which killed 297 people and seriously injured 328 more.

25th November 1944. Woolworth's, New Cross Rd

It was Saturday lunchtime and the streets were bustling. Christmas shoppers, passengers on a passing bus, people queueing for the fishmongers and four clerks in a nearby office were among the 168 people who died when a V2 rocket destroyed the Woolworth's store and its neighbour the R.A.C.S. on New Cross Rd opposite the town hall. The death-toll could have been higher but for the day's one piece of luck: the lines of traffic waiting for the lights to change at the Marquis of Granby were let through just minutes before the blast. This was Britain's worst V2 disaster and its effects were felt for miles around as people realised with horror how close they had been to death. The accounts which appeared in the press were graphic though they gave away no details of location or casualty figures. One Deptford man had arranged to meet his girlfriend near the store. He received his call-up to the Rifle Brigade that morning and had to cancel. There are literally hundreds of such stories.

June Gaida, who was then 13 years old, remembers the day with horror. "I was going shopping that morning for my mother and suddenly there was a blinding flash of light and a roaring, rushing sound. I was thrown into the air. There was noise all around me, a deafening terrible noise that beat against my eardrums and, when I fell to the ground, I curled myself up into a ball to protect myself, and I tried to scream but there wasn't any air. When the noise had faded I picked myself up and I was coated with brick dust, with slivers of glass in my hair. Then I walked towards Woolworth's. Things were still falling out of the sky, there were bricks, masonry, and bits of things and bits of people. I remember seeing a horse's head lying in the gutter. Further on there was a pram-hood all twisted and bent, and there was a little baby's hand still in its woolly sleeve. Outside the pub there was a bus and it had been concertinaed, with rows of people sitting inside, all covered in dust and dead. I looked towards where Woolworth's had been and there was nothing. There was just an enormous gap covered by a cloud of dust and I could see right through to the streets beyond Woolworth's. No building, just piles of rubble and bricks, and from underneath it all I could hear people screaming."

That evening a room was swept out in the town hall for the Council to meet as the chamber had been completely wrecked. The rest of country was edging towards peacetime normality, with cuts in authorised repair work and orders to move to a 'dim-out' rather than full black-out. Such hopeful items seemed sheer madness when they appeared on the agenda that night. The town hall was full of people having cuts dressed and eyes swabbed. Through the broken windows, floodlights illuminated the carnage as the rescue work continued. Rescuers worked for two days and nights, lining up the bodies in groups of six. Despite their efforts, 11 bodies were never found. They included two babies in a pram and two women carriage cleaners from New Cross Gate station who had gone to Woolworth's for tea.

Over the last miserable Christmas of the war there were vague threats of more vengeance weapons and the V2's horrors included a macabre incident at Hither Green cemetery which blasted human remains across Verdant Lane. March 1945, the last month of aerial punishment, saw increased savagery. Two of the blocks at Folkestone Gardens, where George Glazebrook had spent his childhood, were completely destroyed, killing 52 people in their beds.

Eventually the incidents petered out and VE Day (8th May 1945) finally confirmed long-held hopes of the light at the end of the tunnel. When Churchill announced on the radio that the war was over the most memorable thing for many people was not having to pull the black-outs. "We put all the lights in the houses on, and nobody would knock on the door and tell you you were showing a chink of light. That night all London was lit up. The celebration was absolutely terrific; all the windows and doors were thrown open. It was a very warm night in May. All the Christmas bunting was festooned outside the houses, and we got hold of a microphone and trestle tables came from a church hall. Somehow or other we got a party together for the children. Bonfires were lit in the street and it went on for days. The relief was so great." The day was celebrated with jubilation but there was also an undeniable sense of anti-climax. "When the lights went on again – not very brightly – it was to reveal a shabby, run-down country." (Age Exchange, *War*).

SECTION SIX

AND EVER SINCE THEN...

14

Inner City Deptford

*"No crumb of human comfort in
the concrete jungle"* – Molly Parkin

In the ancient world, during the Middle Ages and the Renaissance and even in many 20th century countries, the word 'city' has been associated with wealth, success, culture and opportunity. It gave us the words 'citizen' and 'civilisation'. Yet in our time the phrase 'inner city' conjures up images of disorder, poverty, fear and hardship. The inner city has been called "the cockroach at the heart of capitalism". The idea that the suburban gentility of the outer zone could be universal, if only people would take up the opportunities and work hard, has been discredited over and over again but remains deeply rooted in private prejudice and government policy. Thatcherite versions of inner city policy continue to hide their true aims clumsily behind such 'common sense' prejudices. Their manoevres are not aimed at arresting decline but at fatally undermining Labour's power bases in local government. On the other hand, it is sometimes difficult to identify ways in which Deptford has actually benefited from Labour's long entrenchment in the area. Political parties can have less to offer than the locally-based community activism which has to fight the establishment in order to identify real needs, plan and provide services to meet them, save public buildings from official neglect and encourage community participation in the processes of development. When funding sources are presented as a cake, community organisations are forced to compete for a slice at the expense of others they know are worthwhile.

Building the 'Inner City'

As a historian trying to uncover Deptford during the whole period from the Romans to the Present a chapter like this presents a major problem. Much as I would like to research in greater depth the slum clearances and the building of the major Deptford estates, such a topic is too huge for this book to do it justice. Here all I can do is sketch a few of the factual details and outline some of the arguments which continue to reverberate around planners' offices, the corridors of power and on the estates themselves.

First, let us cast ourselves back to the immediate post-war years when rationing was slow to lift and the world revealed by the end of the black-out was a bleak and severely damaged one. At the end of the war there had been cheering and street parties but it was hard to avoid a feeling of anti-climax and desolation. In the winters of 1951 and 1952, while the old flats of New King St still flickered with gas lighting, hundreds of Deptford people died from diseases related to smog.

In 1947 writer Dunstan Thompson took a train from central London to New Cross. As he walked down New Cross Rd into Deptford he decided "this was not a slum but the next worse thing, a workmen's quarter, a mean grim place...Only the sunshine redeemed it from despair". Turning into Deptford High St he felt "a deepening of the shadow, a darker greyness" and "caught the smell of over-ripe vegetables and rank fish...cheap greasy cooking from the open doors...There were barrows along the kerb and the old women surged about them buying leeks and potatoes. The crowd became so great it was almost like being at a fair or circus, except here there were no high spirits and there was no fun." Thompson had come to find St Nicholas' Church, roofless, burnt out, with its iron gates hanging loosely from their rusted hinges. The shattered tombs were eerie and depressing: "what the bombs had left, the children had smashed." On one a swastika was smeared and later, in a pub on Creek Rd, Thompson listened "to the voices of old women in the next bar talking against the Jews". Thompson's description is mean and miserable but it tells us what outsiders saw in "those grey slums" of Deptford.

At this time many people were living in temporary prefabricated Nissen huts hastily erected in areas where the old back-to-backs had been swept away by the Blitz. Bill Jones remembers his Nissen hut, near Windmill Lane where Pepys Estate is now, with affection. There was cheap fuel, both from the conventional utilities and because the old coal depot at Deadman's Dock had left a huge pile of coal dust which residents carted away in wheelbarrows to feed their open fires. The riverfront position was not always an advantage. The danger of flooding was as real as it had ever been in Deptford and the Nissen hut community took turns to stay on watch during sleeping hours in case a surge-tide took everyone off guard.

Barrels from the Victualling Yard floating down Grove after the flood of January 1928. The flood caused enormous damage in this area both in the Victualling Yard and in domestic houses but no lives were lost thanks to heroes like Mr Leader who waded through the waters to give the alarm.

Many of those on flood duty remembered the terrible flood of 7th January 1928 when Deptford and Greenwich went under for the night. Although no lives were lost in either place there was massive damage to property, including the collapse of a section of Victualling Yard wall 17-ft high and 180-ft long. The post-war night-watch had a brave ancestor in the form of Mr J W Leader who had waded waist high in icy water along Grove St giving the warning from house to house.

Oareboro Rd, prefabs replacing bomb-damaged houses, 1947. These were officially known as EFMBs (Emergency Factory-Made bungalows) and lasted much longer than the round Nissen huts remembered by Bill Jones. There were still prefabs in Reginald Square in the 1970s.

Bill Jones set up a small farm around his hut, fencing off the land to keep chickens, turkeys and rabbits. There was some trouble with Deptford Council but when two men from the Ministry of Agriculture turned up in a Rolls Royce, Bill's little farm was approved as well within their guidelines.

Bill and his wife moved around 1949 into the brand new Council-built Magnolia House on Evelyn St where they set about establishing a tenants' association, one of the first in the country. They canvassed around the big new blocks of Clyde St but found most of their support in the flats at New Cross. Deptford Council were again less than helpful, not giving a hearing to tenants because they believed "the rent collector was master of all he surveyed" (Jones, 1993). Rent collectors were a major feature of Deptford's community life, at least as important and difficult as the police. Everyone knew that if you wanted a flat you should clear it with the rent-man first and then go up to the town hall to apply formally. The rent-man's rules could be petty and irritating. For example, visible washing lines were forbidden so tenants had to string the line below balcony level where the washing was in the way, took longer to dry and often got dirty again.

Magnolia House, and numerous other post-war Council infill sites, were solid brick blocks in a functional 1940s style. Very few of them have been knocked down and, with proper maintenance, they should last many more lifetimes. The estates that were to follow were a different matter altogether.

From December 1965 the press began to carry stories with headlines like 'New Town Scheme for Slum Area'. The "shambles of Deptford's back streets" were to be replaced in a series of major clearances. First off the mark was the ultra-modern self-contained town dreamed up by the GLC Architects' Department for the old Victualling Yard site. Opened in July 1966 by Earl Mountbatten, the new Pepys Estate was "dedicated to the peaceful enjoyment and well-being of Londoners".

Evelyn and Milton Court estates were package-deal jobs built by Crudens Ltd for Lewisham Council using a Danish design called the Skarne system with large precast concrete units, sadly built to lower standards in Deptford than in Scandinavia. High-rise and system building were in vogue and density restrictions were more lax than they have ever been since. The 'open planning' principle of landscaping, enshrined in the concrete of these estates, has been severely discredited but its physical expression is hard to erase and successive attempts have cost central government and the local authority a great deal with few clear, lasting advantages.

Crudens Ltd handing-over ceremony for the first stag of the new Evelyn Estate, 1969. Mayor and Mayores Alderman and Mrs Coomb with Borough Architect A Sutton. The Mayor descrit the first stage of the redevelopment as a "springboard from which shall see the new Deptfor years to come". Crudens built both Evelyn and Milton Court estates.

Why were the estates built as they were? This is too often put down to '1960s bad planning' as if that can explain them away. Deptford Borough Council had not been seduced by high-rise and the area's estates were built late in the 1960s when there were already opportunities for Lewisham Council to learn from the mistakes of other boroughs. There is room for sympathy towards the high-rise planners when one remembers the steep rise of the birth rate in the early 1960s which peaked in 1964. Slum clearance and rehousing programmes were not keeping pace and it seemed the only solution was to build more densely and more rapidly. However, by 1970 it was obvious that the birth rate was dropping again and that, with the mass movement out of the inner cities, Deptford would never be so crowded again. Moreover, it was well known that the space-saving gains of building high were not so great when car-parking and approach roads were added. However, with no provision for ongoing consultation and reassessment, the blocks continued to rise.

Ronan Point in East London collapsed in 1968 after a minor gas explosion. The implications echoed around the new concrete of the metropolis, stirring fear and anger in the recently 'decanted' populations waiting to move into similar tower blocks in Deptford and elsewhere. The four Evelyn Estate towers already under construction were strengthened and Milton Court's eight blocks, three of them 23-storeys high, went ahead to slightly amended design.

We can identify the key elements in the construction of the estates: the local authority (Lewisham not Deptford), architects working for large construction firms and the management of the firms who wanted to build high-rise tower blocks in order to compete in the international commercial building sector. It has been suggested that any local authority wanting to build housing came up against this cartel and found itself persuaded into high-rise. There was also a political side to this 'persuasion'. When the Labour government was elected in 1964 Bob Mellish, MP for Bermondsey and chairman of the London Labour Party was given responsibility for London's housing. He "went round the town halls hectoring and lecturing the councillors to build more and to switch to high-rise and industrialised building" (Taylor, 1993). He found a ready audience in Lewisham.

Nicholas Taylor, a young architectural journalist and Lewisham councillor in the early 1970s, had been writing polemical articles against tower blocks for a decade. Now he looks back at his fellow-councillors and remembers a kind of old Labour machismo which was excited by the scale of the buildings, by their "phallic penetration of the skyline". Whatever contempt we may feel for such attitudes to the building of homes, it would be hard to deny that Canary Wharf appeals (to those who do not hate it) for similar reasons.

Part of Deptford's problem was, as ever, one of outsiders' perceptions. The area was considered by Lewisham planning officers to lack open space. Certainly there were few public parks, British Rail kept large swathes of derelict land behind fencing and it had been half a century since the last market gardens had disappeared. However, Deptford had an enormous number of small private gardens. Nick Taylor points out that "these little gardens and yards, full of washing and children and animals and all the stuff of daily life, were ruthlessly eliminated". The destruction of private space is just one aspect of the 1960s innovation which has been bemoaned by both residents and planners ever since.

Molly Parkin remembered how pleased everyone was with the new Pepys Estate, opened in July 1966, but also that "the backstreets were the same as they had ever been, sprawling, spirited, a chaotic confusion of human warmth, troubles shared, triumphs celebrated". When she returned in the mid-1980s she found "the hell-hole, high-rise Pepys Estate ominously empty with no crumb of human comfort in the concrete jungle, a travesty of what had been before".

Deptford's estates have been a problem since they first breached the skyline. In its early years Pepys was a bastion of the respectable white working class: old dockers in a new town. However, as Deptford's reputation sank and housing stock elsewhere in Lewisham Borough increased, the most 'respectable' of aspirations became to 'get out of Deptford'. Those who were successful in transferring or buying out of the area left behind a battered community of "don't knows, don't cares and desperates". Nevertheless the estate has had a strong identity and this has been predominantly positive for most of its life. Some residents have fought hard against the periodic social breakdowns. Dave O'Hara, whose work on the estate over the years from 1969 until his death in 1992 helped lay the foundations of the bid for Estate Action money from central government, is much missed but other individuals and groups have taken on his positive attitude. Pepys has one of the best youth clubs in South London, a strong arts community and a good resource centre.

When the first part of Evelyn Estate (nearest to Clyde St) was completed in 1969 it proved easy to let to local people. By the time the first part of Milton Court was ready at the end of 1971 "people had rumbled it, they had discovered that Evelyn Estate wasn't quite as bloody marvellous as they had thought. And Milton Court was obviously horrendous." One of the worst aspects of Milton Court, with its dense and complicated layout, was that it retained a main road running through the middle. The dual carriageway bypass planned for Sanford St had not materialised. There was no road at all there because the old houses of Ruddigore Rd still stood in the way. Nonetheless, since the estate plan showed Woodpecker Rd as pedestrianised the flats were built assuming that it did not exist. From the start, therefore, Milton Court had a terrible reputation. The first set of residents moved there in the autumn of 1971. By spring 1972 they had formed a tenants' association. Nick Taylor attended a meeting at the town hall but instead of defending the Council he agreed with residents: "This estate is horrendous; there is a madness in the design." To the horror of Lewisham Labour Group the story made the headlines in the local press. Old Deptford councillors like Bob Lowe and Tommy Agambar "never understood why people weren't grateful for these estates. How dare they form a TA and start attacking the Council when they'd hardly moved in?!" (Taylor, 1993).

The two features of Pepys Estate most heralded at its inception were its massive scale and the walkways separating pedestrians from road traffic. The 1991 Estate Action proposals recommend breaking

The towers of Milton Cou Estate (Hawke, Druid ane Naseby), 1993. In the foreground is New Deptfo Green with Lady Florence House (Epilogue) and two small houses. This area w cleared in the 1970s but approved Estate Action plans involve building ne Housing Association hou on it to make more space within Evelyn Estate. Mil Court's own Estate Actio will involve a major demolition programme.

down the estate into smaller, 'natural neighbourhoods', bringing the raised walkways and the shops back to ground level and reducing the 'over-designed estate' to a more 'human scale'. Similar turnarounds have been seen over the years on Milton Court. The landscaped banks which looked so good on architects' models proved a 'mugger's paradise' and had to be reduced at some cost in the late 1980s. Other features, like the massive concrete bridge over Sanford St which was to lead the estate's children to an adventure playground, were abandoned before they were even built. On Evelyn Estate the notion of 'communalism is best' led to a number of low-rise blocks with communal interior corridors and no individual street doors. With entryphone systems notoriously susceptible to vandalism, the burglary rate in these blocks has been as high as 1:1. The new Estate Action, in line with inner city community safety advice throughout the country, abandons communalism in favour of private or semi-private 'defensible space'.

While Pepys Estate managed to mix destruction and conservation in the old Victualling Yard, Milton Court obliterated an area of small houses with bay windows on both floors, obviously built as flats from the start. In Childeric Rd, where a new road was planned but never built, one terrace survived and was used to house homeless families. The houses of the Milton Court area had looked like comfortable working class homes but they were built later than the good houses on the far side of Deptford Park. The brick quality had deteriorated and they tended to become saturated with water after heavy storms. Jerry-built in the 1880s with 'differential settlement' (different quality foundations at front and back), cracks had appeared splitting the houses in two. Nick Taylor insists that however much we shiver at the horrors of the tower blocks, we should not be sentimental about these old houses with "the Queen Anne fronts and the Mary Ann backs".

Nevertheless "the replacement of companionably unhygienic slums by soulless tower blocks with broken lifts" (Macgregor, 1987) has haunted the memories of Deptford people and planners. Perhaps most upsetting is the admission that by no means all of the streets cleared for the estates were slums. While the Housing Committee were persuaded to save Gosterwood St, Etta St and one side of Rolt St from further Evelyn Estate extensions, there is no denying that the houses on the demolished side of Rolt St were as good as any of the others. How many other houses were lost in Deptford through the ignorance and indifference of Lewisham planners? Councillor Taylor tells of taking other Lewisham councillors on a Saturday morning coach tour round Deptford, a part of their borough some of them had never ventured into. Tenants would hear of the proposed demolition of their houses only when they questioned the Council officers who "walked the streets with measuring instruments and big boots".

It is hard for those who did not see it to imagine quite how disruptive the actual building of the estates was. In 1972, after the completion of the first part of Milton Court, Peter Way wrote in the *Sunday Times*: "The decision to make most of South East London a monolithic end-to-end housing estate was taken soon after the war...The original plan is just beginning to really run amok in the heartlands of New Cross and Deptford. Entire networks of streets now run between corrugated iron walls or smashed-up terraces of decent little stock brick houses. Those inhabitants who linger on sometimes have the paving stones stripped from outside their front doors...Having destroyed a community, devastated trade, and broken up a good deal of workable low level housing the planners have just completed one of the alternatives: an awesome complex in which people are simply refusing to live....Brochures are being sent out to persuade tenants to live in the blocks, which, as every tidy-minded person knows, are much more suitable than a little house in a terraced street with a friendly Irish off-licence on the corner and a street market nearby."

The Loss of the Borough

One of the most important changes Deptford faced in the 1960s was amalgamation with the Borough of Lewisham. Without romanticising the old Deptford Borough Council, we can see that its small scale and insular attitudes were not all to the bad. The enduring class divisions and widely divergent needs of particular areas are difficult to address through the massive bureaucracy of the over-arching Borough of Lewisham. Administrative decentralisation (for example, in the creation of housing 'neighbourhoods' and the concentration of central government funding on small areas) helps to revive local identities only to be disappointed again by the realisation of their lack of power or independent representation. This is a national political question about where the power over individual life-choices should lie and who should be making decisions about the petty but crucial issues of everyday life.

Sir Leslie Plummer was Deptford's MP during the lead-up to the London Government Act of 1963 which merged small boroughs all over the capital. His speeches in Parliament reflected the mixture of intense pride and benevolent prejudice which forms the core of all community identity. The Parliamentary debate of 1962 over the Bill, and especially the Price Amendment which suggested Deptford should be merged with Greenwich and Woolwich rather than Lewisham, brings out many of the issues.

On the wider level, Plummer suggested two major problems. He prophesied that the Act would ossify London government for decades on the basis of information from a Royal Commission begun in 1957. He also voiced his suspicions of the main sponsor of the Bill, Henry Brooke the controversial Home Secretary, who had stated in 1945 that it was his job to destroy the Labour majority on the LCC for ever. Many MPs made this point; that the Tories were manipulating London yet again to make political gains which would rebound on them. The London boroughs had been established in 1899 by a Conservative government hoping to get in the way of the radical LCC. Half a century later they had produced the strongest area of consistent Labour government the country had ever known.

On the local level, both Plummer and the Tory MP for Lewisham West, Henry Price, argued against the Deptford-Lewisham amalgamation. The government had provided four points on which to make the decision: past and present associations; lines of communication; pattern of development; and the convenience of the service centre. Price listed the connections between Deptford and Greenwich (the loss of the St Nicholas' area to Greenwich in 1901 and the inclusion of Deptford in the constituency of Greenwich in 1832). The four provincial town clerks who had prepared the original proposals had suggested that the St Nicholas' area should be taken back into Deptford. Price's Amendment proposed an easier solution: give the rest of Deptford to Greenwich. With fascinating certainty, Price also insisted that "Lewisham has no experience and no knowledge of riverside problems...Lewisham is not, never has been and has no wish to be a riparian [riverside] authority." He suggested that uniting Deptford with Lewisham was "an absurdity...like putting Cleopatra's Needle on top of one of the pyramids".

Plummer agreed but took issue with the treatment of Deptford as "an infectious disease" or "the lost child of South East London". He began "When Deptford was a civilised borough and community, the people of Lewisham were practically running around in woad" and went on to list Deptford's glories – the Dock and Victualling Yards, Samuel Pepys, Grinling Gibbons, Peter the Great. A friendly interjection from a Labour colleague from Lewisham South that it was in Lewisham that King Alfred had burnt the cakes, received the retort: "That seems to be a comment upon the culinary efficiency of his borough. We did not burn cakes in Deptford; we launched ships, and brought an empire to Elizabeth I. We were not common scullions and cooks; we were navigators who girdled the globe and brought riches and treasure to this country."

Plummer pointed out the inconvenience of the service centre. It would hardly bring local government and the constituent closer together when "the people of Deptford will now have to take a 9 pence bus ride to get to the town hall instead of walking there quite easily". In the 1990s, with only two buses linking the whole of Deptford and New Cross to Catford at a cost of 70 pence a ride, the situation has not improved.

Yet Plummer's attitude was ambivalent. However much he despised the upstart Lewisham he had even less respect for "so far-flung and foreign a borough as Woolwich". Colin Turner (Woolwich West) agreed that Plummer's "borough and mine have in common only the tortuous roads which connect them". In the end Plummer took a fatalistic attitude, knowing "that the insularity of Deptford, which has been so important, will be destroyed" but believing that Deptford people would "gravitate more normally – although reluctantly – towards Lewisham than they would traverse the wastes of Greenwich in order to go to Woolwich Town Hall". The only thing agreed upon by all was the desire to remain 'confirmed bachelors or spinsters', to be left alone. Only Lewisham, with its population of 221,000, was in a position to argue that it already fitted the government's specification for a modern London borough. The original plan for Deptford's 68,267 residents had been an amalgamation to the north but the grouping of Camberwell, Southwark and Bermondsey into the new Borough of Southwark had scuppered the scheme and left Deptford a problem child to be fostered out elsewhere.

The strong feelings brought out in the debate continued within the localities for many years after the amalgamation came into force in 1965. Even by 1971, when Nick Taylor was elected to Ladywell ward (which had just become part of the Deptford constituency), there had been little reconciliation. Deptford and Lewisham councillors saw each other as foreigners. Price had remarked patronisingly: "It is not that we object to Deptford or its people. We are very fond of them." The working class backgrounds of most old Deptford councillors and their lack of experience of large bureaucratic borough politics led them into the inferiority trap while Lewisham councillors tended to keep Price's superiority angle with little pretence of affection. There were many continuities of personnel from the old Deptford Borough, but they always became deputies, regardless of merit. Bob Lowe became Deputy Leader, Jim Meader became Deputy Town Clerk, and Deptford became the euphemistic "north of the Borough".

Deptford never did recover its ancient heart in the form of the old St Nicholas' parish, although most recent boundary changes give Lewisham the Sayes Court and Convoys' Wharf areas. Lewisham Council's proposal to run the boundary up Deptford Creek was dropped after heavy pressure from Greenwich and especially from Walworth Rd (Labour HQ) who were concerned about the loss of labour voters in Greenwich constituency which was still held by the Liberal Democrat MP Rosie Barnes.

Community work

We have seen how the churches and chapels of Deptford tried to offer "a bright spot in grey lives". Perhaps part of their failure stemmed from this very attitude. Lives in Deptford were hard and often depressed but they were not 'grey' at all. Only when the clergy began to recognise the warmth and vitality of the existing community would the churches find a new role in helping it through the hard times.

In 1965, after St Nicholas' Hall had been wrecked a dozen times in 18 months, Rev. Robert Miles, known as 'the barrow-boy vicar', went with a team of helpers to the coffee bars, cafes and street corners to ask teenagers why the hall was being wrecked and how the church could win their friendship. The questionnaire they used included "a variety of topical questions ranging from pop music to long hair and fashion, gradually leading up to a challenge on Christian faith". It was unconvincing and clumsy but it was a start.

When David Diamond arrived in Deptford in 1969 to begin his ministry at St Paul's Church he found a battered run-down place with high and rising poverty and crime levels, suffering the early pains of slum clearance and the transition from old terraces to new tower blocks. He came to a beautiful but semi-derelict church, almost completely cut off from its community. On his first afternoon he drew in his breath and went out to "find a congregation". The response he encountered that day later became one of his favourite stories. In the slum tenement corridors of Rectory Buildings a small child looked him up and down before dismissing him with "Fuck off, you vicar!"

Diamond aimed to "open wide the creaking doors and windows of the church and allow the community to surge in". Bingo, football, discos and licensed dances were, to him, morally neutral. He saw it as his job to provide space for whatever activities Deptford chose and in the process to 'consecrate' them as part of the work of God and the parish priest. There were no jellies and funny hats at his Christmas parties; he found a bottle of stout and a game of bingo went down better. He was fond of saying that the resources of the church, with workers and a building in every parish, could equal those of the state and be far less intrusive. His favourite song, 'Consider Yourself At Home' from the musical *Oliver Twist*, was at the heart of his decision to concentrate on the restoration of St Paul's. Although he was criticised for this priority in the midst of poverty he retorted: "St Paul's was the last remaining vestige of Deptford's glorious past and it didn't make anyone feel good to see their beautiful church crumbling."

The much-loved Canon ⸃d Diamond, Rector of St ⸃ul's Deptford from 1969, ⸃ died on 31 August 1992. ⸃nd and colleague Father Owen Beament from All ⸃int's Church said David ⸃as "one of this century's great saints".

A year after his arrival in Deptford, David started the annual Deptford Festival, a determinedly non-élitist extravaganza with street parties, fireworks and 1,000-strong pensioners' outings to Margate or Southend. Twenty coaches would set off from the High St at the firing of a cannon, waved off by schoolchildren who had collected the money. During the 1970s St Paul's hit the headlines a number of times with its youth clubs and parties in the crypt, the Millwall Mass and especially its royal connections. Princess Margaret, who David persuaded to join in the second Deptford Festival in 1971, came back year after year and told Liverpool people in David's old ministry "I just adore the man". David also brought the Queen to Deptford twice:

during her Silver Jubilee in 1977 and for St Paul's 250th anniversary in 1980. At a dinner in Lambeth Palace, David was greeted by the Archbishop of Canterbury's secretary, "Ah, Father Diamond, I know all about your parish. How's this for a bit of name-dropping, I was told about it by the Queen!" When Prince Charles "popped down the High Street" to open the Deptford Enterprise Agency in 1986 he ended up in the Windsor Castle sipping a half of cider. It was the first time the Prince had ever set foot in a pub while on official duty.

David Diamond captured and helped to mould Deptford's humour. When kids came on the scrounge, "Have you got two bob, Farver?" he'd say "I'm the Church of England – not the Bank of England". When someone peered into the minibus and demanded, "What are you doing dressed up as an effin' priest?" he answered "Because I am an effin' priest". When he visited a parishioner in Parkhurst in 1990, no less than 14 inmates were delighted to see their familiar 'Farv'.

David had no time for an introverted church. Friend and colleague, Fr. Owen Beament of All Saints, agreed: "Our job is to look after the community, God will look after the Church." In some ways David was just another paternalist in the tradition of the Victorian slum priests. Yet his peculiar mixture of High Church and low living fitted well with both the glory of St Paul's and the down-to-earth people of Deptford. A typical invitation from the Rector would end: "High Mass; Licensed Bar; Fireworks".

In 1992 David faced an unpleasant ordeal when two of his altar boys were arrested for the murder of Ron Harrison, the former deputy head of Aske's Boys' School. The police had asked for information about a TV set stolen from Harrison's home around the time of the killing and a local woman realised she had bought the set from Timothy Kelly of Howard House, Evelyn St. Too scared to tell the police she spoke to a neighbour who told David in confidence. He spoke to the lad and within three days had arranged for Kelly and his mate Mark Dooley to talk to the police about the TV, though they denied the murder charge. At the trial David was accused of delaying vital evidence. He protested "it has got to be seen in the context of Deptford. It is not the easiest thing to go to the police." After cross-examination David was praised as a 'spiritual and adoptive father' to the boys, one of whom had lost his own dad at the age of 10.

Canon David Diamond died of a heart attack on 31st August 1992, after 23 years in the parish and 10 baptisms the previous day. The news spread fast and there were shocked tears as memories of 'Farv' were gathered and shared. At the funeral on 10th September the High St came to a halt for a procession of clergy, pipes, drums and mourners. Somehow it had been discovered that this humble vicar had "known someone who knew someone in the Privy Council" who gave the go-ahead for burial in the churchyard, despite the 1850s ruling that St Paul's yard was full. Three hundred people filled the church where the Bishop of Woolwich led the service. Many more gathered outside and, as the coffin was lowered into its space in front of the impressive front steps, a group of black lads on the church wall stood up to get a better view as they swigged their coke. It was hard to tell what they thought of him but it seems likely that they were paying their respects as much as any of us. An elderly white woman in an eccentric mix of black mourning lace threw earth onto the grave, saying "That's from the people, David. God bless you. Rest in peace." Peter Fellows, the new vicar of St Paul's from September 1993, faces a challenge and he knows it.

Catholic priests at Our Lady of the Assumption in Deptford High St have built on the work of Fr. James Mahoney who was the parish priest for 22 years from 1916. He was a local councillor for many years and was elected to the LCC with probably the largest number of votes polled by any candidate in its history. The best remembered of Our Lady's priests is Fr. Michael Frost whose Christmas parties for the elderly were surpassed in local memory only by his part in founding the Deptford Street Traders' Association in the early 1960s. Five thousand people were said to have attended his funeral in 1963, stopping the hearse on Deptford Bridge to carry his coffin on their shoulders to the church in the High St.

There were other community agencies at work in inner city Deptford, secular but no more orthodox than their religious equivalents. In the post-war years the Albany Institute had to respond to the development of the welfare state. A new concentration on the elderly included a Darby and Joan Club, the extension of a wartime Pensioners' Meals Service and, in 1955, the first all-day club for the elderly. The Institute building itself remained "very cold and shabby" as the repair of war damage by volunteers and local Rotary Clubs went on slowly. The design of the building was also a problem, with its ground floor full of corridors and the club rooms on the top floor unreachable by most elderly people.

By 1963 there was no youth work at all at the Albany. The Deptford Fund and the Lady Florence Institute asked the Blackfriars Settlement to survey the work of the two organisations. The recommendation was that the two should merge but the management committee of Lady Florence refused, worried that they would be swallowed up. Things did change, however, as the novel idea of 'preventative social services' became widely accepted and volunteer helpers were replaced by paid staff. The basic objective given in the *Annual Report* of 1969 was "offering a total environment in which the Deptford residents can realise and develop potential abilities and interests, and in which they can seek advice and support when and if they feel it to be necessary".

In 1968 the new Albany director, Paul Curno, appointed the 'Combination' as the Albanys' resident theatre group. There was a new emphasis on entertainment as a response to the feeling of cultural poverty after the closure of the New Cross Empire in 1954 and its demolition to build a petrol station four years later. Twenty years after the Empire's closure the Albany team insisted "Never devalue Entertainment. Live Entertainment. We are Deptford's Entertainers. Not Missionaries of Art". In the early 1970s imaginative street theatre productions fitted well with the general chaos going on all around. Commissioned by the South East London Claimants' Union, the Combination staged a show in the local DHSS offices. A row of brightly coloured bowler-hatted clerks high-stepped in, chanting: "We are the men from the S.S./And we come to relieve distress/So confess the truth, now confess/You *know* you could live on less." This was part of a membership campaign called 'Never Meet the Enemy Alone'. There were leaflets to accompany the show and it was followed by a discussion.

In 1974 *Building Design* described the Albany as a private organisation bridging the gap between state and community. Its non-bureaucratic angle allowed it to blur the restrictive categories which fragmented state social services. Children were not a separate 'category of need' from their parents; the elderly could be supported in the context of tenants' associations; claimants may also be single parents or artists or in need of housing advice. The community was diverse and each of its members had a range of inseparable roles.

During the early 1970s the Albany was a crucial part of Deptford. Slowly, however, it became "a haunt of left-wing middle class people who went to the shows to see and be seen". Dressed up in bright colours, or (deliberately) dressed down in scruffy clothes, Albany workers and volunteers were set apart from the working class Deptford community. If David Diamond in his cassock could be welcomed in the pubs, we should not be too quick to say that difference means alienation. However, Diamond had to prove himself and so did the Albany. Some of its workers are remembered as the helpful, generous, caring community heroes of their dreams, but the general feeling remains that the Albany set itself a task beyond its capabilities and was overtaken by political change not before its time was up.

The Crossfield Story

Most of the Crossfield Estate blocks in the old Creekside area around Deptford Church St were built by the LCC in the late 1930s. They remained under GLC management until April 1971 when they were handed over to Lewisham Council. The GLC Housing Department was famous for its grand schemes but notorious on matters of day-to-day housing management and conditions in the blocks were appalling. One woman said "I have lived on this estate for 22 years, I have spent 21 of them trying to get out". Crossfield referrals to Social Services for material poverty were four times the local average.

With advice from GLC traffic engineers, Lewisham Council were planning to turn Church St into a major dual carriageway. Crossfield tenants, some of them living within feet of the proposed road, had not been consulted or even told about the plans. When Albany community worker Ann Gallagher called a tenants' meeting in January 1973, the reaction was instant. Of about 200 people who participated in the campaign, around 170 were women. Their long-brewed anger at conditions was given expression in mobilising support for the demolition of the whole estate. They produced a brochure describing the effects of the road – danger, noise and isolation from the rest of Deptford – and their everyday experience of blocked drains, rats, damp and fungus on the walls. They also took direct disruptive action with a demonstration closing Church St to traffic during Friday evening rush-hour in the middle of a rail strike.

While other councillors had walked out of early meetings, the Crossfield group found weighty support in Ron Pepper, Chair of the Planning Committee, and the two young councillors Nick Taylor and Nick Gregory. Despite concern that demolition was a waste of housing stock (especially since Finch and Congers Houses had already received some upgrading from the GLC and Farrer House was a later and better build of around 1949), these councillors supported tenants in their campaign as well as visiting many in their homes to take up individual cases. Within two months of the first meeting the Housing Committee agreed to rehouse all the tenants on the estate.

A triumph of local activism, but the story does not end there. A group called Student Co-operative Dwellings, started by "an extremely unco-operative young man called John Hands", had negotiated with the Council for sites in the area and eventually built the Sanford St Co-op near Milton Court. Hands and his deputy (a young chap called Nicholas Raynsford, elected MP for Greenwich in 1992) approached Ron Pepper with a proposal to give Crossfield over to SCD. This fell by the wayside but it gave Pepper the idea of using Crossfield to house single professional people. Head of a secondary school in Peckham, Pepper was acutely aware of the teacher shortage in schools crowded with the children of the early 1960s baby bulge. Places at Crossfield were offered to ILEA, Goldsmiths' and Thames Polytechnic. The plan scraped through the Housing Committee and a new community grew up in the blocks: a constantly-shifting population of students, artists, musicians, teachers and social workers. The new Crossfield brought the voluntary sector into Deptford, where its workers lived with the same facilities and often worse conditions than their pupils or clients. Here students had the opportunity to integrate far more than they do in most areas. The estate brought a new middle class segment to Deptford without the gentrification or widespread displacement of working class communities that we have seen in the rest of docklands. It also gave an unprecedented momentum to the development of a radical community arts and music scene. Dire Straits, Squeeze and the Flying Pickets were the ones who made it beyond Deptford but there was also a "proliferation of tiny groups, growing and splitting like amoeba, producing discs from garage studios sounding like they've been cut in a biscuit tin". (*Time Out*, 1978).

With only minimum improvements, the blocks were far from normal standards of accommodation and it was made clear that when families started to form they would be rehoused elsewhere in Deptford. This maintained the rather artificial uniformity of the Crossfield population right through the 1970s. At the end of the Labour years, Lewisham Council flooded the Department of Environment with housing proposals so Government restrictions on new Council building did not finally catch up with the borough until the end of 1981. The steep decline in available property which followed made it almost impossible for people with children to get transfers out of Crossfield after 1982. The situation has come full circle, although in general the better job prospects of the second wave allow them more options than their predecessors. Thus they move off the estate and are replaced not by single people but by homeless families, including a growing Vietnamese community.

The 1980s: Tight purses and new politics

The plan to replace the old Albany building dates back to the 1960s. The 'new building', due some time around 1977, was to be a combined social, recreational and welfare centre, built and run as a joint venture by the Albany and Lewisham Council. Long delays in the expected grants kept the old building going even after the fire in 1978 (Ch. 15). The new building in Douglas Way finally opened in 1981. Carefully designed and very expensive (it cost £3 million to build and had annual losses of around £200,000 in the early 1980s), it occupied an uncertain space in Deptford, both literally and emotionally. The old building was too small, too old, too difficult to heat. Access was appalling, the cafe was cramped and it fronted a major road. Workers and users had struggled to maintain and revamp this crumbling but well-loved building, working all the time towards funds for a new start. The new place was purpose-built, on slum clearance land, airy and open, and in the best of early 1980s architectural style. It lacked both character and roots in the area. Nevertheless it continued to provide information, advice, entertainment and a base for community groups. Instead of Lewisham Family Squatters, face-painting and street theatre, the Albany became home to the Welfare Rights Unit, basic bookkeeping classes and writers' workshops for black women.

Performers at the Albany have included:

Vic Reeves Big Night Out	Nico	Frankie Howerd
Tommy Cooper	Lennie Henry	Maxi Priest
Whoopi Goldberg	Billy Connolly	Los Lobos
Alexei Sayle	James Brown Band	Benjamin Zephaniah
John Hegley	Jools Holland	Phil Cool
Jeremy Hardy	Vicious Boys	Michelle Shocked
Gerry Sadowitz	Kit Hollerbach	Squeeze
Dire Straits	That Petrol Emotion	Curtis Myfield
Flying Pickets	Bo Diddley	Courtney Pine
Linton Kwesi Johnson	Sade	French & Saunders
Christy Moore	Test Department	Gilles Peterson

In the late 1980s and 1990s the Albany was a liability and an embarrassment. With massive and rising debts, a terrible burglary record and internal squabbles which dragged its atmosphere and its reputation through the dust, the Albany came very close to total breakdown. It was held from complete isolation by a small group of people who kept the faith that such an expensive and central resource must somehow be saved. Now a City Challenge 'flagship', removed from the control of the Combination Theatre and with a new management committee and staff, the Albany has a chance to try again. It is in the nature of inner city deprivation that we will always expect the impossible from centres like the Albany. However, if its workers learn from the past and look to the future, while working incredibly hard in the present, we may come to respect and love this building in the heart of our town.

During the 1980s there was increasing talk of an 'inner city underclass'. As Susanne Macgregor points out, "the 'underclass' is what the working poor become when they are not employed". Unemployment was no new problem in Deptford but in the late 1970s it was running to double the average for the rest of the country. Half of these were unskilled workers thrown onto the dole by the loss of industry in the area and by the closure of Surrey Docks. Many others were school-leavers, born in the early 1960s and now facing the implications of their over-stocked generation.

The Skillcentre on Deptford Broadway was first discussed in 1972 but planning problems delayed building work until the summer of 1979 when the £3.4 million contract was given to a Chiswick firm, R.M Douglas Ltd.

The site required "extensive piling" before foundations could be laid because six sewers, two small rivers and Deptford Creek all ran through it (works which helped 'tame' the Creek into mud flats). The Manpower Services Commission, describing the training places that would be available, added "all our market research indicates that there will be a considerable demand for such a centre in the Deptford area".

As unemployment spiralled under the Thatcher government the north-south divide within Lewisham Borough became ever more noticeable. By August 1982 unemployment was 19.1% in Deptford against an average of 12.4% in the rest of Lewisham. Figures from the three north Deptford wards in the 1991 census show average male unemployment at over 42%. No other ward in Lewisham even reaches 30%. In March 1993 another major company pulled out of Deptford. Siemens Plessey Controls left its Grove St plant, making another 60 workers redundant after 200 job cuts in the previous three years. Deptford MP Joan Ruddock and Lewisham Council Leader Steve Bullock took their campaign to save Siemens to Michael Heseltine but found no support at the Board of Trade. Ruddock said it called into question the whole Government strategy for inner city regeneration. With Astra Training Services, in charge at the privatised Skillcentre, going into receivership in July 1993 because they have been "hit by the recession" (sic), the strategy seems already in shreds. Lewisham's bid for Deptford was one of the winners in 1991-2 of a City Challenge award, the government-sponsored competition between councils for money to regenerate deprived areas. However, the £37.5 million City Challenge and over £100 million in agreed Estate Action bids in the area, can make little long-term difference without the provision of employment and a serious attack on the 'poverty trap' which keeps people on meagre benefit, with the brick wall of state bureaucracy wasting their energy and undermining their confidence. Where is Kath Duncan? Where is the Claimants' Union?

Ironically, Millwall Football Club, which by the mid-1980s "was seen as shorthand for everything that sickened people about football", has since 1986 been an important community agent in Deptford. Even before the crisis of falling gates and outright public disdain for football, Millwall was one of three London clubs operating a scheme suggested and financed by the GLC to bring the club closer to the local community. Gary Stempel has been Millwall's Community Development Officer since September 1985. After initial suspicion he and the club became enthusiastic about their dual role in pioneering a change of attitudes.
The Millwall Minders, based near the Den at Monson School, was the first Football League match-time crèche. The club also provided soccer schools, coaching and talks at local schools. Player Wesley Reid admitted that he was not "a big football star" but said "it's surprising the amount of influence a footballer can have...The fact that someone who came from an estate can make it makes the kids listen to me." By the second year of the community scheme, schools began approaching the club asking for speakers to talk about issues such as racism, hooliganism and the life of a professional footballer.

Policing has been an issue in Deptford since the first Peelers appeared on the streets in the 1830s (Ch.10), yet there is also a tradition of police loyalty to the area and individual officers might earn themselves a certain respect if they stayed long enough and proved themselves fair. Booth's researchers at the turn of the 20th century more or less trusted police judgements on the different neighbourhoods. Where they disagreed, the researcher was usually more harsh and patronising than the officer.

Sergeant John Stean started work at Deptford police station in Amersham Vale in 1970. He recalls the tremendous Friday night punch-ups but says "we never used to hurry too much otherwise we'd get there in the middle of it and everyone'd turn onto us. They were all on the floor by the time we'd get there...we'd pick up the pieces and drag 'em in here. They'd be charged with drunk and disorderly, court in the morning, they'd get a bit of a fine and go home." Jayne Walton, who spent a few nights at the station in the early 1970s, remembers the police with a certain affection. "You could guarantee they'd wake you up gently with a nice cup of tea and an egg sandwich. The sergeant would come in in the middle of the night to check you were covered up."

During the 1980s Deptford's estates were policed from 8.30am to 8.30pm by community police. At night they passed over to the Quick Response Team at Ladywell police station. On Milton Court and Evelyn there was a community police sergeant and six daytime beat officers. Pepys had a higher level still, with its own community police sergeant. Half the Evelyn and Milton Court community officers were women, though out of six none were black.

Evelyn's Community Development Manager believes that the reason Milton Court never became the 'Crack City' it was accused of being in the late 1980s was mainly to do with policing. Sergeant Stean, responsible for implementing police strategy in Milton Court, described making 400 arrests in a few months around the periphery of the estate to cut off custom to the dealers near the Spanish Steps pub in the centre. With relatively solid and sensitive community policing the situation was contained. Milton Court remained a terrible place to live and a scary place to visit but it did not explode and in the 1980s that was enough for the police to congratulate themselves. This was the decade of 'crisis management', of riots and unrest, of fine-tuned police prejudice and increased powers.

Irwin Eversley is only the most famous of Deptford's black people to face police harassment. Falklands hero and fireman Eversley was arrested outside his home on Crossfield Estate in April 1989. He was later awarded £20,000 by the Metropolitan Police. The Met continued to deny liability for 'damages' but made the out-of-court settlement "to reflect the seriousness of the allegations".

Community policing has been replaced in the 1990s by sector policing, which means the loss of beat police officers with a personal knowledge of their local area and its people. Sergeant Stean was completely opposed to the principles of sector policing and he had strong support within the police force as well as respect outside of it.

It was a warm October evening in 1990 and everyone was in a great mood in and around the Dew Drop Inn on the Milton Court edge of Fordham Park. It was Mary Oldfield's night off. Her staff were getting on with running the pub and she was enjoying herself, having a well-earned drink with customers. Suddenly, around 10.45pm eight police wagons arrived from Ladywell police station. This was Ladywell's flying squad, all of it, including the dogs.

Eye-witness Richard Walker remembered the incident like this. "The police said 'We reckon you've been throwing stones at police cars, we've heard there's drugs being dealt here'. They weren't there to deal with a small incident; they were there to cause one. The people in the park were calm. The police asked for Mary and there was a big scene – customers, bar staff and the police all mouthing off. They want to search the pub. Mary says 'okay, but you've seen the crowd. I bear no responsibility for it if you go through there'. The police say they'll do her for incitement to riot. Mary laughs and promises to stand stock-still and silent with a couple of hundred witnesses. They arrest her for 'resisting arrest'. Meanwhile they're radioing through to base, checking out the legal position. Brian goes to get her coat, tries to give it to her. The police arrest him for obstruction. Eventually they haul off Mary and Brian and eight others all for obstruction. They pushed everyone back with dogs and scoured the place for drugs. They found absolutely nothing. Nobody deals in the Dew Drop, they wouldn't do that, certainly not with Mary there."

People dispersed. Those charged with obstruction got bail though it was not easy to find 'respectable' references. The case dragged on but when it finally reached Marylebone Crown Court in June 1991 it was thrown out after three hours with the judge warning the senior police officer that he had acted against the interest of public order and of the Metropolitan Police whose Statement of Common Purpose (including "to protect, help and reassure people in London..to be compassionate, courteous and patient, acting without fear or favour or prejudice to the rights of others") was on prominent display in Deptford police station. Costs were awarded against the police, though legal squabbling ate up most of the money. Although the incident was not the fault of Deptford police, it embarrassed Sergeant Stean and spurred him into playing a supportive role to Mary and the Fordham Park festival organisers (Epilogue).

Deptford the Survivor

Deptford's unique character emerges from a complex mixture of new elements with survivals from the past. Totters still work the Deptford streets and pass on the legend that the rag and bone trade began here.

In the 18th century Alphonse Esquiros described a visit to a Deptford rag and bottle shop. Hanging over the door was a "sort of monstrous doll with three heads painted black and crowned with a horse-hair wig...It looked like an idol fetish, cut out of a trunk of a tree by the Congo." On the enormous bone fixed to the shutters was some red writing: 'Make haste and sell me your bones'. A piece of cardboard said 'sell me your fat'. Esquiros was unnerved. A wretched couple hobbled into the shop, coming out within minutes, minus the woman's ragged shawl and the man's cracked shoes, for a glass of gin at a nearby pub. Esquiros made an excuse to go into the shop (selling his silk handkerchief at a knock-down price) to inquire about "the origin of the black figure which from time immemorial has distinguished rag and bottle shops in populous districts".

This was the story he was told. "A young woman one day went to foreign parts in search of her lover. After a few years she returned to England with a black baby. Let us suppose she found it by the road-side, for we must always be charitable towards females. Others say she brought it with her as a speculation, but finding that black children had no value in England, she wrapped it up in a bundle of rags and sold the lot to one of the first shops in our trade that started in our country. It was in this very street, and Deptford, as everybody knows, had the honour of being the birthplace of our trade." The discovery was soon made and the baby girl was accepted out of pity. When she grew up she opened a shop in London and made a

Some of today's market-traders can trace stall-holding relatives back through the generations. Deptford remembers its old faces and places long after they would be forgotten in most areas. Maudie Mears the 'flower girl' was born in Wotton Rd in 1911. Her grandmother used to carry a massive basket of flowers and salad greens around Deptford. Maudie worked in the family florists in Hyde St until she moved into a shop of her own in Evelyn St. Mary Granger, Deptford's 'salad lady', took over the market pitch at the head of Douglas St in 1936 from her grandfather. Her husband, a bare-knuckle boxer, died in 1954 and Mary brought up her five children alone from the proceeds of the fresh produce stall. Although she left the market in 1959 and moved to Downham she was still remembered fondly in 1993 when Deptford traders were prominent at her funeral. These are just two of a score of well-loved local characters. One day we will write their histories in full.

A surviving farrier's shop the old Deptford Market area at the station ramp, 1969. Horses were exercised in Giffin St until Wavelengths Library and Leisure Centre was built in 1990. Ponies are still kept workmen based in the Stowage where they are raced by the rival firms in the streets near the works (1992).

Christmas Eve 1991 was a sad day for Deptford High St. After 58 years of family tradition, Lu's Cafe (No. 187) closed its doors and let the tea-urn go cold for the last time. A group who had a 15-year tradition of Saturday morning breakfast at the cafe mourned the end: "It's not just the food, it's a place to sit alone, to contemplate or meet people, or to chat and catch up on gossip and the rich local history. If the

A Deptford survivor eating jellied eels in Manze's pie and mash shop, 204 Deptford High St. "It's a place to sit alone, to contemplate." (Photo by Keith Cardwell, 1990)

Deptford's high street cafes are important 'community and heritage centres'. Lu's closed on Christmas Eve 1991 but Manze's and Goddard's keep up the tradition while Revival Cafe at No.70 goes for a newer approach but still appeals to local people.

original marble top tables with their cast iron legs could talk, there'd no doubt be some wonderful stories." Another 'heritage centre' is lost and the community historian heaves another sigh! However, there are other cafes in Deptford which continue the tradition, including Manze's and Goddard's pie and eel shops. Further up the High St, Revival Café is a successful new version which has lived up to its name by mixing a traditionally bustling and friendly atmosphere with excellent food and coffee.

Along with the market and the cafes, the other place to find survivors is in the pubs. When Fr. David Diamond was asked for advice by development officials he had one answer: "Go to the pub, that's where you'll find Deptford." English alehouses have been hubs of community life for centuries. Despite the changes of this century which have revolutionised home entertainment (off licences, TV, video, computer games, central heating, soft furnishings), the public house remains an unsurpassed meeting place and talking shop.

It would be good to say the Thames was Deptford's other survival, but it has had a rougher ride even than the old cinemas. Before the war many thousands were employed up and down the river in lighterage (barges which lighten a ship's load for navigating the shallower parts of the river). After the war, moving with the times, lightermen changed over to motor tugs but the Thames still bustled with activity. People felt it would last forever but at the end of the 1960s the industrial river was doomed by containerisation ("the longest 4-letter word in the English language" according to Ernie Murray, apprenticed to lighterage at the age of 15). "Suddenly these great tankers and enormous Japanese-built ships began to use the Channel ports. They couldn't get up the Thames further than Tilbury and it devastated the docks." In 1977 when the Queen arrived in Deptford she came past the corpse of Surrey Docks and through the gate at Drake's Steps into the Pepys Estate. Local historian Joan Read told the *Guardian*: "Deptford desperately needs some industry to come back into it. But we haven't got anything to attract it. You can't sell a view of the Thames." Ten years later "a view of the Thames" in the old dock areas could cost nearly half a million pounds!

15

Racism and Resistance

"It may be that blacks are in the same boat as poor whites;
but we are on different decks" – Tony Ottey

In 1948 H.M.S. *Empire Windrush* arrived in England and 417 Jamaicans disembarked into the country they had been taught to consider 'Mother England'. Soon other ships arrived bringing people from all over the West Indies. Most were skilled workers leaving behind partners, children, family, friends and country to respond to the calls of the British government for Commonwealth workers to help rebuild Britain in the labour-hungry post-war years. Many came for the promise of new opportunities, especially the dream of education. Their schooling had already been thoroughly anglicised. History lessons had taught them about William the Conqueror, Henry VIII and Good Queen Bess. In geography they had traced maps of the British Isles rather than their own islands. They had read Shakespeare and the God of Religious Studies was always white.

They knew the shape and history of Britain but they did not know what was waiting for them in the white communities of the old imperialist nation. British public relations resources had been concentrated entirely on recruitment. Not for many decades did any government give thought to preparing the 'host community' for the encounter. If it were not for Empire and Britain's long history of racism we might imagine that such preparation would be unnecessary. In the post-war years up to 1951 a total of 312,000 European immigrants had arrived on British shores and were accepted, integrated and never discussed as a 'problem'. The stark contrast with their black equivalents is shaming, yet historically it was unsurprising: the British people had thrived on a diet of imperialist jingoism and the myth of racial superiority for over a hundred years. Many of the all-too-familiar ideas of modern racism have their roots in 19th century notions of 'the alien other' against which Europeans judged (and congratulated) themselves.

Racism is an elastic and manipulable ideology, surviving by adaptation to specific circumstances. Its logic is filled with useful blindnesses and justifying amnesia. One of the most tragic outcomes of the imperialist heritage was the division between the black and white working classes. The native working class had long been regarded on two different levels by those in power. On one hand they were 'the salt of the earth', the 'backbone of the nation'. On the other, they were 'a race apart': dirty, stupid, over-sexed (familiar insults from the racist vocabulary). That this convergence was ignored and no alliance allowed to develop is a historical fact whose explanation lies beyond the scope of this book. However, we will see the hardening of this division as many political and social issues, in Deptford and nationally, began to be explained with reference to race.

In the 1990s the situation is complex. Although the ideals of equal opportunities and the 'race relations industry' have become part of the establishment, institutionalised racism continues. On the everyday level studies have shown that massive unemployment has actually lessened racist attitudes among many white working class people who can clearly see that times are often even harder for their black neighbours. On the other hand there are hostile reactions to what is perceived as positive discrimination (eg. in council housing policy) and it is sad that even the indicators of poverty and deprivation within many black communities are held to be self-created. The echo of the High Society types who set up the Albany Institute is ironically strong in such judgements.

During the 1960s it somehow became possible to forget the fact that the influx of West Indians was no refugee flight for which the immigrants should be grateful but was designed to meet British labour demands. Government policy during the 1950s had been one of benign neglect and the shifting of responsibility onto the voluntary sector. From the end of Empire the whole issue of 'race' was seen as a problem foisted on English society from outside, 'imported' with the blacks. Calls for restrictions on immigration were answered in 1962 by the Commonwealth Immigrants Act which finally overrode the old (unequal) Commonwealth partnership, tangling up 'race' and 'immigration' with long-lasting consequences. The perceived 'threat to community' embodied in black immigration was expressed in a variety of metaphors from cultural invasion to racial degradation, from 'taking our jobs' to 'mugging our old ladies', from noise nuisance to lowering school standards. Into this tense atmosphere came a variety of trouble-makers.

In the 1961 LCC elections in Deptford the British National Party took nearly 10% of the vote. In the 1963 by-election independent candidate Colin Atkins campaigned on a two-point programme to stop all immigration and "repatriate all coloureds already here". Atkins insisted "this can be done without hardship. Remember, this is our country, not theirs." In his election address he appealed to Deptfordians' sense of family, of loyalty to locality and nation, of Britain as a Christian country, and to electors' duty to keep 'intact' their children's heritage. Canvassing in Upper Deptford convinced him he could win a third of the votes. Totally disorganised, low on funds and publicly denounced in a joint press statement by the Labour and Conservative candidates, he nevertheless polled 8.5%. The main parties were still strong enough to prevent widespread hostility towards immigrants erupting directly into party politics but Atkins had tapped a nerve in the Deptford community which would reappear periodically in updated forms.

Prominent Conservatives like Enoch Powell encouraged and drew out the latent racism of communities suffering a feeling of dislocation and powerlessness in the face of rapid social change. The threatening black presence was by now coded as 'immigration'. Although in all his many speeches Powell never explicitly described the threat he so heroically 'exposed', he used a language which everyone understood. He conjured up images of 'the alien wedge' and 'the enemy within' and reinforced them with numbers to illustrate the national danger. He predicted inevitable civil conflict, looking over the Atlantic to the civil rights movement in the United States and using reversals of slave imagery without apology: "In 15 or 20 years time the black man will have *the whip hand* over the white man." Describing immigrants as "exotic fare for Mother England's digestive tract" explained away the problem as biological and therefore obvious, natural, unquestionable.

In his 'Rivers of Blood' speech given in Birmingham in April 1968, Powell stressed that the Conservative party believed in equality and no discrimination. Soon he had made clear that "the discrimination and the deprivation, the sense of alarm and of resentment" was not a problem for immigrants but for white people who had been made to feel "strangers in their own country". He went on to deride the new Race Relations Bill which was being debated in Parliament at that time, claiming that it was his white constituents who were denied hospital beds for childbirth, school places for their children and had "their homes and neighbourhoods changed beyond recognition, their plans and prospects for the future defeated".

A respectable and highly intelligent politician, Powell made people feel they could say such things without fear or guilt and that they were not alone. Canvassing for local elections in Lewisham in 1968, Beryl Steele remembers a clear change from previous years; people were now public and defiant about their dislike of 'immigrants'. Powell's speeches and the disproportionate attention he received in the national press popularised racial insecurity and distrust, making a space for repatriation on the agenda of party and popular politics.

In the early 1970s Deptford was undergoing great changes, especially in the sphere of housing. The physical fabric of the old neighbourhoods had long been deteriorating and the new estates were not a renovation of old communities but a challenge to them. The rise of containerisation which killed the inland docks had undermined the identity of the riverside areas and caused many young adults to move down-river to the deep ports of Essex and Kent. The tower blocks never became the 'vertical terraces' of planners' dreams. The decanted populations were dispersed and the notion of community in Deptford all but shattered under the strain.

Deptford's white community was indeed feeling dispossessed and some sections of it agreed with Powell's reading of their situation. Workers at Surrey Commercial Docks, many of them from Deptford, were among the 4,500 dockers who stopped work in support of Powell and signed the 3,000-name petition which was taken to Westminster in protest at his dismissal from the Shadow Cabinet by Edward Heath, Leader of the Opposition.

By 1973 when Sonia Herelle moved to Deptford she was acutely aware of the ghetto being created on Milton Court Estate and insisted that she would not join it. Instead she became one of the first black people to move onto the Pepys Estate, still the bastion of white working class Deptford. She remembers the painful racism, most often expressed as distasteful avoidance but which could easily erupt into overt hostility as a no longer secure community tried to adjust to changes which it symbolised as 'brought by blacks'. General resentment about conditions on Deptford's estates and in its damp and neglected old houses fuelled a scapegoating of the most visible carriers of change, rather than the invisible and unimaginable forces of urbanisation, the death of the docks and the class-ridden relationships between communities and the state. White withdrawal from Deptford – based on a desire to move from a poor area, if not directly racist – increased the feeling of marginalisation of those whites who were left behind. Their resentment often became racist with the understanding that they were trapped with the poverty and the 'problems'.

If 'community' is taken as a 'symbolic construction' which brings diverse people together by giving them a repertoire of shared understandings about ways of behaving, newcomers were bound to be treated with some suspicion since they broke through the physical boundaries without acquiring the symbolic repertoire. However, but for the racism of white Britain, the West Indians who came to Deptford in the early years of immigration could have been involved in a two-way sharing of symbols with the resident population. Instead they were largely shut out of the localised groupings and formed separate communities based on the symbol of common ethnicity. Even this limited interaction shook white Deptford. The very presence of the blacks meant that the white 'community' was no longer based solely on old ideas of locality and class, since they had excluded a group which shared both. White Deptfordians were now, themselves, bounded and defined by ethnicity and the old community could no longer be so simply maintained in opposition with the 'outsiders' of Lewisham or Blackheath.

In the General Election of October 1974 National Front candidate Richard Edmonds won 1,731 votes in Deptford, taking most of them from people who had voted Liberal in the election of February that year. Now a British National Party leader, Richard Edmonds was in custody on riot charges in September 1993 for his racist activities at Brick Lane in the wake of the Tower Hamlets Council by-election where BNP candidate Derek Beackon won Millwall ward.

Partly as a reaction to the 1968 Powell speech and to rising racial tension locally, the Ladywell Action Centre was founded in January 1969. It soon took up cases of alleged police brutality towards black people. Jim McGoldrick, a Deptford solicitor and Chair of the Lewisham branch of the National Council for Civil Liberties (NCCL), and Mike Steele of the Ladywell Action Centre went to the town hall in 1972 to brief party leaders Andy Hawkins and Herbert Eames about the cases. With the NCCL accusing Ladywell police of "a total breakdown between the police and black families in the area", Lewisham Council passed a resolution calling for a public inquiry.

Commander Douglas Randall arrived as leader of Lewisham police in January 1973 into this atmosphere. He was at the centre of more controversy over his description of 'mugging' as "a black man's crime". In the case of Tommy White, murdered for a miserable £2, Randall had argued unconvincingly: "First information indicated this could be a black offence. It proves our impartiality that fairly soon we established it was committed by two white men who were arrested and convicted."

In the later 1970s the National Front caused a frightening tension in the Lewisham area by direct recruiting and hostile publicity. When they planned an open demonstration through the streets of Lewisham and New Cross there was an outcry for the Home Office to ban it. The Council's last minute High Court bid to get the march stopped was unsuccessful and instead huge numbers of police were drafted in, complete with controversial new riot shields and helmets.

1977 was a troublesome year for Douglas Randall. In June Prince Charles visited the Moonshot Club and had a meeting outside with members of the Lewisham 24 campaign (opposing the dawn raids which had led to the arrest of several youths for alleged street offences). Randall received a royal summons to Buckingham Palace along with community leaders to talk to the Prince. Within two months Randall had retired from the force altogether after the 'Battle of Lewisham' on Saturday 13th August 1977.

At one end of the borough that day the ALCARAF (All Lewisham Campaign Against Racism and Fascism) march for peace was led by the Bishop of Southwark and the Mayor of Lewisham. Despite the Mayor's appeal "as first citizen of this borough" for permission to continue the peaceful demonstration, police stopped the marchers at the junction of Algernon Rd and Loampit Hill.

Meanwhile, members of the Socialist Workers Party and other left-wing groups had gathered in Clifton Rise to meet the fascists. This area, where Fordham Park has replaced the old poor-quality housing of Vance St, Snead St, Ruddigore Rd and most of Childeric Rd, was largely inhabited by black families and was the focus of many of the racist controversies of the late 1960s and early 1970s. That afternoon there was a bloody confrontation with many injuries and extensive damage to shops and pubs on New Cross Rd. Police Commander Randall liked to dub the confrontation "a clash between Left and Right", but this was a battle against the explicit racism of the National Front, seriously exacerbated by the overwhelming presence and overbearing tactics of the police.

...ody Saturday, New Cross Rd, 13 August 1977. The ...tional Front march went ...head despite calls for the ...e Office to ban it. Police ...ctics and their protection of the fascists who they ...orted through the streets ...New Cross, were heavily criticised at the time, especially by Lewisham Council who urged local people to sue the Metropolitan Police for damages.

By 1.30pm anti-Front demonstrators at Clifton Rise numbered 2,000, while Front supporters assembled unnoticed in Achilles St. At 2.20pm the police were using truncheons to clear the crowd at Clifton Rise and half an hour later they provided a 2:1 escort for 1,000 NF supporters up Pagnell St to New Cross Rd. With anti-fascists surging towards them, the fascists cowered but the police screamed at them to move on and hand-to-hand fighting broke out. One young lad rushed into the Front ranks, grabbed a flagpole from one of them and broke it in half, holding up the pieces to the cheers of the crowd.

Later Lewisham Council urged residents to charge the police for damage under the Riot (Damages) Act 1886. Deputy Council Leader Ron Pepper said the Council were disturbed about the orders given by senior officers to the 2,500 police on the day and believed that police action had made the conflict worse. Criticised for bringing in the Special Patrol Group, Randall's justification was that it was hard for policemen with 20 years service suddenly to change their traditional role into helmets, goggles, shields and drawn truncheons. "Let's face it some of our older men are not really up to this kind of thing...carrying a shield in the face of an onslaught of bricks." He recommended that if the government expected its police force to make that sort of response then it would have to pay for 100% fitness, efficiency and training: "The trouble is that the force has always been run cut-price." The point was not lost on 'the party of law and order' which got into power two years later.

Commander Douglas Randall retired to concentrate on his other activities as Chairman of the Kentish Alsatian Training Society and of the Metropolitan Drinking Fountain and Cattle Trough Association.

Counterpoint to Childeric Rd was the area around Halesworth Rd where decaying old gentry houses had been brought into multiple occupation. "Just as the jobs that were available to black people were those not wanted by white people, so the areas in which black people worked and lived tended to be those that white people were already moving away from." (Policy Studies Institute survey, 1984). On arrival West Indians with limited capital, barred from council housing by residential qualifications, sought accommodation in the private rented sector. Private lodgings were more prevalent than they have been since but conditions were often dire and tenancies were insecure. With the arrival of partners and children, family households needed larger and better accommodation. The only option was purchase and the incentive to buy was greatest among those of the lowest income group in the worst lodgings. The first wave of purchases followed hard work and scrimping to pay for the delapidated old Brockley houses. Thus black owners took on the worst of the borough's problem housing and the pattern of owner-occupation, increasing against all the odds, had nothing to do with affluence or with good property. When immigrants became entitled to council housing they were already living in areas with poor quality council dwellings. The indirect discrimination of allocations procedures meshed with the direct prejudice of some housing staff to ensure black allocation to the worst of council property. The PSI survey demonstrated that black people's council housing throughout Britain was "markedly inferior, smaller and certainly more crowded; they are more often flats and those flats tend to be on higher floors". The survey considered a wide range of factors and concluded: "Black people came from the former colonies into this country to a position of ready-made disadvantage."

Despite this across-the-board disadvantage and the endurance of 'coloured immigrant' status even of settled black communities, it is not easy to divide up black people's lives into 'problems' and 'solutions'. Racisms and resistances operate in a mutual relation and the forces which create ghettos also sustain helping networks and solidarity among black people. The creation of inner city ethnic communities was not simply the result of white withdrawal and discrimination; it was also a positive response to emotional, cultural and economic needs. "Socialisation and friendship with fellow-islanders were guaranteed. Child-minding under the same roof or in the same street by fellow West Indians was easy to arrange. In times of unemployment, ill-health or personal calumny, help and human warmth were close at hand." (Lee, 1977). While white Deptford was losing its grounding, strong black communities were growing in the same format, with religious and social institutions, shops and informal networks like the 'pardners' (credit clubs). The 'salvation' churches had a central role to play in the formation of 'respectable' black working and middle classes. Canon Diamond believed the appeal of the Pentacostalists was sociological rather than theological. "It was hard enough for black people coming to England but to go to a C of E church and find it all so stuffy and middle class...nice ladies in nice hats...wasn't quite their thing." He saw black churches as offering "a moment of undiluted culture" but was almost smug about his own "amazingly mixed congregation...black, white and khaki, young and old, every nationality, cor-blimey cockneys and one or two nice-nice hat types. We must be one of the most mixed congregations anywhere in Deptford."

Sybil Phoenix says she got to know David Diamond 'through the fights'. "Himself and his curate would be on one side of the road and I'd be on the other side and bottles and bricks would be flying...people were protecting their territory. A lot of the black people would come from other areas of Lewisham and the Deptford kids took umbrage to that, they were coming onto their patch." The Deptford Festival, first held in 1970, was Fr. Diamond's response, hoping to bring the two groups together.

Meanwhile the racist threat continued. In November 1977 the press reported a National Front meeting in a pub where action against the Moonshot Club had been discussed. On 14th December that year the Moonshot's base at Pagnell St was gutted.

Sybil Phoenix came to Deptford from Georgetown, British Guiana (now Guyana) in 1956. She was already running a church club and a supplementary school when she was visited in 1967 by three local ministers who persuaded her to take on the Telegraph Hill Youth Club. This was a small weekly youth club run by two old ladies. Its popularity was expanding rapidly, especially among the young black community and the two women could no longer cope. Sybil took over, the club was renamed the Moonshot and it moved to an old mission hall by the corner of Pagnell St and Angus St. Although the club was mostly black-orientated, it also served the white community in Deptford with a Neighbourhood Club to give parents a night out, bingo upstairs and kids from babies to 18 year olds downstairs.

Sybil explained: "The Front didn't burn me out because of what I was doing with black people or what I was doing in society in general. They were angry that the white people in the area was allowing their children to be brought up by black people." With her work in ruins, Sybil set about raising the money for a new building. She told a radio interviewer, "my name is Phoenix and out of the ashes...." After a long struggle, the new Moonshot was opened to house the many projects which had developed out of the original youth club. With help and input from sources as diverse as Jah Shaka and Sergeant John Stean, it has continued to provide an important focus for Deptford's black community ever since.

Deptford has always been a terrible place for fires and floods, but the blazes of the late 1970s were more malign than the gunpowder explosions at the 18th century Victualling Yard. There had been 15 Rock against Racism gigs, a three-day 'All Together Now' festival, a benefit to Scrap the Sus laws and a highly successful anti-racist show (*Restless Natives*), all held at the Albany Empire in Creek Rd before it was gutted by fire on 14th July 1978. Greenwich police, however, insisted that "the fire wasn't arson. It was either an accident, or more likely natural causes" (spontaneous combustion?!). They made no comment on the scruffy note pushed under the main entrance the day after the fire. Letters cut out of a newspaper said "GOT YOU" and the note was signed with the number 88, which ALCARAF believed was a reference to Column 88, a secret paramilitary organisation on the terrorist wing of 1970s fascism. Evelyn St fire station ruled out a problem with the theatre's lighting circuits since these were virtually new and very well maintained. They were 99% convinced the fire was malicious and the professional way it was carried out made it unlikely that it was started by children.

Three years after the Albany and the Moonshot were gutted Deptford suffered its most horrific fire of all. The joint birthday party of teenagers Yvonne Ruddock and Angela Jackson at 439 New Cross Rd was the scene of a tragedy which sent shockwaves through Deptford, Lewisham and the wider black London community. The fire broke out in the early hours of Sunday 18th January 1981 and within 15 minutes the whole building was alight. People were screaming, jumping through windows and beating their way through the inferno to find friends as the inside of the house was reduced to rubble. Five fire engines arrived but flames leapt from every opening and at first firemen were beaten back by the heat.

Ten black youngsters were killed that night and three more died in hospital, including Yvonne Ruddock and her brother Paul. Anthony Berkbeck, who survived by dropping from a first-floor window, was tormented by the memory of the tragedy. Two years later his body was found at the foot of a block of flats in Forest Hill, the fire's 14th victim. The feeling in the black community after the fire was one of solidarity as well as tragedy. In the following days stunned black youngsters gathered in the Spanish Steps pub on Milton Court Estate. Most of them had known victims of the fire. All of them had knowledge of the vulnerability of black people in 'multi-racist Britain'. The shock of the fire sent them reeling, bursting with emotions from blind fear to blunt fury. With 150 other black people from all over Deptford and Lewisham they attended a meeting at the Pagnell St Centre on the Tuesday after the fire. When Lewisham Police Commander John Smith turned up his words were drowned in shouts of "Go away murderer". Smith thought it was "all rather sad" but he had no idea just how little

Tragedy. The body of a ?nage boy at a window of still-smoking house after the Deptford Fire, 18th ?uary 1981. Thirteen black ?ngsters were killed in the fire at 439 New Cross Rd. ?though the fire was never ?oved to be a racist attack it became a focus of both ?cism and resistance. The ?olved case was closed by the police in 1985.

confidence his police force inspired in the grief-stricken community.

A week after the fire, on Sunday 25th January, around 400 black people marched from the Moonshot to the house in New Cross Rd. Twenty year old Chris Foster addressed the crowd outside the gutted house. In 1978 Chris' brother Carl had been gunned down in a Lewisham street after a terrifying series of gun and knife attacks on black people. There had been no arrests. Miraculously Carl survived but the shootings remained as a backdrop to the fire and the suspicion of police indifference.

The incompetence of Coroner Dr Arthur Davies, who failed to take any notes during the three-week inquest, and accusations from young blacks that police had forced them to lie in written statements turned grief into fury for many of the relatives. The frustration continued for months which eventually dragged into years as the police refused to admit the possibility that it was a racist attack.

The display of solidarity continued and on 2nd March 1981 thousands of black people from all over the country gathered in Fordham Park to show their anger, frustration and grief. More than 5,000 people took to the streets for the Black People's Day of Action march to central London to protest not just at the terrible loss in Deptford but at the everyday racism faced by black communities all over the country. Although the *Mercury* headlined their report 'Day of Dignity', the national press concentrated on the tiny minority involved in flare-ups with police.

Solidarity. Gathering in Fordham Park for the Bla People's Day of Action, 2 March 1981, when 5,000 people took to the streets show their grief at the Deptford Fire and to prot against the everyday raci faced by black people in Britain.

After a year of campaigning by the New Cross Massacre Action Committee the High Court gave permission to apply for a new inquest in May 1982 but by July their hopes were dashed again when the application was rejected. Late in 1983 a report by the Policy Studies Institute decribed police handling of the Deptford affair as "a disaster". It was no longer only a question of how the fire was started but of police behaviour during the investigation. There is still no satisfactory answer to the mystery. Police closed the file on the unsolved case in August 1985. Whatever the truth behind the fire it had a disastrous effect on police-black relations and the bitter taste remains.

A few days after the fire a repulsive piece of graffiti appeared in foot-high letters on a wall in Catford: "13 down, 1,500,000 to go". There were reports of racist jokes about Deptford circulating among the police. Whether the fire was started by racists or not, it became a focus for Britain's long internal confusion over its racist heritage and contemporary struggles.

Over the last 40 years, Deptford's West Indian communities have contributed an enormous amount to its rich cultural diversity. The massive variety of foodstuffs available in Deptford High St is testimony to the two-way sharing of culture which finally broke through the surface suspicions. Sybil Phoenix was introduced to Deptford market in the 1960s. She "would go to a house and they would say 'Oh, we save a melon for you'...they would pick up stuff from the boxes that the traders have thrown out. They would have found maybe one good one and four or five that is not very bad. That's how a lot of them lived, rummaging when the market closes. In fact, one lady told me what to do with soft tomatoes. She peeled them and fry them up with bacon fat from the rinds of the bacon. She use the fat and the top of an onion, a bit of salt and pepper, and you eat that with your bread." Asked "was it nice?" Sybil admitted "I didn't eat it...I put it in my bag!" The old Deptford was as strange as anything the new could offer, but black input has made the forging of an identity based on both cultures a positive and exciting step.

Deptford, like all ports, has a long history of visitors and settlers. Most came to work and start new lives, some fled from famine, political repression or warfare. Community history belongs to everyone and Deptford's history stretches far beyond its borders. A full account of Deptford's multi-ethnic character would mean detailed consideration of its substantial African population, many of whom are ghettoised on Milton Court. It would also need input from the Vietnamese community whose children's memories of refugee camps and boats shock teachers in schools all over Deptford. In the financially strained but socially aware atmosphere of the 1980s the voluntary sector tried to keep up with the changes. While social services struggled with a constantly changing set of circumstances, these were reflected in a local chip shop in the late 1980s when a lone West Indian child appeared bemused at being "surrounded by about 30 Vietnamese kids, all charging about" (Mehmed, 1991).

According to the 1991 census, black people make up over 23% of the population in all Deptford's five wards, with figures closer to 40% in the northern wards. This compares with an average of 13.1% in the rest of Lewisham.

Averages of the northern wards: Evelyn, Grinling Gibbons, Marlowe

White	61.8%
Black Caribbean	13.3%
Black African	11.3%
Black Other	3.6%
Chinese	3.4%
Born in Ireland	3.8%

In 1991 there were 274 Indians, 144 Pakistanis and 111 Bangladeshis. The category 'Other Asian' which mainly reflects the Vietnamese community amounted to 740 people, an average of 2.5% of the three ward populations.

E P I L O G U E

Turning the Tide

"History dying and demolished all the time"

Deptford's special and spectacular history has been neglected for over a hundred years. Those who have tried to recapture the experience of 'history from below' have written general masterpieces like E P Thompson's *Making of the English Working Class* or have followed the prejudices of Victorian social surveys and philanthropy by concentrating on the well-documented poverty of the East End.

There is so much pride in this area, yet so little available to nourish it. Compared with our equivalents across the river Deptford is poor indeed. Stratford City Challenge made history a basic part of their bid for central government money with the argument that community history promotes local identity, respect and "the confidence to take part" in the changes which take us into the future. Lewisham does not even have a museum and Deptford City Challenge have so far funded no project relating to history. Councillors and developers argue that promoting historical awareness does not 'regenerate' Deptford and is therefore not worth funding. If our history had not been treated with such indifference and ignorance we would have less need of full-scale regeneration. As it is, only through learning the lessons of the past and making it come alive for us in the present can we take Deptford proudly into the next century. We have to turn this tide of neglect.

The story of the clocktower

From a window of Daubeney Tower on Pepys Estate in 1981 you could see Rupert Murdoch's empire expanding in old Deptford. The 18th century storehouse, built around the original storehouse of Henry VIII's Deptford Dockyard, was being demolished to make way for more low-rise warehousing for Convoys newsprint importers. In a glorious position on the old building, looking outwards to the river and inwards towards Deptford, was a clocktower. Known locally as Nelson's Clock, it had survived all the upheavals of the 19th century, remained a landmark of the Foreign Cattle Market and even graced the road transport depot which had replaced the market by 1931.

The clock cupola was saved from being pulverised in the general demolition by the GLC, who had it removed first to Woolwich for repair and then in September 1985 to the Ranger's House on Blackheath for £60,000-worth of restoration. Just a few weeks before the abolition of the GLC in April 1986, Deptford's clocktower was donated to what the *Mercury* optimistically labelled the "exciting town centre at the vibrant focal point of Thamesmead". The clock was described by a GLC spokesman as "a landmark for the people of Thamesmead to remember us by". He did not list the landmarks by which the people of Deptford would remember the GLC: Pepys, Trinity and Sayes Court Estates, the decaying Crossfield and the stolen Albury St cherubs. Instead, in response to the campaign by Rev. Graham Corneck of St Nicholas' Church and Deirdre Wood, GLC councillor for Greenwich, County Hall said: "Our plans to give the clock to Thamesmead went through several committee meetings and we heard of no objections. The people of Deptford did have their chance." If the people of Deptford were used to dealing with committee meetings and massive bureaucracies, we would have caused havoc in the planners' offices long ago.

Removal of clocktower to Woolwich for repair, 1983. The clock was saved by the LC when the old dockyard storehouse was being demolished to make way for more Convoys warehousing. It was given to Thamesmead town centre in 1986.

The clocktower in its Thamesmead location looks like any other shopping centre feature. It has no plaque saying where it came from, no date to give shoppers an idea of their privilege: if asked most would probably say it was a reproduction. Deirdre Wood asked Ken Livingstone for an agreement that "if Deptford were in a position to put the clock back on one of its buildings, we would be able to have it back". Are we ready yet?

The Shame of the Libraries

In 1991 the *Mercury* ran the headline: 'Shame of library ruined by scum'. They meant squatters but the destruction of Deptford's old libraries has less to do with the groups who took over the buildings than with the politicians who left them to rot. When the Conservative government introduced right-to-buy for council properties they created an automatic barrier to sales. The local authority would only receive 25% of the actual buying price, the rest would be channelled into Treasury coffers to meet the debts owed by many councils to central government. The right-to-buy means that councils are forced to accept this situation in the homes section of the market. Public buildings, on the other hand, can be left on the disposals list, quietly decaying through neglect and vandalism.

Deptford had a central library in Lewisham Way and two branch libraries at New Cross and in Clyde St. All of them took long struggles to build. They were financed by the great Scottish philanthropist, Andrew Carnegie, on the understanding that they were "for the people of Deptford".

The Old Town Library in Clyde St, built later than the others in 1931, got its name because it was to serve the oldest part of Deptford including St Nicholas' parish. Greenwich Borough Council provided an ongoing contribution in recognition of this service.

In line with the Council's policy of moving libraries into shopping areas, all three buildings were on the disposals list in 1990. They were flooded, burnt out, squatted. Two of them have now been reclaimed for the community. The New Cross Library has been converted into a community music studio with help from City Challenge. The Old Town Library has been renovated, using volunteer workers and 2,000 hours of Community Service through the probation system. Independent surveyors assessed the work as £80,000-worth of renovation for a measly £15,000 of funding. Old Town is now successfully run by a Community Association as an arts and youth centre.

Libraries are not the only public buildings in Deptford to receive this treatment, both the neglect and the community reclamation. Next door to the Old Town Library was a public bathhouse and laundry built before the library and still open for public use until 1988. This unusual and exciting derelict building may yet become one of the most important legacies of our decade. Plans are being developed by local grassroots organisations to renovate and convert it into an International Hosting Centre to offer accommodation at a reasonable price to visiting groups, tourists and travellers.

The Spirit of Lady Flo
The squatters who wrecked Deptford Central Library have been adequately balanced by those who use their talents to renovate and bring public buildings back into public use.

The old Coffee House and Institute on the corner of Arklow Rd was bought in the 1920s by Lady Florence Pelham-Clinton and renamed Lady Florence House. The trust fund she left in Deptford withdrew from the area in the 1970s. The Lady Florence Institute on Deptford Broadway became Champs and is now Futures nightclub. Lady Florence House was boarded up and placed on the Council's disposals list.

In 1991 a group of young artists and community entrepreneurs took over Lady Flo's. They cleared the building out, re-decorated, re-plumbed, re-wired, re-glazed, patched the roof and installed a coffee bar. The group of performers, clowns, jesters, bands and dancers ran art workshops, provided rehearsal space for local groups and organised a series of performance events. They were evicted by bailiffs in April 1992 after the Council ignored their proposal to legitimise the use of the building as an arts centre. Lady Florence House was sold as warehousing. Its windows were breeze-blocked up and the people of Lewisham were bought off for around £80,000.

Many of the Lady Flo's crew have also been involved in organising the Urban Free Festivals held yearly in Fordham Park. At the second Festival in 1991 there were around 12,000 people. By the third the figure had reached 22,000 and 'You Can't Kill The Spirit' had become the biggest free event in London. In 1993 the tiny Fordham Park was crammed with over 30,000 people but there was no trouble. These 'dangerous squatters' liaise with the police, consult with local residents, raise money from the private sector, bring more than £250,000 of expenditure to the area and demonstrate that free festivals and local communities can have a mutually supportive relationship.

A number of other important buildings remain on our skyline, but for how much longer? The Mumfords' mill building stands majestically alone by the Creek where it was once part of a whole horizon of mills. Laurie Grove baths have been awaiting sale for some years. Next door the town hall has been converted for use by City Challenge but its future beyond 1996 is uncertain. In some ways the neglect of Deptford has been a blessing. We have many beautiful buildings in the High St and the Broadway, soot-covered and interspersed with 1960s and 1970s infills but still standing. The High St has not been bulldozed out in the way that most of London's other main streets have been. Other buildings all over the old borough have scraped past the redevelopers precisely because the area was deemed so worthless. The time to save these buildings is now. We need new, sustainable uses for them, generated by 'community enterprise' with the vision to link past usage to viable future potential.

The story of Drake's Steps

The Deptford Steps, which in local legend were the site of Francis Drake's knighting and of Walter Raleigh's gallant gesture with the cloak, were removed during the building of Pepys Estate. There were big intentions to make the most of the estate's historical connections and they were going to be replaced, but (incredibly) the contractors received a major architectural Award for New Housing and further work was deemed unnecessary. The stones from the Steps ended up in storage in a nearby underground garage.

Drake's Steps outside the rum stores on Deptford [str]and. Supposedly the site [of F]rancis Drake's knighting in April 1581. This photo probably dates from the [1]950s before the closure of [the] Victualling Yard in 1961.

Whenever someone new came to work at the Pepys Housing Office they would be given the job of getting these stones removed so the garages could be let. The naïve new worker would call the Council Direct Labour Team or its equivalent. They would meet at the garage. Lewisham Council would have arrived in its smallest van and the response was always "no mate, couldn't possibly shift those". The worker would be told 'you need a specialist contractor, or a bigger van, or six weeks notice'.

This continued from the early 1970s until 1991 when the Steps were finally put back. In that time there was a massive turnover at the Housing Office – this practical joke could have been pulled up to 80

225

times. Local tenants' leader Dave O'Hara finally sorted it out with a stream of complaints that the garages were not in use.

The Millwall move

On 8th May 1993, after 83 years, the Lions played their last match at the Den. The new season opened on 4th August at the New Den with a rather unsporting game against Sporting Lisbon. For the club's supporters, although the move provides better facilities (including 17 food outlets and 365 toilets), it also means another rise in the cost of admission. Long gone are the 1950s days when a match ticket cost 2 shillings (10p) and most fans could afford to go along every week. Another problem with the move will be the loss of trade in the pubs and shops where livelihoods depend on the weekly rush during the season. Perhaps the important issue as we watch the East Terrace come down in Coldblow Lane, is its replacement. Another Fairview 'village' of first-time buyers will soon spring up on the site. The Coldblow cobbles are in danger. Already they are taking the strain of H-reg cars rather than old totters' carts and we are unlikely to see the much-missed Sunday market starting up again.

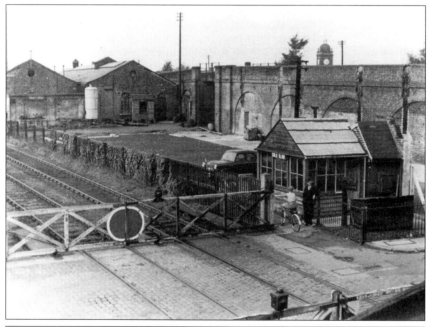

Cold Blow Level Crossin̄ 1958. The dome of the Mazawattee Tea Works̄ above the London & Greenwich viaduct behin̄ the crossing. The Den, hc of Millwall FC from 1910 1993, was to the left of tᵗ photograph. The old cobᵗ have survived, but for how long?.

Alan McLeary, a Millwall player who grew up locally, said in 1987 "the area has been knocked around in the same way as the club. South East London has been a poor relation for years." Fr. Owen Beament, Millwall's chaplain and one of their greatest fans, echoed him: "When the club was promoted to the first division, we felt Deptford and New Cross had been promoted to the first division."

Millwall fans cling to their defiant motto: "No one likes us, we don't care". The fear of the Bristol Rovers players 'legging it' from the pitch invaders at the last Den match was understandable. The distress of Lions player Andy Roberts, led away by police after being stripped to his underpants by souvenir hunters in the middle of the match, made you think maybe the players themselves were not always so happy with their supporters.

Deptford Creek: the muddy heart

The Creek was tamed in the 1960s by having huge quantities of concrete poured into it at strategic points to avoid the flooding which Deptford has always suffered. What it has actually achieved is to hide the old Creek away under mud so that we hardly know it exists. There are a number of proposals for redevelopment in this area, including plans to turn the Skillcentre into a Heritage Centre by spring 1995. Although ambitious, this would still leave a long tract of land including the crucial power station site. Once the East India Company's repair yard and later given a long life as the dockyard of the General Steam Navigation Company, this site has been 'land-banked' by Power Gen because it is more profitable to leave it empty until an upturn in its market value. Power Gen say they are negotiating with Greenwich Council over its development but the process is likely to take many years. Other strips of land and buildings around the area are owned by Thames Water and British Gas and they raise questions about the role of recently privatised public utilities in land speculation. In some ways we can comfort ourselves that the longer they wait the more time we have to decide what we would like to see on those Creekside sites.

Huge amounts of public money are being channelled through the Department of the Environment into the 'regeneration' of Deptford. These form probably the largest concentration of public money in any UK inner city area. Why? It is possible that the Deptford area is a strategically important swathe of what has become known as the Heselbelt, a 10-mile corridor leading eastwards along the Thames from the City to be developed for light industry, packaging, distribution and haulage. The "soft underbelly of South East London", with its high concentration of unskilled and semi-skilled labour, could provide the link between the City, the redeveloped dockland areas and the new Eurotunnel which would make London once again the most appealing investment for home and foreign industry. Massive unemployment and the desperate prospect of the future for many of our school-leavers would make this labour force very cheap and other concessions (demolitions, rushed planning approvals) could be won from a local authority under strain.

City Challenge and the Deptford Gateway

Deptford City Challenge is the most public of these regeneration awards, although the money itself has been skimmed from other sources. With the heavy expenditure focused through Estate Action, many believe City Challenge is "the gloss, the wrap-round", yet it has caused great waves in the area, especially among the hundreds of voluntary groups which have sprung up, expanded or re-orientated themselves to meet the criteria of the 'Deptford Gateway' bid.

Lewisham was not one of the original 15 boroughs invited to bid for City Challenge money. The borough was specifically asked to apply after Michael Heseltine flew into Pepys Estate by helicopter. Instead of the planned 10 regeneration areas, 11 were finally agreed including £37.5 million over five years for Deptford.

It sometimes seems that the very public nature of City Challenge allows Lewisham Council to evade its own responsibilities in Deptford. A short-term and financially limited programme, City Challenge was never meant to take on any basic maintenance funding in the area. When it is all over bar the shouting in 1996 we may find ourselves poorer than ever.

Action on the Estates

The main question in the minds of those involved in developing the Estate Action proposals around Deptford is "whether inherent design faults and the continuing ghettoisation of the inner city underclass can be addressed by capital investment, administered through Lewisham Housing Department, major architectural consultants and big construction firms. Are these not merely the 1990s version of the agents who built these estates in the first place?" (Walker, 1993). The last three decades have clearly produced a stronger concern and cynicism among people living on the estates but two of the most crucial aspects of change – accountability and consultation – seem to have progressed little. Lewisham Council's record of attracting central government investment has been excellent and offers a very real opportunity to develop lasting changes in the environmental and social fabric of Deptford's largest estates. However, their reliance on established tenants' association activists is not a sufficient consultation mechanism. Never have consultants bidding for money to demolish people's homes actually sent anyone round the doorsteps to show and discuss the plans. Are we asking for too much? Former Deptford councillor Robert Lowe would have said we should be grateful for all this money and keep quiet, but look where that got us. "The big boots are still walking round the streets."

> Here then is Deptford, from whose pebbly beach
> Sailed forth the giant armaments to scour the seas,
> To find new worlds, and force the old
> To tremble at the greatness of her name.
> Great in her seaborn sons, but greater still
> In all that made her mercifully just.
> Here Marlowe lived and died, sack-loving, silver-tongued
> And doubt it not that Shakespeare came here too,
> With rare Ben Jonson, to carouse and play
> On Deptford Strond, hard by the Water-gate
> The English game of bowls.
> Then, over all, John Evelyn's honor'd name
> In sweet companionship with Samuel Pepys;
> Sheds such a lustre, that, while England lasts,
> Deptford and they can hold their own
> 'Gainst any name on earth.........Anon.

Here then is Deptford, on whose grimy beach
Two lovers stroll beneath Hays Wharf and wonder
At the way this town still breathes
Against the odds and the stranglehold of neglect...

SOURCES

No detailed references have been given due to considerations of space and level of interest. A full set of references is available at Lewisham and Greenwich Local History Libraries or from Deptford Forum Publishing.

The main published sources for Deptford's history are:

Ellen Chase *Tenant Friends in Old Deptford* (1929) OOP
John Coulter *Lewisham & Deptford in Old Photographs* (1990)
John Coulter *A Second Selection* (1992)
Nathan Dews *History of Deptford* (1884, reprint 1971) OOP
Deptford Into The Nineties *Up The Creek* (1980) OOP
George Glazebrook *Where No Flowers Grow: A Child's Eye View of Deptford 1921–1931* (1989)
Grinling Gibbons Primary School *Deptford's History Through Children's Eyes* (1993)
Father John Kenny *A Part of Deptford Past and Present: The Parish of Our Lady of the Assumption 1842–1992* (1992)

More specific works include:

Rob Cochrane *Cradle of Power: The Story of the Deptford Power Stations* (1985) OOP
Lewis Blake *Red Alert* (1982) and *Bolts from the Blue* (1990)
Peter Gurnett *Guide to the Ancient Parish Church of Deptford: St Nicholas* (1992) and *Guide to the Deptford Parish Church of St Paul* (1992)
Chris Lightbown/Chris Schwarz *Millwall in the Community* (no date, 1980s)
There are also many small published works on particular items such as the canals, the cinemas and Deptford's potteries.

The Age Exchange series of reminiscence publications offer fascinating first–hand information about aspects of everyday life in the last 60 years. They include: *What Did You Do In The War, Mum?*, *Can We Afford The Doctor?*, *Fifty Years Ago*, *Just Like The Country*, *The Time Of Our Lives (Leisure)*

Lewisham Local History Society have published an annual *Transactions* since 1963 which contain many useful articles.

The British Library hold three important collections:

David Showell's collection from the 1840s
A collection of miscellaneous newspaper cuttings 1670-1844
Miscellaneous prints relating to Deptford.

Some items from these collections are to be found at the Lewisham and Greenwich Local History Centres who also have many other sources, including the records of the Deptford Fund.

OOP: Out of print

INDEX

SUPPORTERS

INVESTORS

Josephine Birchenough; *Mark Brayford*; Harry Bowling; *Childeric Primary School*; Deptford Literacy Centre; *Adrian Goodall*; John King; *Deniz Mehmed*; Lionel Openshaw; *Sybil T Phoenix, MBE, MS*; Christine Shearer; *Beryl Steele*; Jess Steele; *Michael Macdonald Steele*; William Michael Steele (Capo); *Richard Walker.*

SPONSORS

Age Exchange; *Kate Allport*; All Saints' Church (Fr. Owen Beament); *Santiago Alvarez*; Sylvia Ashley; *Benjamin Beck*; Andy Benson; *Adrienne Bloch*; Roy Bourne; *Harry Bowling*; Karen Bray; *Mrs G Braybrook*; Clare Brook & Iain Templeton; *Claire Bullen*; Business in the Community's 'Seeing is Believing' Programme; *Catherine Cobham*; Community Desktop Publishing; *Arthur & Joy Cornwell*; Sandra Costello; *Deptford Arts Development Association*; Deptford Green School; *Deptford Pride Video Project*; Juliet Desailly; *Doug Elsley, The John Evelyn pub*; Evelyn Community Development Project; *Kayode Fayemi*; Erica Fitzpatrick; *Marcia H Foster-Norman*; Anna Gelpern; *Goldsmiths' DCC Evaluation Project*; Pat Greenwood; *Sarah Gretton*; Sue & Steve Grindlay; *Emily Growney*; Haberdashers' Aske's Hatcham Girls' School; *Dionne Herelle*; Inner London Probation Service; *International Music Museum (Prof. N McCann)*; Luzia & George Jones; *Steve Jones & Frances Grant*; Mrs Sophie Lake (neé Faulkner); *Chief Inspector John Lansley (Deptford Police)*; Lewisham Council's Race Relations Committee; *Lewisham Local History Centre*; Jani Llewellyn; *London Museums Education Unit*; George Maslin; *Alex McIntosh*; Margaret Murphy; *Musik Minor*; Nixx; *Old Town Community Association*; Tony O'Leary; *Frances Openshaw*; Our Lady of the Assumption (Fr. John Kenny); *Pearce Signs Ltd*; People for Action (SLFHA); *Marsha Phoenix Memorial Trust*; Revival Café & Hales Gallery; *Jim Rice*; Diana Rimel; *Jean Rogers & Roger Cornwell*; Root Sauce Productions; *Jenny Rose*; Round the Bend at the Harp of Erin; *Councillor John Rudd (from Julian)*; Joan Ruddock, MP; *Aranzazu Ruiz*; Dave Russell; *Margaret Sandra*; Shaftesbury Christian Centre; *Dr Jim Sharpe*; Tom Sheppard; *Anita Spence & Marie O'Connell*; Rory Steele (from his brother); *Sonia Steele*; Yvette Steele; *St James' Church (Rev. Frank Hung)*; St Nicholas' Church (Rev. Canon Graham Corneck); *St Paul's Church (Fr. Peter Fellows)*; Councillor Nicholas Taylor; *Nigel Thomas*; William Thompson; *Derrick Turner*; David & Sylvia Walker; *Keith & Jayne Walton*; John & Eva Warren; *Julian Watson*; Beth & Andy Williamson.

GRANTS

Convoys Ltd; *Lewisham Arts Service*; Millwall in the Community; *People for Action*; The *Time Out* Trust.

Exhibition space and promotional support provided by Wavelengths Library & Leisure Centre and Deptford Bookshop.

Cover illustration:
George III and Queen Charlotte Driving Through Deptford, *circa 1785*
by Thomas Rowlandson (1756-1827)
From a private collection, photograph courtesy of Hazlitt, Gooden & Fox.

The picture shows the junction of Deptford Broadway and Deptford High Street with the Centurion pub on the corner. The Old Ship is said to be an invention but evidence from the mid-18th century shows that there was a pub and brew-house known by the sign of the Ship near to the old Tide Mill at Deptford Bridge. This inn also appears in the story of the thief-takers (Ch.6).
The royal coach is on the extreme right, escorted by Horse Grenadier Guards. The Watson sisters, celebrated beauties of the time, are riding by in a vis-a-vis. The space around them would be more suited to the royal couple and it is typical of Rowlandson to put beauty above status. In the basket behind the stagecoach is Jonas Hanway who had introduced the umbrella to a sceptical English public. Below the royal coach the boxer John Jackson is about to enter the fray. The early billboards hanging from housefronts in the centre of the picture advertise Patrick Cotter the 'Surprising Irish Giant' who put himself on show as a freak at Bartholomew Fair and the 'Learned Pig' which had caused a sensation with its mathematical and other tricks in 1784.

This photograph shows the same junction in September 1992, with the Centurion pub still standing on the corner. The dramatic space all around it has since been filled in by City Challenge-funded buildings in a relatively successful attempt to match the elegance of the Centurion. Sadly nothing has been done to renovate the buildings opposite. The anchor at the head of the High Street was installed in the early 1990s. Photograph by Bob Bray.